Beasts in Eden:

The Humane and the Inhumane

Praise for Benoit

"With the brevity of Confucius, the beauty, depth, wit and wisdom of the poet Rumi, and his own succinct, lyrical language, Benoit writes about the human condition. 5 Stars (out of five)"

— Lee Gooden, *ForeWord Clarion Reviews*

[Benoit's] aphorisms have a distinctively late 19th-century Nietzschean feel and flair to them...Even the language itself has a delightfully antiquated feel to it: complex sentences that couch dark, faintly misanthropic observations in an artful formality. Though they may feel like something from another era, the moral musings in Benoit's sayings are never out of fashion. These aphorisms, Benoit writes, "stand alone but they are also a part of the larger whole of the book itself, which argues for an artistic perspective to one's outlook on life."

— James Geary, *New York Times* bestselling author of *Geary's Guide to the World's Great Aphorists*

"Benoit has breached that inner wisdom and offers it up fearlessly with waves of condemnation of the dastardly to twenty slashes for the weak."

— M. Arlene Van Belle author of *A Journey of Healing*

"[Benoit] delivers the perfect combination of creative voice, enlightened spirit, fresh observations, and keen insights succinctly woven into universally true expressions of philosophy...to read the works of Emile Benoit, is to have one's thoughts and emotions stirred by a writer adept at wielding the powerful use of brevity and astute observations to slay the beast of reader indifference."

—U.S. Review of Books

Beasts in Eden:
The Humane and the Inhumane

By

Emile Benoit

Eudaimon Press
San Diego / 2016

Published by Eudaimon Press / San Diego

Manufactured in the United States of America

Typeset in Bookman Old Style

ISBN-13: 978-0-9882277-1-2
ISBN-10: 0988227711

Library of Congress Control Number: 2015937688

Layout/Design by Jerry Urick

Eudaimon Press / 2016

To my three best girls, with much love

LMB

TABLE OF CONTENTS

How to Read this Book

It's important here to begin with a discussion about the language of this book and how the work as a whole should be read. In the first place, I have no intention of proving anything to anyone. Instead, my aim is to provide insight rather than persuasion. I hope to have the reader *see* rather than know something about the humane and the inhumane and the development of human character. The consequence of this reflection, I hope, is to inspire a more conscious appreciation of life and one's own individual responsibility to it. There is no constructive theory to be illustrated in this regard since the life best lived is peculiar to each individual. In fact, this sort of exploration is quite customary. In *Philosophy as a Way of Living*, the French philosopher Pierre Hadot claims that the goal of ancient philosophy was not to construct some abstract, purely objective, theoretical system that speaks of universal principles and dogmatic truths. After all, Hadot argues, most ancient philosophical texts are rather strange, disordered, seemingly unfocused, and quite literary in style and orientation. Instead, he believed that ancient philosophy attempted to utilize rhetoric and imagination to direct someone toward living the best life, a more humane life in many ways. Through the use of literary fragments, dialogue, quotations, figurative language, poetry, aphorisms and other stylistic elements, the ancient philosopher endeavors to provoke a transformation of the self and provide a remedy to some of the worries, anguish, and misery that beset the lives of almost anyone. The wise student then is engaged in the task of creating her own character by employing these texts in such a manner as to produce a kind of depth-therapy for the soul in the midst of all the chaos, distractions, temptations, and difficulties that often arise in life.

So, this present work is designed with the goals of Hadot's ancient philosophy in mind. The writing contained within these pages is deliberately fragmentary, poetic, philosophical, aphoristic, and literary in nature since its overall subject — a life best lived — is so inherently vague. The hope of its intended use is to strike a chord within the reader that might resonate with her somehow, reminding her, perhaps, that the work of character is never complete until she has breathed her last. Therefore, she must continue to divert her attention away from those activities which are merely vain obsessions and neurotic concerns and direct it, instead, to perspectives which instill a profundity of spirit.

Earlier I mentioned that I hoped the reader would "see" these perspectives rather than adopt them as dogmatic truths of any kind, but the use of the word "see" isn't quite correct. It is not an act of the eyes that I hope to inspire but imagery of another kind altogether. Imagery itself is the attempt of an author to deepen a reader's understanding of a text through the use of figurative language that appeals to one or more of the five senses. In other words, it's an effort that is of interest to the bodily senses, the quite physical attributes of seeing, hearing, feeling, tasting, and smelling. However, there is a different kind of imagery that is also a physical feature, a more subtle one — even one imperceptible to some. It is the imagery that appeals to intuition, imagination, and insight.

The East has traditionally employed this brand of imagery in its writing for centuries. The pithy maxims of Confucius and Zen Buddhism can serve as fitting examples, but they are hardly alone in this regard. The West remains enthralled with the fragments of Epictetus, Cicero, Marcus Aurelius and so many of the other wise spirits from antiquity, to say nothing of its appetite for aphorisms. Contemporary westerners mine the larger works of its authors — both dead and thriving — in order to find some short phrase or paragraph that illuminates and inspires by its very brevity, providing a more concise and precise expression of the larger idea. There arises a pleasure of the human psyche when challenged with maxims of this sort, a pleasure of the intellect that is not necessarily directed at reasoning or logic — and certainly not theory. It is the pleasure of mindfulness. We read: "The unexamined life is not worth living" and the mind is immediately seized by the insight — agreeable or not. A great feeling arises from the encounter with such expressions, a sense that something noble has awoken within.

Perhaps an ancient parable might best demonstrate how such insight might then be used to improve one's life. The fable begins, as most stories do, with five blind men gathered around an elephant. Each man inspects a different part of the elephant. For example, one man might examine the tusk and report the smoothness of an elephant while another man holds the trunk and determines an elephant to be quite rough. All five men, though they will describe entirely different features of the elephant, remain correct in their individual assessment. The elephant *is* smooth and rough and tall and all sorts of other various qualities. Yet, notice that no one individual will achieve a proper understanding of the elephant as a whole. Only if the blind men come together and compare their own unique perspectives will they arrive somewhat closer to the "truth."

The short pieces that make up the contents of this book — artistic in nature — should be similarly read, as various perspectives all directed toward understanding the enormous mystery that is human existence. There is no one definitive interpretation possible for these brief fragments because it is the reader's own reflection and imagination which brings ultimate meaning to this form, yet, simultaneously, there still exists a single interpretation which is intended to immediately excite or inspire the mind to awaken. It is through this process of individual confrontation with ideas that the reader eventually — through practice — begins to understand the self and develop the roots of true character. In the words of the German philosopher Friedrich Nietzsche:

> "[T]he relief-like, incomplete presentation of an idea, of a whole philosophy, is sometimes more effective than its exhaustive realization: more is left for the beholder to do, he is impelled to continue working on that which appears before him so strongly etched in light and shadow, to think it through to the end, and to overcome even that constraint which has hitherto prevented it from stepping forth fully formed."

There is much in this book that is purposely incomplete and likewise "etched in light and shadow." It is the reader now who must create a more nuanced and individual interpretation, forming meaning from the seeming chaos, and thus arousing the development of character and humanity.

The Inhumane

Attempts at Definition

1

The zombie is an appropriate symbol for the contemporary man, he who often acts *as if* he were a creature possessing human consciousness and sentiment. This "zombie" largely sleepwalks through his life and pays little regard to others around him. He remains blissfully ignorant of the world and indeed seems to intentionally delude himself with entertaining forms of distraction in order to evade having to experience the pangs of consciousness. In this manner, he isolates himself from both the human *and* the animal, creating a distinctive living thing that is something of an anomaly in nature — the beast, a creature most vicious, vengeful, and foul.

2

In general, we are born with the potential to achieve some of the most noble, virtuous, and inspiring of deeds — great works of art, profound scientific and philosophical theories, genuine acts of kindness and benevolence, feats of staggering ingenuity, and all forms of deep reflection and insightfulness. Yet, within the breast of all people also rests the potential to accommodate, and then perhaps unleash, one of the most brutal, repugnant, and vicious of beasts ever to have existed on the planet. So, the most urgent campaign against the external forces of the inhumane must be fought primarily within the conflicted psyche of every individual.

3

Man has not become more brutal in the modern age, he is merely better at keeping a record of it now.

4

The sage must take a stand — in fact, she will draw quite a few lines in the sand over the course of her lifetime — against the true threat to humanity: that ancient element of the human character which seems entirely drained of conscience. This barbarian appears throughout human history and is only ever momentarily quelled when the greater mass of men refuse to abide his barbarism. In his own heart, too, man cannot allow the inhumane to creep into his actions. Otherwise, as goes the individual, so goes the species as well.

5

Civilization should be humanity's response to brutality. It should exist as a testament to the better nature of man and tirelessly gather its forces to oppose all forms of violence, ignorance, stupidity, fundamental certainty, and idiocy in all its many guises. Instead, it often serves as one of the more brutal aggressors in a world already quite comfortable with staggering cruelty.

6

Men have through the ages attempted to disguise the brutality and cruelty of their character with the superficial masks and other accoutrements of culture. He may, for example, make a show of his philanthropy or take pains to know all the finest wines while secretly a violent cretin in his home. This is, of course, quite different from cultivation or development of any kind, though such men often imagine themselves to be rather cultured indeed.

7

Moses stands up against the brutality of slavery with a cruelty of his own — evidenced by his unleashing destruction upon the enemy. So, in order to bring an end to the inhumane practices of the Pharaoh, Moses obediently summons the merciless plagues of what seems to be a rather ruthless conception of a deity.

8

Except in those cases where aggression shocks the conscience of a reasonable person, it is often the highest hypocrisy to stand victorious in battle over one's opposition while charging them with war crimes. If a war was waged, everyone who participated engaged in something barbaric, ignorant, and short-sighted — no matter how much the victors might like to excuse themselves. This is the very nature of war, so to imagine one combatant as more ethical than another merely demonstrates a prejudice that borders on the delusional. The very name of war itself suggests a legality and a final justification for the unleashing of human brutality. There exists no rule of law in such jurisdictions. All are guilty and will pay some consequence.

9

Mankind is often only two degrees of separation removed from the brutal savagery of the barbarian.

10

Nature remains silent and stoic around the brutalities of

the world. She sits with stony indifference upon her majestic throne and has nothing to say about the unspeakable way that men treat one another or the moronic designs that they pursue. Nature is even mute with respect to her own destruction as men continue to inject her veins with poison and litter her features with debris. Nature watches as men are led to their execution, lifting their eyes to the sky for some sign that she may pause and gasp at their extinction. Yet, she will not so much as sigh. She has witnessed this grisly scene far too many times over the centuries and has grown desensitized and immune. The seasons revolve unchanged and life continues in much the same manner as it had before. Only man may truly concern himself with the suffering of humanity and his sympathy often appears quite selfish and narrow, even rather apathetic at times. His understanding of another person's sorrowful condition is generally prejudiced by his own unjustified arrogance and the appalling sense of entitlement that inspires and strengthens his every conviction.

11

The cross, Christianity's symbol of divine sacrifice, is more appropriately a reminder of mankind's brutality rather than an indication of his transcendent nature. This vulgar and inhumane condition of violence and revenge, it seems, is chronic in every age in a variety of forms.

12

In his depiction of god — the morality of god, the character of god — man often proves himself to be a brute once again.

13

He who denies the inhumane in his own nature often does so with reckless savagery or, at best, cruel indifference — as if this aspect of his personality were somehow an unwarranted insult. In this manner he wishes to abolish the inhumane and promote morality through actions quite cruel and callous.

14

To a certain extent — short of brutality — a government must enforce a "civilized" morality upon its people. This may, of course, seem intrusive or even treacherous to we who already possess an inner restraint of our more beastly characteristics. Yet, a quick look around at men as they are — and not how we might wish for them to be — will reveal that these restrictions often seem quite essential in preventing brutality on a far greater scale.

15

Nature is often cruel enough without man further contributing his own merciless brutality.

16

Men have for centuries attempted to justify certain barbaric sports or actions as necessary for the release of poisonous sentiments within the heart of the populace. Yet, more often than not it is the spectacle of the sport itself which inspires these infected passions.

17

Injustice, properly understood, serves as a kind of affront to the beauty of human nature. In other words, a person who acts unjustly offends not simply his victim and humanity as a whole, but also the very notion of life as anything more than a cruel, relentless, and terrifying encounter with the cold, fierce stare of Nature.

18

War shamelessly reveals the quite painful and cruel reality that all men are ultimately expendable and endowed by their creator with certain inalienable flights of fancy.

19

The government that must resort to cruelty and unprovoked aggression in order to maintain the peace and preserve its rule, immediately and unequivocally forfeits its own legitimacy.

20

Civil disobedience, to be at all possible, requires at least a slight concern for civility. Gandhi's crusade would have ended much sooner had he been met with unmerciful cruelty first.

21

Man is not particularly worthy of respect nor possessed by dignity simply because he sacrifices himself for his beliefs. His sacrifice, in other words, does not confer special consideration for the assessment of his character. The Nazi continually gave up his very life in the pursuit of a repugnant goal based upon a narcissistic delusion. Man's sincerity is largely inconsequential if his aim is inhumane. The crusader, too, who so wished to save the souls of others by burning them at the stake must be judged now as a cruel, ignoble, and inhumane creature no matter what he might have otherwise believed at the time.

22

No man should dare aim to become who he is entirely. After all, a great many fools exist in the world and a great many barbarians, too. These characters should not be encouraged to remain ignorant, cruel, and self-righteous creatures. They must instead become inspired to something greater, as the acorn develops into to the oak. Yet, unlike the acorn, a child will not simply flower and flourish unaided by the other trees in the grove. He could as likely grow into a squat crabapple as reach the height of the oak.

23

Man has long extolled the virtues of liberty and a love for all mankind while simultaneously enslaving his brothers and eradicating his enemies. When man is not being vicious and cruel, it seems he busies himself with hypocrisy.

24

More often than not, Nietzsche's noble warrior takes on the characteristics of a *lower* man rather than the higher. The warrior's *lack* of morality brings about a kind of cruelty that at least matches the ferocity of extreme religious spite. While the noble warrior's goals *may* be more worthy of admiration, his attitude toward other lesser souls reveals a lack of compassion that generally borders on the inhumane.

25

Men often excuse themselves for finding a kind of humor

in the misfortune of others. Yet, the jokes, titters, and guffaws of the outsider to some tragic event are not simply the means by which he attempts to cope with a difficult situation, but are an expression of his inner cruelty as well and an example of the delight he takes in trampling the lilies of the field for his own twisted and ignoble pleasure.

26

The drawing and quartering of criminals, a practice that is now widely considered quite cruel and inhumane, still shares a disturbing foundation with modern notions of the death penalty. The latter at least *attempts* to make the procedure humane by making it more sterile and moving it away from the public streets. The effect, of course, is a procedure that is certainly less painful, exploitative, and bloody. However, the cruelty and ignorance of the act persist and these characteristics form the bedrock for all manners of execution.

27

The Puritan conception of evil was rooted so deeply in his nature that he became shameful of everything. The contemporary individual, on the other hand, perceives evil from the opposite extreme wherein it only arises when most obvious or seemingly impossible to otherwise forgive. The Nazi, for example, can be easily recognized as something quite vile and repugnant. So we contemporaries proceed with no shame or guilt whatsoever because we certainly know that none of our actions actually reach the level of such an absolute and extreme notion of the inhumane. It is this superficial understanding of malevolence that shields us from the uncomfortable truth that many of our own instinctive needs, in fact, possess some element of cruelty to them.

28

There do exist, it appears quite obvious, evil-hearted men who in some bleak region of the brain seem intent on spreading hate and destruction. For them, nothing can be done but lock them away from the rest of humanity or banish them to one's enemies. After all, these men seldom ever change unless it's by their own design and this rarely occurs for the most atrocious offenders. State execution may resolve this predicament, but it causes many more. Killing, no matter how righteous, always infects the blood of those nearby and merely multiplies the amount of spite and cruelty in the world.

29

The conflict between good and evil is a struggle within the human heart rather than some great cosmic divide.

30

Nietzsche's madness was famously recognized when he threw himself atop of a fallen horse that was being whipped to rise. Nietzsche pleaded for the whipping to cease, apparently unable to bear silent witness to the animal's suffering any longer. Yet, it is Nietzsche here who is characterized as the madman — as if the inability to withstand cruelty in this world were a sickness of some kind while brutality is considered something more understandable.

31

The cruelty of omission is sometimes the more subtle

expression of our inhumanity. The kind word withheld, for example, fails to serve its purpose of countervailing the inhumane as a whole.

32

Nature is full of such staggering regularities that the entire universe appears as an ordered system that we might predict and control. However, while certainly orderly and predictable at times, Nature is also wild and unmanageable, irrational, and oftentimes quite cruel. Mankind, too, exhibits these qualities, but with the additional faculty of thoughtfulness that distinguishes him from the natural animal.

33

The artificial speed of contemporary society causes us to perceive Nature, including our own, as something far too painfully slow and methodical for us. We grow impatient that life itself does not provide for our immediate needs and gratifications and this frustration often leads to fits of cruelty, vengeance, and ferocity.

34

Our morality hasn't changed much over the centuries. Justice, humility, reason, generosity, and compassion — among an abundance of other virtues — remain as important to humane existence as they did in Socrates' time. Still, man remains as cruel, violent and intentionally ignorant as ever before, although he imagines himself now tamed by government, science, technology, and mindless entertainment. Yet, we should not be lulled into a false sense of accomplishment since these methods only temporarily subdue our more ubiquitous animal instincts. Besides, they generally leave our spirit quite uninspired which then eventually results in a crisis of sorts, an overwhelming uneasiness that never leaves us — unless of course we have already deadened our inner self. We desperately need the spiritual benefits of art and the humanities but we shun them nonetheless. Still, the resources of culture and humane civilization are an inheritance and not something that we have earned. Thus, they can be squandered too. Truly noble and profound civilizations must be renewed again and again with each new generation. In order to achieve such renewal our individual character will require cultivation as well as a commitment to the persistent quest to sharpen and refine its own more natural tendencies. Yet contemporary man appears quite contemptuous of such an obligation and remarkably unconcerned with the consequences of his failure to develop his soul.

35

The very notion of the objective man, the idea that someone can essentially remove his spirit from any particularly passionate deliberation, is itself something of a prejudice. While objectivity — or the pursuit of it anyway — is a wonderful tool and even works to eliminate bias in many circumstances, it can also serve to rationally justify cruelty and viciousness.

36

In many ways man's cruelty arises from the sentiments of his morality. His determination that someone is "evil" or has broken the moral code provides a justification for punishment of some kind. It gleefully sanctions retribution and reprimand, dispositions of presumed superiority which grant someone an allowance to express his inner vindictiveness. In order to punish a "criminal," for example — he who has transgressed the moral law — the emperor or the herd or the judge might — as has occurred — lock the offender into the hollow crucible of a bronze bull and light the fire beneath it. The resulting screams of these "delinquents" creates a kind of music by which the dance of hollow justice is arranged.

37

Evil often arises because of an indifference to the good rather than an ignorance of it. Though ignorance too can produce a kind of evil that struts around the public square in the brilliant light of day, spreading great misery and sorrow while the unaffected remain blissfully unaware.

38

A dormant volcano is often mistaken for a mountain precisely because men are generally ignorant of what lies hidden beneath the surface of the rock. The same is true of man and the interior aspects of his own self.

39

Tolerance eventually will lead to acceptance over time. While this quality is quite necessary — even virtuous — for dealing sensibly and fairly with the many varied and differing beliefs and actions of others in the world, it can also simultaneously welcome and encourage the existence of great evil if left unchecked. One may become, after all — out of sheer habit — tolerant of many subtle forms of cruelty and brutality.

40

Evil frequently arises from some form of "group think" which may pragmatically accomplish much in its time, but often merely serves to eliminate — or at least suppress — the individual moral instinct. We must then stridently oppose surrender of our own ethical responsibilities to the ideology of the mob.

41

The brute criminal demonstrates an immorality operating primarily on a physical plane whereas the more insidious evil of ideological fundamentalism functions at the level of the spirit. The former destroys the body while the latter destroys the soul.

42

During times of war, man disappears into the deserts, forests, and jungles of combat, emerging as something of an anti-man — not merely an animal at all but openly changed nonetheless — vicious and unpredictable with a newfound opportunity to inflict the kind of evil that previously he kept concealed in his breast. He is a contemporary, of course, yet he so much resembles the warrior men of old.

43

The evil that we do is largely the consequence of some insidious brand of hubris. Most of us think so highly of ourselves as individuals that we listlessly forgo the individuality of others — viewing the interests of other people as generally inconsequential by comparison. Yet, the primary focus of any ethical view must begin and end with the notion of humility — the humbleness of intellect, talent, and power of any kind. Otherwise, man begins to imagine himself as something of an authority in matters where his ignorance holds sovereignty rather than his wisdom.

44

The beast with whom we must daily contend — the true struggle at the heart of all conflicts involving the human animal — is the creature known as ego. For every kind word whispered in the ear of its host, ego will demand a sacrifice in return.

45

The inhumane is not simply the presence of some aggression but also the forsaking of restraint.

46

Proud ambition and an ignorant sense of entitlement are salacious qualities of character and of far greater interest to the mob than more fragile concepts such as humility or gentleness of heart. The more lurid elements, of course, ultimately find expression in a culture seeking vapid entertainment and possessing a reckless indifference to what truly matters in life. After a while, these traits become so engrained within the consciousness of entire civilizations that we begin to *yearn* for things most disastrous to our overall health and well-being.

47

The contemporary individual rarely thinks beyond his own subjective experience and so fails to produce any significant contribution to humanity as a whole. Instead, he is something of a volatile and ignorant brute, unable to free himself from the restraints of his own mind and too immersed in the pleasing balm of egotism to generate a purpose for his life that might transcend the trite and the banal.

48

Leaders often lead nothing but their own ambition to make of themselves the icon of a movement, era, or idea. They are, for the most part, great egoists.

49

The reason that the majority of men imagine they possess such an abundance of rights is due to the vast overestimation of their own character and value. After all, many men are little more than children who believe they are mature enough to handle thought and weaponry. They even seem deluded enough to perceive of themselves as the guardians of "lesser" spirits though they generally have the greatest difficulty administering to their own lives. Children, after all, make lousy parents and even worse leaders of humanity.

50

Man is so addicted to the spectacle and drama of his existence that when there is not enough to suit him at any given moment, he will invent it for himself instead. This is the impetus behind mankind's obsession with the masculine sports of war and physical competition. He is not yet evolved enough to relinquish his natural ambition of eliminating competitors, so he remains devoted to external victory with very little sign that he intends to cease the violence in his heart. Of course, recent history seems to show a somewhat circumstantial tendency for mankind as a whole to be less violent overall and this is certainly encouraging news —

debatable though it may be. The sublimation of hatred and aggression into some quality more civilized is quite a valuable tool for the improvement of character, but we should be careful not to shower man with too much praise since his egotistical lust for competition could seduce him to a state of Hobbesian viciousness once again. The "natural" competitive passion fuels the majority of mankind's most unnatural acts.

51

Man will often go to great lengths to avoid being deceived in his daily interactions. He must, for example, quickly discern whether another person is truthful or untrustworthy. Otherwise he may be led to ruin by some unscrupulous soul intent upon seizing an advantage. So the cautious man arms himself against deception and sends out spies to capture some semblance of the truth. Only then might he hope to make an informed and somewhat confident decision about what he must do. Yet, he is not as suspicious and guarded about his own personal deceptions. His mind promptly deceives him because it knows the weakness of its host, the ego. The unconstrained ego of man is just that element of his character which so adamantly opposes *any* unfavorable comparisons. So, it fashions a grand overall deception for the individual man himself in order to justify those conclusions already preconceived.

52

The person confined in a prison cage is an animal sentenced, but for strange circumstance, by his fellow beasts.

53

It's a contemporary habit to perceive of freedom as a virtue and repression, a vice; however, inhibition is quite often a necessity in any civilized society. Few would wish, after all, for the rapist to freely satisfy his most primal desires without restraint of any kind. If someone is raised without limitations, he has hardly been raised as a person at all. Instead, a peculiar sort of beast is formed — one quite removed from empathy or understanding — that far exceeds the animal kingdom in both aggression and intentional ignorance.

54

War demonstrates the true nature of man as a creature quite capable of the inhumane, if not entirely committed to it at times. War itself is the collapse of the humane into something brutish and beastly — a state of being that only man might achieve since the animals are incapable of stooping to feats that shock the conscience to hear.

55

War relegates man to the status of beast, a rank below the animals, no matter which side he may defend. Societies, of course, will attempt to instill patriotism into the hearts of its citizens in order to perpetuate the idea that a particular war is just and its participants heroic despite the atrocities that inevitably arise. Yet, man often finds it almost impossible to maintain the dignity of his better nature while engaged in such horror. In order to survive he feels he must, instead, unleash those elements of his personality which are the most vicious.

56

The same precautions should be employed when engaging mankind as when encountering a wild beast — a tiger or a bear, perhaps. While man may not be *always* such an immediate threat, he is nonetheless something of an animal himself and proves himself as dangerous as any lion through his masterful use of cunning and deceitfulness.

57

The human race must develop and maintain, as a collective and individually, some means of sublimating its aggression. Politics is one attempt to civilize such destructive instincts, but the hostility here is only barely beneath the polite facade. The base competition of the beast is only minimally removed. In fact, the more man engages in competition with *others*, the less he will participate in the more necessary struggle with himself. The resulting creature will be one who is quite antagonistic and only superficially civilized.

58

There are some who would have us believe that the will is an evil thing — as if man's desire leads primarily to his ruin. Yet, there would be no art without desire, no love, no invention, nothing to animate humanity much beyond the day. Man without desire is barely a person at all and he reflects this bland homogeny in the emptiness of his eyes, like a broken colt being led in from the ring, or a businessman on his way to work. Of course, the wild and passionate beast — metaphorically speaking — threatens our humanity as well and does at times break free in a panic or a rage from the rational boundaries meant to safely contain it. The *trick* is to humanize our animal passions and channel them into something designed to arouse our better natures.

59

Man often takes civilization for granted — especially during times of comfort and prosperity — assuming that his kind have always treated one another with kindness and deference. He sometimes forgets his duty to protect and nurture the very concept of culture and civility. Thus, he must reexamine and ultimately renew his commitment to these notions of the higher man, the more humane creature, on a daily basis. Otherwise men will fall to more practical concerns or distractions and eventually enslave themselves to some superficial pursuit in the end. He may forget his duty to his fellows entirely and even begin to believe he has no need of culture and civility — at least until he encounters the beast that arises from such a pale and rotting soul.

60

These old men who grumble, complain, and sneer at life are generally not the product of age but of a character that has been rotting for quite some time. The corrupt old man is often merely a greying version of his quite contemptible younger self.

61

If someone wishes to spend his days in degradation and depravity, whoring every great impulse in his soul for the benefit of some small change and a smile, then by all means he should do so. A life with significance and purpose, no doubt, is not for him since he is intent upon enjoying his life as something of a child's toy. He indulges himself in every impulse and satiates almost every desire while the sage seeks to control these impediments. After all, the sage craves the development and deepening of her character as well as the grounding of her soul to the hub of universal consciousness. This is too great a task for the lesser man, accustomed as he is to the weak and lazy nature of his spirit. The inhumane often arises from this deadening of the soul.

62

The relative ease of someone's life, his freedom from significant poverty or suffering, leaves him happy, no doubt, but without the benefit of much character. He is instead a fragile shell that will crack almost immediately upon contact.

63

People do not only reveal their true character during times of crisis and tragedy but often when they are engaged in the daily grind of living too. One brilliant moment of boldness though does not create the brilliant man.

64

While we might *imagine* ourselves unique by nature, we are truly only distinctive from the animal to the extent that we cultivate a humane and civilized character, a more wise, reflective soul that constantly seeks opportunities for intellectual, spiritual, and artistic growth. Yet, few spirits subject themselves to the necessary rigor and sacrifice — the struggle with uncertainty and self-doubt — required of such a well-examined life. After all, the instinct and intuition of the animal is sufficient for most as long as they receive their daily bread.

65

There is little hope for mankind as a whole if each of us isn't willing to improve upon the nobility of our own character, to enlarge the scope of our own perspectives. The very existence of humanity — though not the existence of the human *animal* — is greatly imperiled by the ignoble individual who reprimands the collective for failing to sponsor virtue more.

66

The soft-hearted and good intentioned progressive is not ashamed to expose his sympathies and speak publically about his naïve belief in man's inner goodness because he generally feels he's had little experience with man at his very worst. However, the staunch and stubborn conservative is only too aware of the dark capacities in man since he himself possesses so many of them in his own secret character.

67

Vices — those individual habits or actions (or lies) which distract us from the betterment of our disposition — can be insidious and inhumane precisely because they erode our commitment to noble ideas.

68

In the act of judging others, we are often guilty of a quite maddening species of forgetfulness — the sort which conveniently overlooks so many of our own most obvious deficiencies in personality and temperament.

69

Contemporary man continues to sharpen his deceitfulness, make pettier his desires, shower his ignorance with merit, and perceive himself to be the most enlightened of all. These he will do partly because it's something of a tradition with his kind.

70

Much madness can arise from an overabundance of the sane and rational. It might take little reasoning, for example, to derive a number of good, rational arguments for the killing of any creature.

71

Without emotion participating in the process of thought, we might quite easily justify the slaughter of innocents using that terrifyingly "objective" aspect of our reasoning.

72

There exist so many contradictions in the world because mankind often perceives and understands the cosmos through the lens of logic alone. The imperfect nature of logic itself eventually leads to a contradiction of some sort. Logic, after all, must rely upon the abstract nature of words and numbers to convey its objective "truth" so it remains susceptible to a variety of differing interpretations.

73

The use of reason or rationality to explore the understanding of a madman is similar to the notion of utilizing a match to illuminate the contents of a black hole.

74

An occurrence can't be considered inhumane simply on the basis that it arises from man's animal instincts. Instead, any act is inhumane if it fails to live up to the standards of an intelligent, reflective, rational, and empathetic being — the kind of creature that exemplifies the *best* that mankind has either thought or done.

75

Restraint is integral to the notions of balance and stability. The muscles of the body, for instance, must limit the movement of the legs to prevent a person from falling over. Similarly, the emotions must be restrained at times so as not to lose one's reason entirely. Yet, so many fools — those most immature — perceive freedom to be merely an absence of restrictions, a coarse justification for all sorts of self-indulgent idiocy. They imagine restraint as something of an enemy to liberty rather than a necessary component of it.

76

Absolute freedom is merely a free fall from some great height without the benefit of a parachute. In short, it's suicide.

77

The search for freedom at all costs, oftentimes freedom for the mere sake of the name, is itself a kind of slavish routine that subjects the individual to the rigid demands of an obsession.

78

A rather unfortunate condition of most moderns is that they generally possess the necessary independence to freely run their lives to a remarkable extent but they lack the ability to wield that freedom with any kind of understanding, insight, or wisdom. Therefore, they ultimately resemble a dangerous animal recently paroled from the zoo, terribly overwhelmed by the sudden atmosphere of possibility.

79

The person who wages an endless and indiscriminate battle for more and more freedom will, in the process, lose the war to liberate his own mind.

80

The Greek and Roman philosophers often aspired to only desire those things which were essential to the human being — both body and soul. After all, they reasoned, most unhappiness stems from man's inability to regulate the passions in one form or another — usually desiring instead to pursue that which is beyond his own individual needs and abilities. Modern man, on the other hand, celebrates the person whose passions largely *define* him, often at the expense of others. These two eras appear to be the mirror image of one another in this regard. The first gaining freedom through the restriction of passion while the second enslaves man to his passionate addictions.

81

Hatred, anger, and greed spread their cruel disease outward into the world like a contagion.

82

Men often believe that they can gain some kind of revenge over their enemy by killing him — as if killing another person somehow pins a ribbon of immortality upon the killer. Yet, it's more often the case that the murderer, whether justified in his actions or not, will be unable to free himself from the memory of the person he killed — unless, of course, the killer no longer possesses any discernable characteristics of the human within him at all.

83

The historical anomaly of the sexual revolution was that the masculine finally achieved the liberty to express all of its most bestial urges over a feminine power too easily swayed by its own instinctual drives. Eventually this unleashed a pack of human dawgs upon the world — still roaming in hordes today, they resemble no great improvement over the caveman at times. It will take a truly feminine ruler to restore justice and civility once again.

84

Contemporary society has spent the last forty years attempting to "free" itself of most value judgments in the name of toleration. Yet, the effect has been to release the hounds upon the butterfat. What remains is mostly chaos and wild confusion. While man today may have become more tolerant in public as compared to his ancestors, his private days often continue to be hidden away in horrors too unspeakable to mention.

85

A troubling weakness of any "free" society that takes equality seriously is the inability to recognize its most truly significant members amid a crowd of lesser fools. This generally leads to corruption, incompetence, and an eventual erosion of trust in all public institutions — and in all of humanity for that matter.

86

The most damaging myth of Auschwitz is not a question as to whether the horrors there actually occurred or are fictitious, but the notion that we imagine such atrocities as little more than isolated incidents — unfortunate anomalies within the otherwise impeccable moral character of man. However, Auschwitz stands as a monument to the brutish charm of ideology and self-delusion, a tombstone that might just mark the death of man altogether.

87

Given the horrors of the Holocaust in the last century, it should be of no surprise that so many *German* philosophers found generosity and pity to be — for various reasons — detestable.

88

So many of our own contemporaries attempt to distance themselves from the horrors of the Holocaust, as if such murderous rage were not already lying dormant in their own heart.

89

The idea that man is disposed by Nature to live honorably and well is as mistaken as the notion of man as someone fundamentally sinful and rapacious. Instead, we are all born as animals and must therefore be trained well if we are to live as something more.

90

As animals can participate in acts of the humane, so too

can the human sometimes degenerate into something far more animalistic.

91

When a despot has finally been removed from power, the violent overthrow is generally quite bloody, noisy, and confused. The entire region becomes enveloped in the dust kicked up by those arriving to bear corpses through the streets. Yet, when the madness ends — as all madness does eventually — and its ferocity has abated — the stricken bodies now laying quite harmlessly armed and silent — there will arrive a terrible stillness, a recognition of an inhumane presence in the world. Vengeance it seems, though momentarily an invigorating feeling of glory, is nothing more than an animal's need to survive which leaves the humane in us with nothing much to do but weep.

92

The more we *live* like an animal, the more likely we are to *act* like one — only worse.

93

The common man is not much more than a domesticated animal — sometimes dressed in a suit and tie — but always on the hunt and never much concerned with what occurs beyond the confines of his perceived — often instinctual — interests.

94

At different times in our lives we must remove ourselves from the goal-driven obsessions of everyday living if we are to reap the benefits of human consciousness. After all, no one can meditate about which goals are proper to pursue if actively engaged in an earnest hunt to achieve them. In the rush to accomplish these feats we often act reflexively and without much conscious awareness of ourselves or the world around us. We are, in other words, pushed along by the waters of a raging rapids while possessing the delusion that we can steer our course. Yet, under such conditions we are not much more splendid or excellent than any of the other species in creation.

95

It's a statistical fact that the severely ignorant reproduce at a much higher rate than those who are more wise and cautious. Eventually, this small detail can reverse the very evolution of humanity. Unless the ignorant can be inspired to act more humanely or small contingents of wise and thoughtful souls sustain themselves somehow during these ages of oblivion, the human race — at least as a species distinctive from the animal — will perish from the face of the earth.

96

Man, too, can be tamed — as can the tiger and the elephant — but this hardly affords him special status above the animal.

97

The contemporary man finds the sexual and the sensuous in everything he perceives just like any animal. His psyche — still rather impulsive and undeveloped — remains fixated upon the primitive concerns of the mammal, the allure of instinct. As long as he allows himself to be manipulated by nature in this manner, he will fail to cultivate a uniquely human perspective — a spirit enlightened by the mind and the imagination to possibilities hitherto thought the domain of the divine alone. A person devoted to bread, water, money, and lust is consumed by issues too distracting to expect the evolution of his spirit as well.

98

Man is a relatively scarce species in a world overabundant with animals and brutes.

99

Our own unconscious mind is often thought to be something that is, while dark and mysterious, nevertheless tempting in its overall appeal. Yet, the unconscious hides in the shadows for a reason, since monstrous can be its form. All of the gruesomely natural propensities of the human soul lie collected there as limbs upon the animal. Its eyes are fashioned of past deeds sooner to be forgotten. Its stomach is a lascivious pit of appetite — unquenchable — which might steal ripe souls from their living trees and eat them raw.

100

Man, in defense of his own atrocious nature, will often refuse reason and insight in favor of the more pleasurable pursuits of frivolity and distraction. He hides from the light of his own good sense to frolic in the shadows with his animal drives.

101

The only thing self-evident about mankind's "natural" state of equality is modern man's unwavering belief in it.

102

Contemporary man has so fetishized the sexual urge that it no longer even resembles anything human. Further, his impulse to destroy and dominate is given heroic worship while any bad behavior is often excused as the product of some unfortunate circumstance. He views any form of censure to be an infringement on some fundamental right, yet he is more than willing to censure others when they oppose him. In fact, his entire relationship to the world is an attempt to establish his power in some fashion. He has retreated, it seems, back into the caves and jungles of *natural* man.

103

Man enslaved by his instincts is oppressed by unseen forces in opposition to his own more conscious — and moral — will. This is the tyranny of the "natural" man.

104

Man finally emerges from the primordial ooze and arrogantly proclaims himself worthy of rights and special treatment due to the naturally superior stature of humankind. Yet, since men are often entirely unwilling to conceive of some perspective beyond the human in general and their own blind self-interest in particular, their perception is necessarily compromised. Mankind's notion of superiority then is largely perceived through a lens soiled by delusion and prejudice.

105

We can lose our instinct for self-preservation when fragility, suffering, and danger become merely vague abstractions — so far removed from our everyday encounter with life as to prove almost entirely meaningless. We have grown, it seems, quite complacent with our longevity and our good fortune — imagining them both to be, fallaciously, long.

106

We can often grow quite hostile to our own fate and so attempt to *take* what Nature does not immediately intend. The results are generally disastrous because we are rather ill-prepared for a future which we have largely bullied into existence. Greek tragedy arises from conditions such as these and yet we seem to yearn for these fortunes nonetheless.

107

Contemporary man's overall attitude toward existence—the manner in which he perceives of life in general — is often one of profound disrespect, a resentment perhaps that Nature doesn't care for him more. He displays an outright disdain for the sacred and so engages in religion and politics instead. His hatred of all things complex and mysterious produces in him a love of the superficial and so he scorns the very notion of depth itself. Yet, the person who would choose to allow his life to deteriorate in such a way — the greatest of all blasphemies — should have no fear of missing some eternal reward for his misdeeds. His life will be punishment enough.

108

If man cannot control one of the most primal and forceful aspects of his instinctual nature — the drive for sex — he will find he has great difficulty governing much of his life as well — slave as he can be to instinct.

109

A person releasing himself from the shackles he's borne for years will likely just as readily chain himself to another in the process.

110

Justice does not exist in Nature because it's a social construct existing solely in the mind of man. Its responsibility rests with man alone and arises because of something within him that yearns for it. Perhaps it's nothing more than the ardent insistence of a weak and pitiful creature who demands that others consider his safety as well as their own. Regardless, justice is a particular perspective shared by a particular group of people at a particular time. It evolves as people evolve to a certain degree, but it is *not* progressively improving toward some ideal concept of perfect justice. Instead, it's gradually reimagined and modified to meet the expectations of its most recent supporters. While the living may sanctimoniously believe that they are more enlightened than their ancestors, the fact remains that what they consider justice is often little more than prejudice writ large. Unfortunately, it's the kind of prejudice that is so unconsciously engrained within any of our own particular understandings that we are often unable to perceive of it as anything other than something true and eternal.

111

Even among the greatest civilizations there were only a few men who lived truly virtuous lives. The vast majority of men in any society are, and have always been, — at least instinctually — selfish, violent, easy to anger, impatient, and arrogant to the core. So, such men need guidance and wisdom in order to overcome their very natures. Yet, their notion of justice and morality will be heavily influenced by whatever was presented to them in childhood, which can lead to blind devotion toward some wicked regime — or the unfortunate creation of one. The greater mass of men generally waste their days and years in conversations destined to speed them to their graves. They exchange the finer things in life for those which most amuse and openly mock the person who attempts to live according to some higher principle than ignorance, indulgence, and debauchery. They laze about their day like a 13 year old boy and pray that they are not taxed too strenuously by anything in particular. All of this and more, of course, can be observed in any age, but the sheer number of indifferent, base, and immodest men in contemporary society makes the truly great man hard to see at all — immersed as he is in a sea of inhumanity.

112

There's a fine balance that must be maintained between our need to stretch out and perhaps exceed the boundaries of our nature from time to time and the necessity that we accept life as it is presented to us. Quite often we may refuse our own true destiny and push against the fabric of our fate to such an extent that we leave a deep tear in it. This rip in the spiritual structure of our lives precedes the collapse of a particular destiny that had been waiting for us all along.

113

Suicide is the childish rejection of fate while at the same

time sealing it forevermore.

114

Contemporary entertainment has led many to perceive of life as something with a definitive moment or two that ultimately determines one's fortune — true love united, evil destroyed, the hero's return, etc. Yet, no such moment exists when destiny is decided once and for all since fate itself, like life, is continuous— only death has the final say.

115

The balance between our own acceptance of fate and the desire to enact our will upon the world is quite difficult to maintain even for the wisest among us. It should be little wonder then that mankind as a whole has so badly failed to keep its poise over the centuries — after all, few of us seem to show any prolonged tendency to sacrifice our self-interests to anything other than our own happiness. The vast majority of us seem to desperately need the parental authority of law and religion to civilize our instincts and surrender our superficial desires.

116

Vengeful men tear at the world with all their might in the vain and bitter hope of striking a significant blow to life — a blow so fierce at times that they imagine it might somehow frighten death.

117

"Order, even at great cost!" is the mantra of the living dead. It is they who so desperately wish for eternal, universal, and unchanging moral laws to exist, so much so that they begin to rigidly fashion their own —

generally those better suited to a particular ideology. These principles are the invention of a mind that desires sterility, order, and ultimately death.

118

The more consistently we deny — or otherwise distract ourselves from — the overwhelming issue of our own death, the less likely that we are to live at all — at least with any awareness, wisdom, or understanding.

119

Death is such an unknown, an entirely incomprehensible possibility, that we are unable to imagine it properly. Even the most imaginative genius cannot truly conceive of a world without her in it. So, when we attempt to perceive of our utter demise and eradication from the planet, we often forget to eliminate our consciousness too. Instead, we imagine our awareness still present in the world, removed from its body and waiting patiently for a good seat at the funeral.

120

Apart from pleasurable literary contributions, happy endings do not truly exist in the world unless death brings to an end a life lived in absolute and appalling misery.

121

A humanist generally cares for and believes in the sanctity of the human being, but he is often less concerned for the humane treatment of other creatures as well. The humanist, in other words, usually possesses a prejudice for his own species or tribe and this subtle form of bigotry can ultimately manifest itself in some profoundly inhumane practice.

122

For any human to rank superior to an animal requires more than just the protracted suffering of one's mother in the birthing room. It requires education, and cultivation, and patience, and love, and so many other virtuous contributions, both great and small, and each in the right proportion, that most people simply spurn the whole process, choosing instead to laze about the day in a kind of self-imposed intellectual stupor.

123

Modern man so often hastens himself to death, rushing towards it as if he were late for an appointment.

124

The speed and hullabaloo of everyday life — set, it appears, at the rate that contemporary man enjoys it most — allows one to race through life without having to confront death but once. Yet, in this very refusal to truly face the reality and finality of death, we likewise — and to the same extent — generally fail to perceive a higher state of existence, the opening of a spiritual dimension of thought.

125

A terrible silence underscores all the music of the spheres — the fragile melody of death lightly moaning beneath the noisy dissonance of the living.

126

The mountaineer who seeks to scale the very heights of

human achievement and sit atop that peak, above his peers, shall find no tears among them if he should fail. For his victories are largely perceived as their defeats.

127

War is an explosion of the masculine powers upon the earth — so loud that entire nations become deafened to the cries of the feminine and her sisters.

128

Society still forces the feminine instinct to contort and conform to the strong-arming of the masculine. The world would be better served, however, to allow the feminine the freedom to rule on her own terms — without having to resort to the masculine tendency to coerce.

129

War provides a peek into an ugly reality of life, a reality quite contrary to the experience of someone raised during times of peace. War suggests that all men are expendable, little more than plastic pawns in some tragic game played by peevish fools befuddled with power and ideology. War renders life itself meaningless, dismissing it as something largely insignificant unless sacrificed to the larger cause. War welcomes the inhumane and even serves as a catalyst to keep it flourishing.

130

A peaceful world with no significant war or conflict is as much of a utopian dream as the notion of some perfect union between the lion and the lamb. It must be passionately encouraged nonetheless.

131

There are certain people for whom war is an arena in which they excel primarily because civilization is a burden to them. The complexities of justice are transformed to decisions of life and death in a war zone and such warriors find these easy distinctions illuminating. In addition, the battlefield allows for, and even promotes, viciousness, deceit, and indifference. So, if a person were already prone to such conditions, he would find much to satisfy him.

132

"My son is not a murderer," claim the mothers who would send their sons to war. Yet, men's hearts are more than capable of performing actions quite unimaginable to her.

133

The soldier who hoped to achieve immortality through the memory of mankind, if he could awaken one hundred years after his own death, would find it strange to note that his sacrifices went largely unnoticed. No doubt he too marched off to war awed by the reality of commerce and the delusion of propaganda. Yet, if we were to abandon the notion of immortality altogether and perceive of life as something finite and fragile we might be more inclined to finally begin treating each other well — with sympathy and compassion.

134

Democratization and the global reach of technology make it more important than ever for us to think for ourselves. However, the vast majority of us rarely contemplate either deeply or critically about much of anything. Thus, the inhumane resumes its reign into the new millennium and the old war with enlightenment continues unabated.

135

The historical trend toward less overall world violence is a result of the expanded role of governments to tamp down upon the beastly urges of man and remold them into a passion for nationality, sports, and other silly amusement. While certainly a more humane outlet for these volatile energies — far preferable to outright violence and cruelty — there exist even greater heights for which we might strive. Nevertheless we seem quite content with remaining lobotomized and domesticated instead.

136

The administration of the death penalty demonstrates that even the most "civilized" among us can act as cruelly as any murderer. Those who would so haughtily condemn others to die and allow such punishments to occur while maintaining a sense of morally superior indifference are not much less callous than the killer who soullessly buries his victim alive. A murderer, after all, has his own hubristic reasons and justifications for his actions — tragically flawed though they may be. He, too, feels somewhat blameless — or at least left without a choice — given the circumstances of the crime. The executioner meanwhile is generally motivated by revenge which he then coldly rationalizes as an act of justice. He will not even allow suicide for the condemned, almost salivating to carry out the deed himself.

137

Sometimes hate is all that remains of one's memory.

138

Violence is a form of monosyllabic communication used primarily by those who have no other resource from which to draw but the rock and the pitchfork. These men express themselves in explosions and bloodshed because they feel they have no facility with words. Besides, the development of good character that arises from — among other experiences, no doubt — a comprehensive education in the sciences and the humanities which should then inspire a more curious and open heart and mind, a more thoughtful and generous spirit, generally proves to be a less efficient and more time consuming solution to conflict than simple, violent eradication. In other words, the viciousness of the beast is more easily accessible.

139

Any governmental system that accentuates competition over cooperation will ultimately succumb to the oppression of the sociopath, whom it favors.

140

Politics should be left to those who enjoy a kind of slavery to the mob's caprice. After all, no one generally leads a group anywhere it doesn't already wish to go. Unless, of course, the beast possesses weaponry.

141

An obsession with maintaining one's good name is a peculiar kind of slavery to the perceptions of the mob.

142

The base materialist would ask us to follow insecurity and vice to their logical end: fulfillment — often by any means necessary.

143

The history of mankind is plentiful with examples of man the fanatic. The 20th century, however, seems to have molded these ideological extremists — all competing to gain some imaginary foothold. Wisdom in such an era — the perception that resides between the extremes and the seeming duality of Nature — appears as a kind of weakness to fools who are so certain of their convictions. In this circumstance, wisdom is barely audible among the din of shouting partisans.

144

The fundamentalist seeks to force a commonality of thought and belief, a conformity with those perspectives which more closely resemble the instinctual drives of a golden-mantled howler monkey.

145

Too many systematizers and theorists are little more than extremists and tyrants themselves — forcing life or knowledge to fit neatly into the prefabricated world of their own ideology.

146

Contemporary man often resides in a state of suspended adolescence which drives his fickle urges and causes him to remain almost entirely anxious and eternally dissatisfied. We should instead rise to the heights to which our best is capable and resist the passionate lure of our less mature instincts.

147

Fallow youth is not some disease from which all of us will soon recover. On the contrary, some of us live with it for the entirety of our lives.

148

The faster a society functions, the more those within it begin to suffer from the sickness of continuous motion.

149

One entirely instinctual element of the human personality is the social perspective of the herd. Man participates in the herd mentality whenever he would have all men — or at least a large contingency — act as *he* would act or conform to the norms of the collective. In fact, it is often criminal to do otherwise. The norms, however, are too frequently prescribed by means of some great traditional ignorance or the thoughtlessness of the mob. Rarely are laws duly considered by the sage in power anymore. Instead, the philosopher king has devolved into an ideological politician.

150

Man often gladly receives and accepts the opinions, beliefs, and ideals of any group with which he affiliates because he greatly appreciates that in the group these opinions, beliefs, and ideals are absolved of his responsibility.

151

No society can maintain justice and nobility within its

borders when its citizenry is composed of mostly wicked men — no matter how sublime a nation's origins.

152

Contemporary society cannot accept the blame for the majority of mankind's childishness. After all, man has for centuries acted like a childish fool. Even Homer depicts two "great" men, Agamemnon and Achilles, locked together in a stubborn, immoral, and immature confrontation about what each believes should be their due — namely the attractive slave girl, Briseis. In each case, justice is perceived as obtaining some advantage that is fundamentally both selfish and cruel.

153

Man often seeks to find some cause in which he might happily surrender his will. He feels the terrible burden of mature responsibility and the struggle of indecision inherent in any conscious choice. If he does forfeit his will — relinquishing it to god, to country, to spouse, to drink, or to whatever he might choose — it is as if he were born a child again. In fact, this has been his secret wish all along: a return to immaturity and the simple-minded life.

154

The golden age of the philosopher was essentially usurped by the storytelling narrative of religion because most of us are far too intellectually lazy and spiritually vacant to reach an understanding of the world that isn't authoritarian.

155

We can often appear quite *incapable* of insight or moral

understanding at times, more apt to respond like a cornered wolverine than a creature possessing any great humanity.

156

The thinkers who considered Christianity as some grand monument representing the best in Greek thought were a naïve bunch who spent their energies misinterpreting Greek ideas and endorsing those translations that best suited their purposes of persuasion. While this early Christian, to his credit, did analyze Greek thought as something of a literary piece, his ancestors received these texts as universally fundamental to any conception of truth. This confusion leads to a kind of religious understanding more appropriate for young children than sophisticated minds.

157

We must generally pay with increments of our soul for refusing to follow the divine within ourselves. Yet, since so many of us value material existence above spiritual abstractions anyway, the loss will not *appear* too significant — at least not to those who are so afflicted.

158

Much of our past greatness is merely the expression of a great imagination.

159

Even the ideal of Eden itself appears as a place not much different than the blight of some city ghetto without the devoted care of true, artistic gardeners who tend to it.

160

The contemporary political conservative bleats and whines against the oppressive authority of those who know far more than he ever might about any particular subject, yet he bows like a child on his knees before the imagined authority of some omniscient Papi.

161

If we began to truly imagine our every action as a sacrifice given to the world for its betterment, our actions might just become more considered and thoughtful.

162

We may no longer even perceive of the divine in the abstract anymore. Once an image attaches to an abstract idea, it often becomes the idea itself — similar to what occurs when a photograph comes to represent a memory. The image becomes the idol of worship and the original urge toward the spiritual is lost — perhaps forever — in the quest for concrete truth.

163

All "religion" first developed and then elaborated upon the notion of the humane within the domain of men. These were the early voices of the most ethical of us at the time. Yet, as times have changed, fundamentalist religion remains antiquated at best. It is now somewhat marginalized precisely because it stubbornly refuses to waver in its understanding of divinity. The religious have become violent or ignorant in their beliefs. Now, more often than not, religion expresses — or at least has come to symbolize — something of the *in*humane.

164

The religious fundamentalist is often the first to presume that his view should hold dominion over the thoughts of all others. Yet, what weak-minded "deity" would require an absolute, unalterable, and uninspired perspective of the universe while simultaneously creating a cosmos that is infinitely complex, variable, and beyond the ability of any of us to fully comprehend? We only conceive of a static world in order to *avoid* the "divine" rather than describe it in any way. The fundamentalist imposes this spiritual monstrosity upon the earth in a desperate attempt to make this delusion true through the recruitment of others to share in the mirage, thus coupling it to legitimacy.

165

Man proves himself a liar and a fool if he declares to definitively know the absolute truth of anything. It is his lack of intellectual humility that leads him to believe so conclusively in his own convictions, but it is a decided lack of knowledge that would have him claim to understand any truth as such. He is the anti-Plato, wise only because he *imagines* that he knows.

166

Comfort, security, and certainty are all means by which we often attempt to return to the womb and retroactively refuse the gift of life altogether.

167

For the human mind, the world and the things within it seem to exist as some variation of true or false — right or wrong — because our mind is constituted to understand existence in this manner. This does not mean that things actually exist in this way, only that we perceive it as such. A sin, of course, is committed if we begin to imagine that our perceptions should be forcibly adopted by the majority.

168

The person who fails to compromise when a greater need arises — particularly those concessions to moral necessity — betrays all of humanity with his stubborn pride. He imagines himself, poor fool, to be the arbiter of his fate, the rational creator of his fortune. He truly does not believe that character paints his destiny.

169

The more ardently we desire our world to be a utopian paradise the more violently must we press all of the messy, chaotic, irrational, complex, and otherwise wonderful elements of existence into the mold of the perfect ideal.

170

A good sign that one is dealing with a fundamental extremist is the man's inability to laugh at himself. He is, after all, the serious hero of this drama being created and staged within the opera house of his own mind. Yet humor undermines this solemnity and generally reveals him as someone rather foolish instead.

171

The fundamentalist is a fundamental failure as a human being, long ago having surrendered the fear of uncertainty to the cowardice of the ready-made truth.

Such a missionary does not inhabit a character as much as merely dons a rigid mask.

172

The contemporary man is bombarded by sensations to such a degree that he confuses them for reality itself and so lingers too long among these lotus trees thinking them to be a holy fruit. Meanwhile, divinity often passes unnoticed through his heart as he grubs after the next great sensuous experience.

173

Righteousness is often the state of being most closely associated with delusion and hypocrisy — both conditions of monumental significance to contemporary hopes for peace.

174

Many innocents have been literally and metaphorically nailed to the cross in the name of justice. Christ, for instance, and even Socrates to a certain extent, were both "crucified" by civilizations greatly concerned with notions such as the good, the just, and the righteous. This should serve to humble any society that believes it can ever truly imitate the ideal of justice. The best it might accomplish is to treat everyone the same under the law, but, as with all human enterprises, this is often fraught with inherent uncertainties which can never be entirely resolved. For example, a great many "criminals" are driven by forces outside their own control or consciousness, so who might know enough to say with absolute certainty the guilt or innocence of anyone else? Thus, the death penalty demonstrates a civilization's lack of understanding and displays an ignorant and appalling arrogance in the face of the mysterious abyss.

175

In many cases we must rely on the assessment of others to determine the nature of our own understanding of reality — colorblindness, for instance, is a perceptual disagreement about what makes something "red," or "green," or "blue." We must verify, in other words, what our senses perceive lest they deceive us in some way. We must gain confirmation of the world from those around us, our contemporaries. This is true of our beliefs as well. Yet, so many of us in the contemporary age imagine ourselves to be autonomous and self-sufficient, offended by the very notion of our own dependence.

176

The five senses, of course, are extremely important to us. Our life certainly seems to be impossible without at least a few of them; however, we often forget that without deep, reflective thought *about* these sensual experiences, they would possess no significant meaning whatsoever.

177

There are two very distinct — though intertwined — worlds thus far discovered in human history: the realm of thought and the kingdom of sensation — the abstract and the concrete. Thought is an expression of the abstract while sensation is more of a physical interpretation of concrete, tangible experience. The humane belongs primarily to the kingdom of thought as the mind breeds moral principles and lofty notions meant to raise man to nobly meet the challenges of his character. The inhumane, on the other hand, often arises from the despotic command of the senses, the tyranny of the material world.

178

Eros is more often a puerile little sprite — prone to fits of caprice and outright villainy — than something of such profound enormity that we can hardly contain ourselves from fixating upon it.

179

There will come a day when we will have to tell our children of a sky that once was blue, radiant, and spectacular. We will have to account for what mankind has done to the forests and the oceans and the other creatures with whom we share this earth. We will have to bear witness to the devastation that we have created and the misery that we've spread. It may be too late by then, of course. The fragile planet will have already begun to crumble away.

The descent

1

These are the dark ages, no doubt — despite the glittering of lights and the glamour of stars being photographed along the boulevards. These are the dark ages because the shadows are upon the walls already. Another great civilization is about to fall because it has become too greedy, ignorant, and lazy to sustain itself. While voices may cry out a warning of the coming devastation, they cannot be heard amid the roar of the crashing wave.

2

Glitter, glitz, and glam inhabit the unworldly scene of spectacle — resembling the natural world in image alone while possessing none of its profundity. Yet, we will often abandon our souls to these shadows on the wall, sparing ourselves, perhaps, the pangs of self-consciousness, but impairing the more genuine destiny of our lives in the process.

3

Men are far too overly concerned as to whether they might succeed at some particular vocation, but seem to have little concern at all for their status as a humane and reflective individual.

4

It is with the greatest difficulty that we accept, if we ever come to accept it at all, that we each are to fall like so many dry, autumn leaves. Instead, we expect an endless spring or summer without even a hint of frost upon the air.

5

It is no longer a rescue to save a drowning swimmer from the same shallow waters for the hundredth time. It becomes, instead, a peculiar way of life.

6

Contemporary man is generally an assortment of short-sighted individuals who go about their lives squinting at everything in the distance and misinterpreting the shadows cast by a falling sun. Yet, most of these men are entirely unaware that their vision is in any way impaired, impeded, or impossible.

7

It's not always quite so obvious to know if we have slipped into the shadows from a virtuous life. In fact, it's sometimes too late when we discover that we have indeed fallen far from the path of a good life and into the abyss of vice and ignorance. Those who mock the idea of such a possibility are often the first to fall.

8

Humanity has evolved and developed in fits and starts rather than through some fluid, linear, or rational narrative. Man may progress in his civility one moment and then prove himself barbaric in the moment that follows. In this manner we as a collective have risen from the ignorance of the animal to the understanding of the sage many times over the centuries. Similarly we have fallen from the heights of divine accomplishment to the dregs of human despair. It is the plight of the lonely individual to wrestle with these forces of history, these dizzying contrasts of good and evil, love and hate, and all the many more. These are the same forces that we may find within us too.

9

The planet earth can be seen as a rather curious vessel, a ship of fools sailing through the darkened cosmos as a beacon of light with no sense of direction.

10

The pleasure that many of us receive in deceiving ourselves and in being deceived by others means that there will remain a large contingency of fools who sit watching the shadows dance upon the walls of Plato's cave while remaining steadfastly obstinate of ever leaving the place.

11

We often imagine that truth eventually rises out of the dark shadows of the unknown and into the light of day as something akin to an evolutionary path of fate. Yet, more often than not, such "truths" are merely the concentration of some unfamiliar prejudice.

12

The existential suicide is *not* metaphorically trapped, as David Wallace Foster contends, in some fire-engulfed high rise that forces him to jump rather than experience the horror of the flames. After all, the average suicide is not confronted by a genuine physical threat and generally faces no such urgent choice in electing to die or withdraw. The actual conditions of our existence are not so dramatic, or as clearly delineated, as Foster imagines. Rather, the existential suicide is trapped in the *belief* that he is faced with a similar dilemma as the poor soul in the high rise. He *imagines* the flames and jumps because he feels this to be his circumstance when, in fact, the fire is born entirely of his own imagination. His mind has created a mirage that supports the distorted perspective of his own worldview. He perceives only the dark side of the moon and so concludes the entire planet to be in shadow.

13

We should be as wary to wander into a darkened jungle as to linger among his fellow humans in the broad light of day. In fact, there are times when it might be in our better interest to face the hungry tiger instead.

14

To the great, wide, infinite galaxy, the earth is but an infinitesimal speck upon which a stubborn fungus continues to grow and flourish: the thorny ego of man.

15

In the contemporary world, we have made it so that we must sin simply in order to live sometimes.

16

We often mistake evil as a rather permanent state of being that can be easily recognized in the eyes of those possessing a blackened heart. However, great evil is oftentimes the result of a mere weakness in character conjoined with some unique and unfortunate circumstance. In fact, evil results from a certain blindness in our character, our refusal to examine the depths of our own prejudice which then reveals itself — sometimes horrifically — under certain historical conditions. Yet, generally there will be no outward sign of evil on the face of any one of us for it resides much deeper within, a latent darkness in our soul that we will not admit. In such cases, evil is nothing more than sheer possibility.

17

The truly good man is difficult to find. He's not simply some homespun cliché such as "the man who provides for his family and helps out his fellow man" or "the man who provides service to the community." He may be all these things, of course, and more, but the good man, through some act of individuation, separates himself from the crowd. He must then proceed as something of a lonely satellite, orbiting the rest of mankind for his own space in the sky. He is alone, but he need not despair if he is well-read since all of antiquity travels with him. These great ancestors, too, persevered against the vast darkness of their age to splash their talent upon the canvas of the world and demonstrate something unique and wondrous about the species "man." However, these men exist on the periphery of contemporary life. Others, though human by appearance, choose to follow their own natural — though generally not shameful — tendencies, mocking all the while those who attempt to rise above them. These creatures lack the proper foresight to notice the slow development of habit formed by indulging in their less reputable traits. Such men are typically not much more than children left unsupervised. The wise should remember that while Einstein tinkered for years alone in his workroom, the majority of his contemporaries bickered over pastries and other such nonsense. Only the future can generally perceive the true genius because her peers usually find her somewhat odd.

18

We will generally only serve the common good if we imagine our own good intertwined within it. Yet, it often requires a sharp intellect and rich imagination in order to properly recognize the association between one's own good and the good of others. It requires an ability to comprehend paradox and abstraction as well, an aptitude, that is, with complexity. Unfortunately, these seem as traits quite uncommon indeed for a species disposed to apathy and inertia.

19

The notion of evil as a consequence of good gone terribly awry assumes a goodness to human nature that is generally nonexistent without consistent labor, wisdom, and guidance.

20

A nation — essentially an idea that any collective agrees to, or is forced to, share — is incapable of morality since it has no conscience. It's only as good as those who inhabit its borders and even then it must necessarily provoke some brand of evil on the unfortunate souls left out of the entire discussion: the others.

21

The agents of the inhumane are difficult to perceive. One cannot simply identify the enemy by the colors of their uniform. In fact, our own worst enemy is generally ourselves. Evil is, after all, quite often cloaked in the garb of the familiar as that of the strange.

22

The definitive contrast between good and evil can discourage the inhumane condition of indifference that sometimes arises when we attempt to raise ourselves above the notion of morality itself. In other words, our attempt at transcendence beyond moral ideas themselves generally leads to some greater immorality. The sage, of course, knows that all is one and true transcendence arrives with the recognition of this fact.

23

The materials of materialism are usually not anything destructive in themselves. Many *things*, in fact, should be prized quite highly and sought after with a committed — though restrained — passion. The evil that arises from a faithfulness to materialism is found in the heart of man — in his obsession with the things of this world and his utter indifference to that which is not so readily available to the brute senses of instinct.

24

Evil, almost without exception, arises from the "truth" of some ideology — any notion that has arrested the mind and enslaved the identity of man. Individual acts of evil generally serve the needs of a particularly rigid brand of intellectual idolatry.

25

We moderns would find it quite difficult to be led out of slavery today — or even to conceive of ourselves as enslaved. After all, we do so entirely loves our chains.

26

Evil could be eradicated from the world if each of us were to spend the majority of our time reforming *ourselves* instead of others.

27

The root of all evil can be found in ignorance of one kind or another. The difficulty, however, is that it is impossible to eliminate something which is itself an absence. Ignorance is always lacking some important element of a proper understanding. It's in need of additional features if it might evolve into a virtue of any sort. In this manner, ignorance is subtracted through addition.

28

The wrong is often right under certain conditions as good can be evil in a particular light. The trouble is that we must learn to properly perceive these circumstances and for that we must surrender our perception to the imaginative realm of possibility. We must, in other words, accept that very little in our world is as concrete as we would like to believe. We must be willing to suspend our desire for certainty.

29

The person who does not believe in the existence of genuine evil — seated especially within the confines of his own heart — is so naïve about himself and his world that it borders on the childish.

30

The ignorance of the mob often allows it to feel quite righteous in its crusade against its enemies and the certainty with which it wields this "intelligence" often releases devastation as a consequence.

31

Our inability to predict the consequences of our actions does not excuse us from the immorality of our deeds. After all, we can only plead ignorance if we have applied due diligence in our attempting to know.

32

Once we abolished slavery in most of the civilized world,

it seems we then turned quite diligently to the pursuit of enslaving ourselves with industry, delusion, hypocrisy, and willful ignorance.

33

"Divinity" is desecrated through no impurity or corruption but by the continual refusal of mankind to recognize divinity as such. Generally we are woefully ignorant of the divine and look to the heavens like a child for comfort. Yet, the further we stray from our own depths the more distant will seem the concept of divinity altogether.

34

Perhaps the most detrimental aspect of the contemporary character is his inability to truly understand the world from the perception of someone only slightly different from himself. Unfortunately, he is also often shamefully ignorant of his own condition and unwilling to make even the most half-hearted of efforts to rectify the situation.

35

No one can be held responsible — at least not rationally — for deeds performed in a state of ignorance. Yet, we must know as much as others believe we *should* or they are apt to ignorantly stoop to some cruel form of punishment in revenge.

36

An individual life is a well-constructed narrative pieced together from the various fragments of experience while those pieces that do *not* fit are promptly banished and forgotten.

37

There will be no peace among men until they can recognize the depth of their own ignorance and so begin to reject ideology altogether. Science — the newest of creeds — can sometimes create the illusion of a more comprehensive understanding when it has merely served to change and multiply the questions. This is not the fault of science, of course, but it does accentuate the faults inherent in the judgment of some practitioners — they who are so desperate for certainty.

38

Egoism is an expression of profound ignorance. After all, man can think so highly of himself only if he ignores or refuses to acknowledge facts about himself which refute this conclusion. The adulterer, for instance, may pride himself on his punctuality to such a degree that he feels somehow superior to others simply because of this one feature of his personality. His pride, of course, seems rather odd in the face of his more significant failings.

39

In stark contrast to the naiveté of John Stuart Mill, we generally do *not* know better than others about what best serves our own interests. In fact, we are often quite wrong about such things, blinded as we are by prejudice, ignorance, and pride. Therefore, to trust our own opinion is often to endorse the proliferation of error.

40

The apocalypse will not arrive by sin but through some means of ignorance — the foundation for almost all the shameful displays of man.

41

We should be ever skeptical of our own character and motives for acting lest we begin to imagine ourselves as somehow inherently good, righteous, and pure. They of such moral certainty find it quite effortless to point their fatted finger at the evil of others but remain entirely ignorant or deluded about their own rather significant faults.

42

Far too many men imagine themselves speaking the truth when they are, in fact, only discussing the rationalizations for their own ignorant, uncritical, and childish beliefs.

43

It is not desires or passions which are responsible for our unhappiness but the excess of these qualities. However, it is more than simply these which humanity must learn to balance in life. Excess in all its many forms is something that must be modulated. While the excess of pleasure may seem, at least to the individual receiving it, something quite desirable, it should be obvious that eventually there will be a limit to such delight. After all, even excess itself, if left unattended, can lead to greater excess. In addition, the excesses of a single individual may significantly affect the lives of those who are entirely innocent of these kinds of overindulgences and are forced by circumstance to pay the consequences regardless. Thus, there seems to be some sort of a moral responsibility involved in choices that may appear otherwise isolated. Of course, no one can expect to be aware of all the many possible consequences of their choices, but we often choose ignorance in order to continue our excesses with a muted conscience.

44

In the vast complex universe of inner and outer space, a person who is aware of only one great thing — however deeply — is ignorant of far more than can be reasonably excused.

45

Americans in general continually suffer from the delusion that they hold sway over fortune somehow, as if their fate were something of a choice that they can either recognize or refuse. Often they equate providence with a decision about one's career and domestic situation, but those choices are mostly incidental since it is character which ultimately determines destiny. These men are filled with hope and expectation, but they remain ignorant of themselves and their world. Americans are regularly shocked by tragedy and failure because they do not prepare themselves, in body or in mind, for dreadful consequences — having either experienced so few in life or in desperate retreat from an exposure to so many. In any case, these souls often perceive society as a secondary caregiver who will provide comfort and security during times of greatest need — much as they view their god. Bitter disillusionment is often delayed in perpetuity for the American because they have so many means of distraction from reality that they are able to keep hope incessantly alive. Yet, when bitterness does arise, it is often understood — bizarre occurrences aside — as a kind of disease that man brings upon himself. Further, any mistakes made in their youth, Americans believe naively, can be easily put behind them with age. And, at least on the surface, they appear to be correct in their assessment. They do survive quite nicely with a smile and a handshake, happily chittering with their neighbors about the weather or the latest fashion to hit New York; however, they rarely live with any sense of insight or wisdom. Such men also may begin to endure mysterious pangs of consciousness and depression — though these should not be seen as punishments of any kind. They are instead symptomatic of growth and the budding awareness of a spirit that can keep silent no more. Of course, even this voice can be overwhelmed by some pleasant noises.

46

We moderns reject history and the influence of our ancestors at our own peril. Yet, we do so quite regularly nonetheless. We believe ourselves so unique in time that our ancestors cannot possibly have much to teach us. In fact, this is a rather common weakness of our kind — that the majority think themselves superior to those who did not know enough to survive the past. It seems we simply find it too difficult to imagine ourselves at the blind mercy of fate. Or else we know it all too well and our ignorance is a choice we make to keep ourselves distracted.

47

Rousseau's idea of a "noble" savage is ludicrous. Everyone must, of course, sacrifice certain freedoms on the altar of society. These sacrifices though generally enable us to lift ourselves above our baser, brutish nature and enjoy the more subtle aspects of cultivation and culture. The noble savage meanwhile is only noble if he remains completely isolated from other people who might otherwise serve to bring out the brute in him. Even in total isolation though, he appears less of a noble and more of a child — immature, unsophisticated, and prone to tantrums or some other extreme. Ignorance and nobility are hardly synonymous with one another.

48

Montaigne once remarked that we should not trouble ourselves as to what we should do when it becomes our turn to die since Nature will inform us sufficiently. Of course, this is true of most significant decisions in our lives as well. We may agonize over what to do, research all the alternatives, and lay out an entirely rational plan for how we should proceed, but it will ultimately be a kind of Kierkegaard-Ian leap of faith that propels us to move forward. It is our character that will reveal the way. However, a lack of it, too, will cause the ruin of far more than just ourselves.

49

Events that contradict the precious chronicle that we have created for our lives will generally be met with despondency, depression, and despair until we either incorporate this event into our own historical fiction or alter the overall narrative significantly. Madness can quickly overwhelm us otherwise.

50

The day of reckoning will soon enough arrive when mankind's children will have to pay for his luxuries, his ignorance, and his somnambulistic indifference.

51

No one can ever truly know what's best for him or her because we remain so unaware of future consequences. Yet, few of us will attempt to lift our own veil of ignorance to any significant degree so that our fate at least somewhat reflects the intuitions and intellect of its agent. Instead, most of us simply assume that what's best for us must be necessarily whatever happened to have occurred.

52

In times of profound immaturity and great confusion, sexuality usurps the very nature of love.

53

Only young or otherwise immature minds will mock items of great significance and only then because they don't truly understand them.

54

A nostalgia for one's childhood is often masking the more insidious desire to return to a state of ignorance or oblivion wherein we might escape the more mature realities of our existence.

55

There are no truly simple ideas in life, only simple people.

56

It is perhaps true that once we mature we must put away our childish things. Yet, this means we must put aside our literal belief in gods as well, derived as they are from a childish understanding of the cosmos.

57

Humanity, it seems, has returned to infancy in its old age.

58

The child truly engaged in play is generally participating in life at the very height of her creative powers. She chooses the game for the most part and agrees to abide by its rules — sometimes amending them as she proceeds — but she possesses no grander scheme than to live the present moment in the splendor of the self-directed life — no matter how difficult that life may be. She will only abandon her play of necessity and then only for a brief respite before she will be drawn to it once again. However, when the child has grown and begins to put away her childish things, she may mistake this creative urge as some immature impulse and dispose of it dismissively. She might just as well lay her soul open to a butcher's knife and sell the divided pieces to the highest bidder.

59

When — or if — we come to realize that the vast majority of our contemporaries are essentially little more than mad children with most of the entitlements of adulthood at their disposal, we must learn to tread lightly around them, just as we might smartly elude a pride of hungry lions lounging on the rocks above.

60

Conformity, it should be noted, is not maturity. In fact, it is a brand of immaturity in that such a stance attempts to shirk the responsibility of true maturation by uncritically surrendering one's development to the familiarities of tradition.

61

The ideal of a more global governance will ultimately fail because no institution can possibly maintain control over such a large contingency of children.

62

Man seems greatly offended by any deity who has no personal attachment, affinity, or concern for him. Such a person possesses the ego of a child who demands that attention should be paid and the insecurity of the animal who remains always on the alert to safeguard his life. Only maturity and evolution can bring about a change in him, but religious fundamentalism retards this natural development and keeps man chained to his childhood, praying in vain that life provide something more satisfying to his desires.

63

There are some who believe that if something isn't easily achieved then it is largely unnecessary. The thinking is that fate will eventually provide any individual's destiny so there is no need to wrestle one's character into existence. While surrendering to forces outside of one's control is perfectly appropriate in many situations and even quite noble and wise in others, the compromise of one's humanity all too often results from the conformity to the authority of providence.

64

The majority of us, like little children, seek simple answers to complex questions. After all, we begin our search with the decided prejudice that simplicity lies beneath the surface of nature. So we content ourselves with simple thoughts and simple lives. Yet, it is the failure to recognize complexity — an inability to make sense of abstraction — that often doom our efforts to better ourselves in any significant way.

65

Ignorance is generally the fundamental cause of most evil in the world. Of course ignorance is also a treatable condition that can be greatly improved with even a modicum of patience, effort, humility, and understanding. However, the vast majority of us generally refuse to endure the necessary struggles with consciousness and ego that such progress would entail. Evil requires very little strength of character and even less comprehension of our responsibility toward the development of our own better nature.

66

Man often worries that he will be a burden to his children in old age because he secretly worries that he is a burden to them now. Sadly, it is too often true.

67

Translating a poetic text — primarily religious material — into more "readable" or "clearer" prose strips a work of all its vitality, rendering it "easier" to read but impossible then to fully understand. If a text has edified humanity for generations but no longer fuels that need because we are too illiterate or lazy to comprehend it with any depth, then it must wait until its audience returns — assuming we do not extinguish ourselves altogether. Meanwhile, what remains are rather banal and lifeless platitudes and stories which inspire only very small children or like-minded fools.

68

The fear of failure arises from the child's desire to remain a child, a babe in the mother's arms. What we ultimately fear, however, is maturity and separation. And this terror remains deep within the memory of every individual when we stumble forth to undertake some unfamiliar task.

69

Serving oneself while not simultaneously attending to humanity as a whole imitates the attitude of the young child who perceives that he resides at the very center of the universe and possesses no duties toward his family at all. Yet, no one achieves wisdom without maturity and maturity only arrives when sympathy — the virtue of selfless concern — has sufficiently bloomed.

70

There are so many children today who stoop to pray though they have long since grown away from religion. When lacking a suitable alternative, we often choose to remain rooted to our traditional custom. Hypocrisy doesn't terrify us nearly as much as an encounter with the unfamiliar.

71

The person who believes himself to be fortune's blessed child — generally concerned with little more than the operation of his elbow — is in many ways able to do so only because others allow it.

72

The vast majority of us don't possess the virtue of perseverance or the faith in anything other than a childish divinity. We essentially believe that *we* are all who matter.

73

With few exceptions, "God" has always been on the side of those with the largest armory. The true divine, however, doesn't take sides. Even humanity has no special influence with eternity.

74

If the dinosaurs had possessed the mental and physical capacities necessary to express themselves through art, their god, no doubt, would resemble the dinosaur in all its glory.

75

Any religion attempting to justify the suffering of children or innocents as some divine "plan" for the overall good has lost its moral authority to the anthropomorphic and proves itself so hopelessly addle-minded that it will soon accept any explanation as long as it sustains belief in the institution.

76

How we understand the "divinity" of our universe will often determine the nature of our society in many ways. The vicious, superstitious, and generally misogynistic aspects of any society based on strict religious orthodoxy is generally a reflection of the stringent, patronizing, and vengeful god from which such civilizations are founded. The staunch atheist meanwhile resides at the other extreme. He perceives a material universe that is essentially empty of spiritual significance so his culture is generally empty as well, centered upon bringing he and his friends closer to as much pleasure and contentment as they might be able to receive in one lifetime. Yet, even this contemporary malaise and confusion about the world arises from a rather confused and inarticulate conception of the "divine."

77

We often envision great individuals as "divine" or possessing some unattainable, ethereal quality as a means of shirking our own responsibility toward obtaining greatness for ourselves. After all, there does not appear to be anything particularly heavenly about us on the surface. Yet, the divine lies within.

78

There is no need for us to pray at the feet of some divine entity, but this will require that we find strength and spiritual subsistence on our own. Our "higher power" slowly arises from within — as it does for all — as soon as we begin to faithfully commit ourselves to its proper expression. Most will retreat from such work as they demand nothing more from enlightenment than what religious tradition already provides. They walk, in other words, along a path that was meant for someone else, attending services in some outward show of righteousness when, in fact, they exist in a state of existential limbo that *needs* to pray but has no real passion to do so — these are the reluctant atheists.

79

Family — whether biological or contrived — is the only protective unit for the individual. It is the first and last refuge for the solitary soul who is too weak to survive on his own. However, the slow decay and corruption of human character largely poisons the family field as well, allowing ogres to rule as kings and loosing savage beasts upon the nurseries.

80

From the perspective of a "divine," the concerns of men, at least the vast majority of them, are inconsequential and petty. We imagine that this little speck of dust upon which we reside — immersed, mind you, in the infinite expanse of the universe — possesses some unique significance solely because of our presence on it.

81

The black plague wiped out 40% of the European population. The dinosaur, that awesome creature of such enormous height, disappeared almost entirely. Yet, mankind — historically ignorant and fearfully deluded — wildly imagines that climate change does not offer a similar threat. We have become, after all, rather complacent and overly confident in the power of our technology to solve somewhat irreversible complications spawned from previous technology.

82

The religious fundamentalist lives according to one particular philosophical view precisely because he does not perceive of it as a philosophy at all. Instead he believes his religious tradition to be the only true perspective through which one receives redemption and salvation. If man is able to tolerate another religious faith nearby it will be generally due to similar goals of the two traditions. Yet, if the fundamentalist were to merely unclench his hold on the notion that his religious text is the only one that ultimately matters, he might see that a literary understanding of these ideas provides greater insight than a literal one. Of course, it also requires a passionate commitment to the labor of understanding.

83

The uncultured man is generally quite inhumane in some aspect of his existence as well. Only higher culture can reform him in any way, but he is often too enamored of politics, cartoons, and his own baser instincts to make much of an effort to change.

84

As the physicist has little respect for the theoretical opinion of the student who cannot set up a basic algebraic equation, the sage, too, cannot be expected to seriously consider the metaphysics of the religious fool: the fundamentalist.

85

Tongues often lie to coerce the ear into blind belief.

86

The fundamentalist has so rationalized and justified his actions with egotistical half-truths, delusions, and outright lies that he can't help but ultimately imagine himself as righteous. Therefore, he possesses no guilty conscience for any immoral deeds. After all, he has perfectly legitimate reasons — at least sensible to his own limited imagination — for perceiving of them as something honorable.

87

Pain need not be judged as an evil in all cases. For example, pain can serve as an early warning for disease. So, the recognition of pain as a kind of evil is a matter of human perspective to a certain degree. In fact, it would seem that through techniques such as meditation or hypnosis particular individuals can even train their minds to feel no pain at all, consciously eliminating the very will to live. Ultimately this is the fate of all literal religious doctrine. What was initially a great spiritual insight about the human condition — essentially that suffering is largely a result of one's perspective — becomes little more than a means of existential suicide.

88

The greatest danger of all evangelical religion — politics included — is generated from its tendency to encourage and inhabit a singular perspective. All events, actions, and claims are interpreted and understood in relation to but one unruly narrative.

89

The replacement religions of the crumbling Western facade all seem to spiritualize our desire for extraordinary material gain. The "power of positive thinking," for example, has spread its metaphysical contagion over a legion of fools who all hope to parlay its simplistic message into winnings more tangible than thought.

90

In many cases our entire spiritual context is framed by one narrative and incorporated into a single book. This is the myopic tragedy of much fundamentalist religious understanding in the contemporary world.

91

We all are artists in the sense that we must *create* a meaningful narrative for our lives and oversee the virtuous construction of our character. However, the fundamentalist, refusing such a calling, merely receives the established narrative into which he was born and awkwardly traces his life over it.

92

Fundamentalist religion — that communal tyranny — impoverishes true spirituality by subverting those most sublime and mysterious elements of the spirit with simplistic notions that any child might comprehend.

93

The contemporary religious devotee does not seek existential comfort or understanding from his tradition as much as he wants it to provide an escape.

94

There is nothing wrong with our finding comfort and consolation from a great many sources as we merrily move through our lives. The problem occurs when we imagine these reprieves to be some lifelong ambition rather than a momentary respite along the way. Often we become so enamored of them that we slavishly seek their favor to the exclusion of all else. In the process we lose touch with life itself and soon find it quite difficult to tolerate even the slightest twinge of self-consciousness, uneasiness, or grief.

95

Religion has become hopelessly lost in the defense of its metaphysics. Instead of serving to inform life with meaning and significance through metaphor, religion appears more concerned with its own severely proselytized ideology. The priest of the industrial age seems to fancy himself as something of a scientist while assuring his herd of the corporeal existence of some intimately personal god.

96

Religion ascends from a sense of helplessness while the atheist arises from arrogance. The former knows too little of the universe while the latter makes assumptions beyond what the evidence shows. Eventually though, even religion itself can grow quite arrogant.

97

Symbols such as "numbers" or "god" do offer a more clear representation of some particular abstraction perceived of the cosmos. Yet these symbols are then too often reconstructed in the human mind as something quite *physically* true.

98

The irony of the contemporary world — one of them anyway — is that the common religious man, he who should be most familiar with the benefits and the profundity of poetry and art, actually knows the least about these concepts while fancying himself something of a scientist too. He is the most arrogant of men who imagines he knows the truth with certainty — the very consequence of an overinflated ego.

99

The primary reason for the formation of most religious doctrine is to justify some group's imagined superiority with respect to what it feels is the moral thing to do in any particular situation. Religious texts are in this sense one of the first attempts of our creating a codified manifesto.

100

The original text of any particular religion has been altered considerably through translation, so even the significance afforded the words of the text — in many cases the work of zealotry — can often lead to inhumane interpretations.

101

Eastern and western man must unite to create something of a new global culture which recognizes *all* religious perspectives — the atheist and the naturalist too — as quite valuable interpretations of experience. This can only begin if we imagine religious manuscripts as purely metaphoric, sacred in the same manner that all great art is sacred.

102

If we haven't the imagination to perceive of ancient spirits inhabited in the dancing of the leaves or the twinkling of the stars then we will never understand our life in any truly profound manner at all. We will be, instead, a most excellent candidate for some putrid brand of ideological zealotry.

103

In "killing time" man incrementally murders himself as well, often without even noticing the slow decomposition of his spirit. He gathers together a wild host of revelers and blowhards, each more entertaining than the last and each promising to release him from the ever-pressing burdens of time. While he *should* surround himself with wise, noble, and trustworthy souls to deepen and enrich his remaining time, he is instead attracted to the garish, the deceptive, and the inferior because these are more amusing.

104

We cannot and should not liberate the soul from the passions. After all, passion fuels the spirit's concern for things outside of itself. Instead we must learn to regulate and control those passions which take possession of us to such a degree that we become a kind of slave to their caprice, those passions which almost entirely obscure one's ability to reason much at all.

105

The desire to lose oneself in some blissful thought or action is a somewhat spiritualized mask that hides a secret desire for death. We are only ever truly alive when we are blessed with awareness and perspective, both qualities sadly absent from the more "blissful" state of death.

106

The selling of our soul is a rather common occurrence in the modern world. In fact, we often strike the deal without even realizing that we've done so. In most cases, we will gladly surrender something immaterial in exchange for the opportunities of wealth and possession — unless, of course, we prize our spirit more than colorful strips of paper. However, more often than not, we remain committed to the notion that "making something" of ourselves requires a significant amount of capital.

107

The human being is the amalgamation of body and spirit, the physical and the esoteric. The entire world is comprised of illogical paradoxes as well as rational and observable patterns. For example, light exists and acts as both a wave and a particle simultaneously until it is observed. This defies the very notion of what it means to be a singular identity. So too is man fundamentally comprised of two separate natures, oftentimes in conflict with one another — the physical and the meta-physical. Much of value has been gained in the scientific and mechanistic drive to improve mankind's corporeal existence — although, no doubt, more still needs to be accomplished. Yet, man has not achieved nearly as much prominence in the development of his spirit and has even seemed to regress at times with respect to ethics, degenerating over the years from a creature of sometimes quite noble intent and sophistication to a crass and boastful twit supremely disillusioned that his ego isn't God.

108

It is a necessity, at times, to hurt a person's feelings or wrinkle his pride. It strengthens his spirit and tightens his resolve, eventually showing him his place within the greater universe. Otherwise he might develop into quite a tyrant, imagining the planet as little more than his enduring plaything.

109

Contemporary man immerses himself in the horrid minutia of existence because he hasn't the skill or inclination to lift his spirit above the hyper-dullness of everyday experience.

110

We should imagine our future self and so compose the content of this character like a musician places notes upon the staph. Ultimately it will be our vision of this future that will guide us. Unfortunately, most of us only perceive of the future as some material goal, ignoring the pleas of our spirits altogether. These will be truly the hollow souls, the creatures of cruelty, the beasts of war who fight with their claws for the simplest of possessions.

111

The propaganda of popular culture often praises our animal instincts as fine and noble characteristics while virtues are perceived as cruelties of a sort, tyrannical shackles on the fullness of human expression and experience. The popular sentiment generally agrees with Terence that nothing human can be unfamiliar or odd. Yet, while we may understand human behavior as humans ourselves — and so familiar with the many failings of human character — such knowledge should encourage prudence and restraint rather than the reckless release of our mostly pitiless instinctual drives and dispositions.

112

The true individual of character acknowledges no law or lord which would prescribe some truth beyond the understanding of her own mature and reflective conscience. Alas, this is not the way of all of humanity, fascinated as we are with being told how we should live. Instead, the vast majority of us know our conscience only as something quite removed from our own experience. It is a cultural remnant, or an heirloom that has been passed down for generations, though no one remembers exactly when the first die was cast. So, it becomes no longer a vital element of the human spirit, but survives as something of a human artifact. There are only but a few spirits anymore who remain committed to the pursuit of integrity and the development of virtue. The rest simply want to step into the waistcoat of a garment already tailored to the specifications of someone else.

113

If we dedicate our heart to something that is mostly outside the domain of our own deep and unique interests or concerns, we will make an adversary of our own spirit.

114

The notion of free will is a concept that imagines man to be something of a king who reigns over all of — or at least some of — the diverse serfs of his personality. We then infer that others possess these powers as well and a whole system of external laws and statutes are established to ensure that order is maintained. Those rulers who are unable — or unwilling — to properly manage the unruly forces of their realm will find, as Nietzsche noted, no shortage of executioners from outside the kingdom. Yet, our own unconscious empire is the most difficult to regulate with so many corrupt and deceitful forces at play. In fact, a "wicked" individual is more likely to commit some crime against himself long before he infects others with his damaged soul.

115

If you intend to inflict your will upon the world, expect storm clouds to gather as the world prepares its inevitable response.

116

We possess ideals so that we might live up to them rather than hold them up as universal truths of any kind. The dogmatist, that sad fundamentalist fool, imagines his ideal to be quite unquestionably true.

117

Infidelity arises from an unstable heart which so fears its impending age that it must find some means by which to convince itself that no vitality has been sacrificed in the everyday living of life. Eventually such a soul may realize that he has been dying slowly for years and his many attempts to escape this reality generally leaves more than a few people (many of them children) in a state of quiet agony.

118

A lack of fear often correlates with a lack of intelligence as well.

119

An extreme and rigid Stoic — that man who so hopes to

successfully rid himself entirely of all attachment and desire — does not fear death precisely because he experienced it so long ago. His body may continue to breathe, but his spirit has putrefied.

120

The ultimate goal of the Buddhist is to kill oneself while still alive.

121

A person who feels a sickness in his soul — a rather common malady in the contemporary age — is generally suffering from some misperception about himself or the environment in which he lives. Oftentimes, the misunderstanding arises because he overestimate his station in the world, possessing an ego which imagines itself as something ultimately priceless and irreplaceable.

122

As with individual suicides, a suicidal society has lost its sense of perspective.

123

The contemporary man often finds modern life hopelessly complex and despairs that it should be so. His cries to "simplify!" largely go unheeded — even by himself. He yearns desperately for days long past. Yet, alas, he is a sad prisoner of fate, a poor victim of circumstance — (as are we all). These laments are largely states of mind brought on by a kind of mental slavery chained to the idea that life is merely some foolish, simple pleasure — an Eden quite misunderstood. So man pursues this utopian dream hoping to achieve relentless contentment or transcend the earthy realm altogether in the hazy bliss of some resplendent "heaven." In any case, the pursuit is doomed to fail for anyone but the most simple of creatures.

124

If primitive man arose from his cave one day and came out into the open air, he would be forced to admit an entirely new perspective, a view in many ways less reassuring than the more established luxuries of home. It should be no surprise then that so many of these creatures would no doubt spend the vast majority of their days attempting to return to the comforts of that enchanted grotto.

125

Boredom is a state of mind and not a state of being. Yet we seem to imagine it as some sort of existential plight, a burden we're made to bear for which we seek relief from a variety of ineffective sources. We entirely ignore the many opportunities that boredom affords for reflection and insight.

126

There is no essential difference in the inherent value of sand and gold except within our mind and here the greater value is determined by how much more appealing we rank one above the other. We will often esteem those things which are the most difficult to obtain, making possession of them all the more extraordinary in our view. Yet this is purely a matter of perspective and only generates the force of "truth" when others agree to value such things as well. A child, for instance, quickly learns that a thing discarded by the majority of others — trash, essentially — possesses little value at all and so she adjusts her desires accordingly, believing the majority of us will know what's best for her.

127

Overweening pride can only arise with a momentary or eternal forgetfulness of our place in the universe. We are, after all, but a speck upon an already infinitesimal planet within a galaxy that is not much more than a light fleck on the limitless canvas of space. In such a context, our egotism seems patently absurd.

128

The fool who boasts of his great luck and the many comforts he now enjoys does so from the pretension of the moment — sadly oblivious to the clouds gathering on the horizon.

129

The man of certainty is often quite forgetful that almost every word he uses to construct his golden conviction — no matter what the doctrine — possesses various degrees of meaning, each thought tainted by at least a drab of ambiguity or paradox. Man should then develop a solid foundation of many diverse perspectives besides his own if he is to have even a slight advantage in the quest for understanding. The person of certainty, however, cannot be bothered with such heady work. He is far too busy hiding himself away in an attempt to limit the number of views available to him. He desires homogeny as a means to banish his own self-doubt.

130

The scientific perspective is damaging only to the extent that it might provide a convenient — evidenced-based — justification for some inhumane or beastly conclusion. The scientific *method*, however, — that slow and careful process of reasoned, thoughtful, and open analysis — should prevent the cruelest of deductions from arising in the first place. Yet, we must never forget the significance of intellectual humility or the devastation too often wrought by hubris.

131

The work of all true art is to stimulate thought and inspire new vistas of perception. Otherwise, art will at best only serve to entertain. And it is this attribute of art that seems to continuously rouse our sentiments so entirely.

132

We all view the world through the refracted lens of the senses which must of necessity interpret an image by bending it a bit. In this sense, all of our truths are more than a little bowed.

133

Nietzsche's philosophy did not move him to madness any more than religion generates cruelty and ignorance on its own. Oftentimes we commit this error of perception because we like to experience life from an armchair, judging cause and effect from the perspective of someone in the know when, in fact, we know quite little.

134

Many political prisoners of the postmodern world are

confined, not in prison, but within the walls of their own mind — held captive by a series of traditions and perspectives that dominate their age, unwilling to acknowledge even the possibility of such a cage.

135

No one should waste a single breath in argument with a fool who refuses to admit to any truths that might somehow weaken his position. Such an interlocutor has no concern for what is wise, or just, or true. He's merely preoccupied with etching his perspective into limestone.

136

The vast majority of us wait impatiently for the acquisition of some external thing — love, possessions, honor, etc. — to bring peace and contentment to our lives when a slight change of perspective could produce an entirely different state of being altogether.

137

One great difficulty of the simple golden rule — doing unto others as you would have them do unto you — is that it assumes we can possibly *know* — without significant prejudice — how we would wish to be treated in similar circumstances. The vast majority of us find it nearly impossible to truly understand the complexities inherent in any particular situation. We are barely able to understand our own reasons and motivations for acting, let alone those of someone else whose experiences we don't share. How might we know how we would wish to be treated if we were someone other than ourselves? And is such unbiased objectivity even possible? Further, there will be times when such golden dogma may actually lead to some great immorality. We are quite skilled at deluding ourselves after all and we often believe that *our* perceptions matter more than any other.

138

Artistic perception, because it is so immersed within the duality, contradiction, and paradox inherent to human language and consciousness, cannot help but notice the bittersweet nature of existence as a whole. This is generally the mood of all great art: a touch melancholic. However, many of us choose to ignore such insights nonetheless, preferring a life free of reflection and deeper thought. In this manner, we quite willfully and assuredly live the unexamined life — a life which we imagine to be blissfully happy as a result. And it is, no doubt, because we believe it to be. This, too, is bittersweet as often our own unique individual character is compromised in the process, doomed to an existence of eager short-sightedness and superficial understanding.

139

Mankind as a whole so readily relies on pat stereotypes because the species is generally too limited in its perception of complexity.

140

The notion of surrendering to one's fate depends upon one's ability to recognize the distinction between destiny of the inevitable and fate arising through the complex process of choice. Most of us are too quick to simply bow before *any* force that stands in the slightest opposition to our own desire. We quit and call it fate, praising ourselves for our sheepish wisdom. Although even we are not so cursed as the fool who ignores his duty to necessity and fate altogether. He often forces himself into situations where he does not generally belong, thereby disturbing the equilibrium of the natural conditions and inspiring a great deal of misery as a consequence.

141

Humanity generally praises those actions which seem most unbound by the strong and persistent pull of self-interest. Yet, such an evaluation requires quite special knowledge that is beyond our comprehension. So, we are entirely ill-prepared for these types of assessments because we rarely understand our *own* impulses, let alone those of our fellows.

142

A 21st century retelling of the Emperor's New Clothes reveals a new ending to the story. As before, the emperor is sold "invisible" clothing by a pair of tricksters who wish to take advantage of his vanity. He, of course, is too proud to admit that he doesn't see the clothing and all of his advisors follow his lead. However, the original tale has the naked emperor smugly parading about the town until a boy tells the crowd that the emperor is indeed exposing himself, at which point everyone begins to laugh and the emperor is mortified. The new ending, on the other hand — the one which seems more appropriate to the current age — would have the crowd direct its scorn at the boy since most would share in the king's illusion. And delusion is something that does not easily fade. We generally don't abruptly cease the habit of lying to ourselves when we are confronted with the truth. A mob, as well, is not prone to change its perceptions just because a child announces some alternative. Further, the more desirable the lie, the more we are likely to desire that it retain its legitimacy and the more diligently we are likely to labor for it to remain so. In most cases, if he's not ignored altogether, the boy would find the crowd laughing at *him*.

143

Existential misery is a symptom of our inability to perceive of life beyond the scope of our own individual, and so quite personal, condition.

144

Surrender and retreat are necessary elements in any life. There are, of course, times when we should *not* surrender or retreat, but these opportunities only rarely present themselves and when they do, most people duly rise to the occasion. Far too many lives are lain to waste on a battlefield, however, when, instead of withdrawing, soldiers become immobilized by the fear of public scorn. Only survivors describe this as courage, the dead often refer to it as the carnage of the ignorant.

145

The world goes mad in times of war, a state wherein the surreal becomes quite commonplace and the inhumane is perceived as something of a virtue.

146

Instead of feeling compassion for the suffering of another, too many modern men seek to assign blame instead — it is, after all, far easier than the pursuit of understanding. Many oftentimes dismiss empathy itself as a kind of weakness that buckles the knees of judgment. Yet, without compassion we will generally perceive of others — especially our enemies — as willfully orchestrating their own undoing and so deserving of whatever fate has dressed for them. This is the portrait of the dead man, one who no longer retains any semblance of the humane in his character.

147

It may be true that what doesn't kill you only makes you stronger, however, frequent suffering may nevertheless cause you to *wish* that you were dead.

148

If perceived through the lens of some particular glass, even the most righteous representative of man can appear as someone cruel, cunning, ruthless, and insignificant. None of us then should have need for crowing about our achievements since only a pitiful kind of fraudulent certainty allows us to do so. We should instead gather the seeds of this understanding and sprinkle them around the globe to encourage the blossoming of humility.

149

Mankind is often idealized because of fear or psychological necessity. If we were to truly perceive humanity as it exists in reality — not the exceptions which merely prove our own prejudice, but an honest critique of the character of those who exist at any one time on the planet — we would find that the truth is closer to our nightmare than our ideal. This finding should give us pause lest we discover that we, too, are a chosen representative of the unconscionable.

150

The self is only a prison if we perceive ourselves to be so caged. The bars of this penitentiary then are constructed by the inmate himself. Yet, such a warden is also the most aware of just how best to hold this particular criminal. Likewise, he's quite familiar with how to free himself as well.

151

The rationalists have always imagined that they could engage anyone in discussion and eventually reach agreement about most important decisions through the process of reasoning. While this may work quite well for some conversations, it quickly fails when less tangible notions such a virtue or morality are concerned. What one person endorses, another disdains and both generally have good evidence to reasonably sustain their views. In such cases, persuasion is often impossible since the prejudice of our own beliefs can usurp the authority of reason.

152

To punish anyone with death reveals some of the most atrocious hubris imaginable, a sense of moral certainty that favors rationalized vengeance over the more subtle requirements of authentic justice.

153

There are many entirely logical and seemingly ironclad arguments that justify a whole host of depraved conclusions which then lead to repugnant acts and beliefs steeped in the mythology of universal and fundamental Truths. True reasoning, however, is not some purely objective exercise. Reasoning, instead, employs the heart in the service of the intellect.

154

The realist arrogantly imagines that his expressions and beliefs are somehow associated with the real and the True. In order to do so, however, he must first confidently fabricate an understanding of what constitutes truth, which is, of course, another lie.

155

The hungry man cares not a whit for morality or law. After all, a vegetarian pacifist can tear open the flesh of an animal with the same enthusiasm as the sadist if his belly is empty enough. The thirsty zealot will also discard all of his rigid principles for a small drink when the urge to live becomes too strong. This is a truth of the animal. Yet, when we are advised to know ourselves, we often dismiss this instinctual aspect of our personality as something of an inconsequential remnant from our distant past.

156

If the truth be told, the weary nurse, tending to an irritable man's deathbed, is generally annoyed that he was ever born in the first place.

157

Neither the pessimist nor the optimist can be definitively proven wrong since each finds ample evidence for the "truth" of his own proposition — conveniently failing to observe the many instances in which these predictions were disappointed.

158

The abstract — that weighty mass of undifferentiated everything — is like an ocean in which all of us fish for meaning. We pull some image, thought, or conception from this great reservoir, separating it from its context and its home, and hold it up in joyful triumph — imagining we have somehow seized the truth.

159

So many fools adamantly deny their secret wish to be ultimately deceived, imagining truth to be their desire instead. Yet, their actions — the manner in which such people live — usually demonstrates otherwise. A comforting lie can blissfully endure and flourish, providing its believer with a whole lifetime of meaningful distraction. Whereas the truth is not so easily categorized or understood, oftentimes requiring great patience and persistence merely to enlarge the scope of the inquiry. Unfortunately, this approach toward understanding often requires more toil and suffering than most of us are willing to bear.

160

The most difficult truth for the warrior to accept is that — despite the prolonged, overwrought, false protests of his countrymen — all of his sacrifices will be forgotten and, over time, will become little more than a historical narrative in which he is mentioned as a rather ambiguous generality. So much for the fame, glory, and immortality of the warrior hero!

161

The fool doesn't permit his mind enough freedom and flexibility to adapt to the abstract complexities of life. Instead, he remains stubbornly devoted to universal principles and truths which are the easiest to digest, but which lack nourishment of any kind. Such a person desires that everything be reduced to its simplest terms in order to drive out the confusion of paradox entirely. It is his wish, after all, that he not be compelled to tax his intellect too severely.

162

It generally doesn't take long before the revolutionary finds himself seeking asylum from those forces which he helped bring to power.

163

As Spinoza would no doubt agree, the entire universe might simply be a tiny quantum particle of something considerably larger and more complex than itself — a paramecium on the backside of some great colossus perhaps. After all, everything else in the existence of which we know can be reduced to lesser particles, so there is no reason to imagine that the universe itself isn't a smaller part of some larger whole. However, the majority of us will often dispute such a thought because we do not wish to consider ourselves again relegated to the status of something "lesser" — a truth about our nature that Galileo uncovered long ago.

164

The physiological, historical and cultural factors that inform our relationship to the world add to our quite common delusion of normalcy — the belief that tradition somehow informs the truth, that the mundane trumps the extraordinary, and that order will always prevail.

165

The contemporary man of luxury generally will have the greatest difficulty managing the real hardships of life because he has become somewhat unaccustomed to such struggles. He has grown out of practice with the more profound — and sometimes more disheartening — truths of existence and has dedicated himself instead to its more prolific illusions.

166

We often imagine that because something makes sense to us, it must be therefore true as well.

167

The heart untrue to itself will be rarely true to others.

168

We often infer significance when something possesses none at all and ignore that which is most significant.

169

The voice of reason and restraint in an age gone mad is often ignored or persecuted as itself a kind of madness. Insanity, after all, is merely some irregularity of a more common pattern, but intensified to such a degree that it becomes difficult to dismiss as merely inconsequential.

170

The faith of many rationalists is a kind of reason that excludes imagination and emotion almost entirely.

171

We are all moral in some aspect of our existence and this often allows us to feel somewhat justified in dismissing those behaviors of ours that might seem otherwise quite heinous and inhumane. As long as we can explain away our actions as a product of some rational sense, we can still imagine ourselves as a decent, honorable, and even ethical person — though perhaps with a few "weaknesses." Yet, while a justified claim of self-defense may protect a person from the law, his conscience is usually another matter.

172

Mankind, with an almost religious faithfulness, believes that the entire cosmos is organized in the same manner in which his mind is organized — with reason and coherence and laws. This is, it seems, our most ardent dream: that the universe make some coherent sense. Yet, we are ill-prepared for those elements of existence which are less explicable, those aspects of life with an intricate complexity that is beyond the human mind to completely understand — death, for instance, or love.

173

We groom a path for the inhumane just as much when we "objectively" detach ourselves from a difficult situation as when we passionately engage in an emotional melee.

174

One of the fundamental errors of Enlightenment thinking is that it assumes all of us — or even a large majority — would employ reason in similar situations and in such a similar manner as to arrive at the same conclusions. Many use reason, however, to justify rather dubious or downright irrational claims. Rationalizations often fuel the very identity of an individual — the delusions of his existence which inform those experiences that define his character. He considers himself a "good" man, for instance, because he is able to rationally defend himself against all those times when he acted otherwise. His talent for rationality often only serves to solidify his prejudices.

175

If you attempt to reason with a starving man, expect to be promptly eaten.

176

The story of Adam and Eve is not some cautionary tale about the ill effects of ambition, but of the persuasive influence of rationalization.

177

The simple possession of reason and consciousness isn't enough to bestow some special dignity to human existence without the development of a strong — seemingly *un*natural — moral temperament as well.

178

Philosophy has been transformed over the years from a love of wisdom to a love of minutiae. Perhaps this has occurred because of the 20th century philosopher's devotion to reason and logic rather than wisdom.

179

The narrowing of the mind is a much more debilitating

condition than the hardening of the arteries. Its consequences are generally more lethal too.

180

Even the most influential contemporary philosopher — the successful ideal of today's professional — subsists in the attic, playing with his theories and concepts like so many childhood toys, knowing but a little as to how any man, including himself, should best live his life.

181

Philosophy without action is only so much blustery wind gathering storm clouds to rain upon those poor souls beneath.

182

There is a poverty of mind which is often associated with external poverty, yet it afflicts the rich just as readily as the poor. It is an insufficiency of depth and wisdom stemming from a superficial and generally material understanding of life's project.

183

Sometimes a great tragedy awakens us from the superficial slumbers of pleasure, wealth, and fame. Yet, more frequently this opportunity to acquire wisdom is lost in the unchecked grief of mourning, the existential lament that eventually we all must surrender everything.

184

The fool imagines a virtue to be an acquisition of sorts, a quality that one possesses forever, regardless of circumstance. A person is "honest," for example, or "devoted" and the fool begins to twitter about the supreme merits and morals of such an individual. However, most good judgment about virtue depends upon an understanding of the more subtle nuances of any particular situation. Honesty, after all, resembles more of a character flaw when used as something of a weapon.

185

The notion that *nothing* is worth dying for misunderstands the entire purpose of human life. Yet, to die for *anything* — a view generally held by the rabid patriots and war mongers of any nation — demonstrates an eagerness for destruction and death. It will require wisdom to navigate between these two extremes, a wisdom often found lacking in the greatest majority of men.

186

The din generated by the cacophony of fools who populate the world at any particular time is often too great for the individual of true integrity, wisdom, or genius to be heard at all.

187

Heaven is the "place," for lack of a better word, where fools are seated on pedestals. Our lives, instead, should be primarily dedicated to the raising of our awareness. Otherwise, we may be the richest soul in all the world, but have no notion of it whatsoever.

188

Freedom can become a kind of slavery when we obsess about emancipation from our own natural limitations. It is the fool who, seeking fundamental liberty, cuts his rope rather than using it to help raise him further up the mountain.

189

If a person were to use a small scrap of fish in order to defiantly tease a hungry grizzly bear, few but the very naïve would expect that man to remain attached to his extremities for long. In fact, we might even root against the survival of such an individual, hopeful as we are in the notion of natural selection as a fair administrator of justice. Yet, contemporary societies often reward these kinds of hubristic feats of foolishness in war and business while extolling the virtues of an overly aggressive self-regard in one's personal life, leaving many with the impression that such deeds are actually virtues of a sort.

190

There can be no faith in the progress of man until man can prove himself to be progressing toward the humane in some fashion. Otherwise, he merely changes physically over time while remaining the same old fool he has been for centuries.

191

After the appearance of the 20th century dictators — and the likelihood of those beasts yet to come — we cannot afford to ever trust our kind again — at least not entirely. Nor should we trust ourselves entirely either. We are animals, after all, and often wild ones at that. Only a fool allows a wolverine access to the nursery, no matter how tame or submissive the creature seems on the surface.

192

Indifference to reading and knowledge in general isn't much better than deliberate misinterpretation. The fool who chooses not to read or learn, he who is only mildly curious about the world, often supports the forces of the inhumane by adding mass to a voice that should hold no weight. Why do such fools believe that others should take them seriously? After all, a groundhog, with the benefit of a skilled interpreter, might offer just as sound an opinion on any subject as the fool who can't be bothered to contemplate much. In any event, it would be unwise to allow either of them access to positions of influence.

193

The ridiculous edict that we should love all of our "brothers" and "sisters" is an optimism brought into the world through the mindless chittering of fools. The human race, of course, is more than capable of perceiving others (and even animals) as brothers and sisters — at least conceptually — and feeling passionate about abstract concepts such as justice and brotherhood. Yet, to actually feel *love* for a stranger is the overly sentimental act of one who seems addled by a mental disorder of some kind, perhaps someone who is too immature for the sad austerity of life. In any event, it is not the type of person familiar with a notion of love as something complicated and profound. What is necessary to prevent the spread of the inhumane, instead of some false affection, is a better understanding of other people and ourselves.

194

The title "man" is often used to excuse some shameful act committed, presumably, from human weakness. The adulterous husband, for instance, who conducts secret affairs while his wife is sleeping. "I'm but a human being!" arrives his cry if caught "how might I be faulted for my very animal nature?" Yet, such a plea assumes that we are *only* an animal and cannot be expected to achieve sophistication in any way. While this attitude may be true — sadly — of the vast majority of human fools who populate the earth, there is still hope that "man" exists somewhere in the universe.

195

We can pray from now until doomsday in order to wrestle some control over our existential condition. However, alas, we show ourselves to be but sad fools raging against the wilderness, eager for any illusion that might provide comfort of any kind.

196

The modern age of detached cruelty, unchecked perversity, and the assimilation to repugnant virtues only helps to prove the ancient maxim that character is destiny — in ages, as well as individuals.

197

Whoever lives without shame at all exists without much of a conscience as well. Shame shocks our awareness and pesters us to act more humanely. Many virtues generally arise from this struggle to survive some disturbing realization — perhaps we have indeed acted shamefully. Though we certainly might *imagine* ourselves as individuals possessing the virtues of character, we should verify such assumptions through an honest and comprehensive evaluation of our own thoughts and actions.

198

We are often more concerned with our possessions rather than the development of our character and our virtue because we measure each using the currency of materialism. Yet, virtue cannot possibly participate in such a manner since it bestows only immaterial and priceless — indeed, quite irreplaceable — treasures.

199

The mere appearance of virtue is not a virtue at all but often an experience that occurs according to the dictates of the situation. A person seems brave, for instance, because he is forced by circumstance into confronting a state of affairs that he has no choice but to face boldly. He may, in fact, *be* brave in his character but he will be required to *act* in such a way if he is to truly possess the virtue. In other words, his virtue will be kept a secret without some virtuous deed to confirm it. Still, authenticity remains an issue in determining ethical behavior since actions alone are not enough to knight a person with character. After all, we may defend our words with actions that are entirely insincere.

200

Any virtue can readily become a vice if we are careless in maintaining our balance. If we fail, for example, to feed our children while generously bestowing our life's entire savings on the poor, we might be rightfully questioned as to our motives *and* our morality. Not only have we neglected the sacred oath to protect our own child, but even our future duties to the poor are compromised since we no longer have the means by which to benefit them. In one rash moment our generosity becomes a vice and the forces of the inhumane proclaim victory once again.

201

We, of course, speak quite eloquently and sometimes even profoundly about the virtues which designate "man" as something unique and significant in the universe. However, in practicality, these lofty notions fail to inspire most of us to truly surrender our attachment to security, property, vengeance, and entertainment. We will hail, instead, some exceptional individual for her possession of the higher virtues and then conspicuously claim, without even a hint of shame, that everyone possesses them in kind.

202

We contemporaries often assume that we differ greatly in character, temperament, and condition from our ancestors because the era which we inhabit is so distinctive from their own, an age now gone forevermore. We imagine ourselves as something of a new species then, evolved from the lower incarnations of humanity to our present state of enlightenment, as if the evolution of mankind progressed steadily along some imagined stairway to the heavens.

203

Character is what truly matters in one's life and it develops mostly due to the struggle to find one's place in the world. It is not the mere presence of suffering that generates character, of course, or the poor would be quite significantly more virtuous than the rich, which they are not. Instead, one must labor to transform one's misery — from whatever source — into something beautiful and perhaps even useful at times. In this manner we give purpose to our anguish. Otherwise, suffering is essentially meaningless and prone to engender quite violent expressions of jealousy and resentment. Yet, as any society rises to opulence and increases its access to luxury and entitlement, the descent of character soon follows — not of necessity, of course, but simply from forgetfulness and an animal desire for ease and comfort.

204

We often interpret our blind and random luck as some talent of our character and so begin to believe over time that we somehow deserve —and therefore are entitled to — the privileges of our own good fortune.

205

We usually desire to be remembered in our best moments, but our conduct or character can often influence others to remember us at our worst.

206

If we are unkind to our own children, it would not surprise anyone if we are likewise unkind to others. Yet, the hypocrite or the charlatan — the all-to-common character of contemporary times — is often privately a beast and only publically wearing the mask of someone posing as humane. These are the most dangerous of creatures since they are only too conscious of their own misdeeds and so shamefully employ deceit as a means to keep them secret. These people exist as something of a snake-ish organism, full of cunning, venom, and ruthless resolve but hidden beneath the tall grasses so as to hunt without humane censure of any kind.

207

Even a fool would not wish for a life of ease and luxury — where almost every need is immediately satisfied — if he knew the true cost of these commodities. After all, failure and discomfort are oftentimes remarkable instigators of creative thought. Furthermore, though no one wishes for a life of overwhelming difficulty, a life of tremendous luxury possesses far too little hardship to produce a person of character. The great soul must learn to persist and flourish through hard times — which arrive to all eventually — and remain patient for fate to unravel itself. Otherwise, the character who arises instead is something of a partially developed, perpetually naïve, noble savage who imagines himself a king.

208

While it is certainly true that, as Epictetus states, "a person who will not stoop to flattery does not get to have the flatterer's advantages," it is likewise true that a person who will not stoop to murder will not receive the killer's advantages either. These are the kind of sentiments reflective of the beast in man, he who is inclined to best proliferate his own self-interest without much thought as to the consequences of his actions upon others. Such a beast may, of course, receive even a plethora of benefits initially, but over time these will serve to bring him misery. After all, purely animal man must forsake his *human* nature and he does so at his peril. The same is true, of course, when he pretends that he is purely genteel and civilized. In either case the imbalance of his true character leads to despair and wretchedness.

209

The human male has for thousands of years attempted to control his own beastly and carnal drives by forcing women and others to hide themselves or quit their entirely innocent temptations. The male in general is far too weak and pathetic — it appears — to do much of anything other than escalate the level of coercion he employs. In general, many today are still too aberrant, ignorant and violent to limit their own character.

210

The only creature that must be hunted and hounded without relent is the beastly monstrosity of Ego, the worm within our own character. The inhumane is often a product of Ego run amok, some imbalance of personality. So we must confront the Ego at every opportunity and refine its needs into virtues of some kind. Those who refuse to do so merely add to the ferocity of the Ego beast. They feed it and allow it to gain strength and legitimacy. They deny the creature's impact on humanity as a whole and dismiss its violence as something altogether natural.

211

Even the most pristine and glorious city in the world — populated by only the most noble and civilized of creatures and steeped in great art and culture — will revert to barbarism under the right conditions. Any society is first concerned with brute subsistence since those who are starving or threatened will not likely concern themselves with culture in any way. They will be far more concerned with sustaining their survival. However, once these basic conditions are met, civilization may then follow afterward. Yet, culture does not simply materialize when people no longer worry about their daily bread and water. It additionally requires that each of us commit ourselves to the development of a civilized character, a more humane incarnation of a creature who might otherwise be a beast.

212

We are not as much of a social animal as we are a pack animal. Our sociability often merely serves to help define and cull the herd.

213

The long fight for greater independence has led many liberated neurotics to now staunchly refuse the validity of any superior authority, trusting primarily their own individual judgment instead. This sort of fundamental hubris often impedes the development of character since it allows us to imagine ourselves as something grander than life itself, engaged in some great struggle for freedom and progress. As a result, we only come to understand what we already knew: the affirmations of an inflated ego.

214

Imagine madness itself as merely the imbalance of some

particular aspect of our character. In this sense, addiction can be a kind of madness; love can be a form of madness; obsession, ambition, and desire can be all manifestations of madness. The entire contemporary age it seems is quite mad indeed.

215

Sexuality as a primary source of identity generates from an obsession with sex in general in a century that desperately seeks to find some acceptable term that definitively labels us as either one thing or another — a simplistic means for understanding any human being. Any particular role in a society can serve as a convenient mask as well, often supplying us with a ready-made existential identity without our having to forge one for ourselves — a labor quite difficult and demanding under the best of circumstances.

216

The person who imagines himself more deserving of basic respect than the vast majority of animals already reveals an arrogant feature of his own beastly character: the drive to dominate and reign, to subjugate life and Nature to the urges of his own foolish and instinctive self-interest.

217

Too often in the contemporary situation do we interpret the expression of emotion as a sin — something it is *not* normally. Emotion *can* be sinful under certain conditions, of course. For example, we may release the highly pressurized gas of our own anger and frustration on those around us, thus passing the poison on to others who, no doubt, become themselves somewhat noxious.

218

The infantile preoccupation with the body often stunts the development of mature character. This is not to condemn sensations per se or sensuality in any manner. Yet, a delight in one's senses is very different from indulging in them to the exclusion of much else.

219

Misguided wives, by their husband's pale sins, have themselves been cast, time and time again, amidst the hells intended exclusively for the sinner.

220

Hardship molds character but cruelty often deforms it into shapes quite unrecognizable.

221

It is generally possible to trace the development of any severely violent, aberrant, or detestable behavior committed by a female of our species back to an original inhumane act at the pleasure of some masculine force in her life.

222

One of life's more significant challenges is that, in order to survive, a living organism must exist as itself in opposition to those forces that would wish to make it into something else, or kill it off entirely. In order to escape this strenuous state of affairs we will often simply surrender and accept whatever condition is required of us. We then successfully avoid this great, ancient struggle of life in exchange for the composition of our character.

223

Rudeness is one symptom for the disease of bad character. Impertinence is another. Yet, the nihilist will celebrate these as if they were among the highest achievements of man.

224

During the Holocaust, the German people in general remained so loyal to the demands of the status quo that they became something of a new contemporary monster — the sickly, pathetic, fearful, and all-too-common creature of moral ignorance and indifference.

225

Autonomy is actually the *fear* of most us. We may cry to the heavens to bring us more freedom and individual sovereignty over the course of our lives, but ultimately we will often bend when required to stand and actualize that gift. It depends upon the character of a person whether they will benefit from autonomy. The murdering psychopath, for example, should have his freedom restricted to a large degree while the artistic genius should be provided more freedom than even most heads of state.

226

Men quite often — and for reasons despairingly natural — freely exchange liberty for slavery if the latter pays well enough.

227

While all of us share in notions of justice, freedom, and

virtue, we are divided as to what these notions entail. We might disagree, for example, about what justice *is* but concur with the more superficial conclusion that justice itself is something worthy of pursuit. Yet without an open and reflective mind — along with a great deal of reading and experience — these noble ideas will not take root deeply enough within our character to be able to withstand the strong gusts of fate that storm into everyone's life from time to time.

228

The difficulty of acquiring freedom is that as soon as we free our foot from the source of its entanglement, our other foot becomes ensnared in the process. To free this foot will then capture a hand. To free the hand may require the tongue and so on. Thus we should consider what we are willing to surrender as carefully as we decide what we should achieve.

229

The spirit searching for freedom is often seeking escape rather than redemption of any kind. What we sometimes desire is the liberation of our spirit from the world.

230

If we spend our days seeking to deny or destroy the unpleasant and burdensome existence of our past, we will find that this obsession has stolen the present and the future from us as well — stacking insult upon injury. The more time that passes in this pursuit, too, will only serve to increase the dire consequences.

231

The contemporary hermit generally doesn't live amidst the empowering "independence of solitude" as much as he lives in hiding.

232

The slippery slope of freedom must be carefully tread or entire nations can sink in the mire of individual passions. If few are willing to sacrifice to the needs of the larger community, there will ensue a return to tribal law wherein we are only willing to commit our support to a small contingency of incestuous spirits. This will precipitate a freedom *from* government, of course, but it will also create an even greater need for it as we will devolve into beasts once again, threatening the efforts of the humane to near extinction.

233

The fool who seeks to entirely free himself from the rules and restrictions of nature can quickly find himself a slave to his own unchecked and capricious appetites.

234

The rabbits hopped to court one day, demanding equality for all the little critters of the forest. The lions in attendance, of course, promptly made a meal of them.

235

The release of all repression — America's cultural ambition it seems — creates an exhilarating rush of freedom for a time at the expense of the more sobering conclusions of wisdom. Icarus — the boy who flew too high and fell into the sea when the sun melted His waxen wings — is the ideal symbol for our age of impatient accomplishment as well as the reckless and thoughtless accumulation of experience.

236

The fervent patriots of freedom, the "free" fundamentalists, are often those who would most enjoy the *elimination* of much choice in their everyday lives — replaced by a rigid conformity to the "proper" and traditional way.

237

The modern soldier — at least in practice — is generally the tool of big business rather than a defender of noble ideals.

238

Everyone is a criminal amid the chaos of war as immorality is rather the norm, so to accuse anyone in a war zone of breaking the rules of peacetime is always going to seem as something of an ignoble hypocrisy. Yet, many nations brandish such accusations as a means to assuage the guilt of their own unconscious complicity in wartime slaughter. While there are certainly *just* wars, most are quite unconscionable, laying waste to the claim that man is anything but an appalling monster.

239

If young men had any experience with the horrors of war, they would never let old men send them off to fight.

240

The tremors of war are such because the cruelty of man is allowed to roam unleashed upon the countryside. These forces of cruelty do not subside when the conflict has abated, but they do find new expression in the activity of the every-day.

241

We often surrender our wills to what we refer to as the randomness of fate in a thinly veiled attempt to rationalize our own ineptitude as some inevitable principle of destiny.

242

While Nature may be indifferent and cruel, it is a great sin — a sin against humanity as a whole — for man to be so. The very notion of humanity is of a collective greater than our own individual natures, natures which can so consume us too that we become, or remain, something of a beast — that organism which ranks beneath even the worms.

243

Family life — or sometimes even private existence — is often plagued by horrors far more gruesome, cruel, and alarming than might be found in public life. The cause of these atrocities is almost exclusively masculine by nature.

244

Eros is generally beneficial to us in its feminine form alone since the masculine expression of Eros is often merely the sheer exhibition of power and brutality — forces best left leashed unless they are needed in times of extreme duress.

245

The very best things are understood by the fewest number while the worst are known to almost everyone.

It should be no wonder then that we so often display characteristics of the brute.

246

In many respects, the "simple" life is generally the existence of the animal. We long for such an idealized sense of reality — a more simple existence — because the burden of being human and the duties it entails are sometimes too much to bear. It is far easier to merely subsist through brute instinct and the sensual rewards of immediate gratification.

247

In order to relinquish the many prizes of immediate gratification, that force to which every animal is subject, we often require some greater reward as compensation for our patience.

248

When faced with a fierce and violent beast who will not relent its aggression, one can ethically resort to savagery as a form of self-defense. Yet, such a creature, once unleashed, will be difficult to tame again.

249

Meanness, unkindness, and hostility of all kinds are individual salvos in a larger war against humanity and the humane. The person who shoots an aggressive look of disdain toward their fellow human being may not have fired a fatal blow, but they have nevertheless joined the fray with the temperament of a soldier for the inhumane.

250

It makes little sense to talk of human rights if we are confronted by a hungry grizzly bear. We have only the right to survive at that point and — to be sure — such a right is in no way guaranteed. Our rights, in fact, are entirely meaningless without the concerted effort of others to defend those same rights whenever seriously challenged.

251

Imbalance generally presents itself as something of a psychosis in the life of anyone who has lost their footing.

252

How does one discern the humane in any single individual? We must first hear or read another person's thoughts and juxtapose them with their actions. The insights derived from the comparison will generally lead to the proper conclusion about that individual. If these facts cannot be assessed, for whatever reason, it's safest to assume that you are dealing with an ignorant and indifferent beast.

253

A sage should keep her own counsel about matters of great importance. If the mob hears of her disdain for their most precious commodities, they are likely to move to silence her in one way or another. The group is always threatened by the outsider who holds no allegiance to them other than as a member of the same general species. Herein we often revert to our more bestial nature and ostracize any individual who does not conform to the "rules" of the group.

254

Nature most patiently waits for all of us to die.

255

When we identify some pattern in nature and bestow a name upon it, we believe that we somehow understand it better than the madman who still defends the thesis that little green fairies created the design.

256

Nature has no concern at all for what we deserve and even less for what we earn.

257

Contemporary man is generally accustomed to having many of his desires and silly wishes indulged as if they were sanctioned by royalty. In fact, he is quite often taken aback whenever Nature does not conform to this expectation. It can even cause him great confusion and distress. At such times the contemporary media rushes in to fill the void, striving with an obsessive fervor to satisfy each and every whim that blows through his conscious as well as unconscious mind. Yet, these diversions only satisfy briefly — if at all.

258

We often imagine ourselves to be far more independent than Nature actually allows. We forget, it seems, that we are surrounded by others who could at any time decide to be easily done with us forever if we do not meet our obligations to the group — whether these duties be reasonable, wise, and inspired or idiotic, naïve, and banal matters little to the mob, compliance is the first requirement.

259

We are the great protestors, the great complainers of the world. We live perpetually unsatisfied for most of our existence while remaining indifferent or ungrateful for much we have been given. Instead, our all-consuming passion becomes fixed on obtaining those things or qualities which we do not yet possess.

260

Nature's response to excess is generally restriction. The reverse is likewise true: too much constraint and there will come an explosion of excessiveness. After all, nature's role is to function as something of a fulcrum to maintain the equilibrium of life. Humanity, on the other hand, seems dedicated to extremes and the tilting after windmills.

261

We must continue to prune nature, uprooting the weeds from the concrete and mowing the grass so that it doesn't overtake our home. If we fail to accomplish these tasks routinely, then nature has a tendency to envelop us over time and conceal the entirety of our existence. Such is the tension inherent in all of existence: the fight to maintain equilibrium. The fool who works against this most necessary and fundamental symmetry does so at his own peril. The entire planet is now quite sick from just such a reckless disregard for the overall harmony and balance of the organism.

262

Nature is not particularly kind to those who stray too far from the groove in which they have been set providentially.

263

We have fewer significant choices in our lives than we might care to realize. While we may luck into some situation that brings us vast riches, we may find ourselves living in abject poverty as well, sometimes within the same month. The person who believes he has some manner of control over his existence often pushes so hard against his fate that he tears the fabric in the process, frequently with tragic consequences. However, the person who assumes that she may at least choose her *attitude* about events discovers that great happiness ensues when she eliminates her concern for particular consequences. In general, the person who persistently laments that events don't meet his expectations will find his entire life is lacking as well.

264

Humanity as a whole is far too reactionary and thus needs the calming insight of the sage to provide context and understanding to any particular situation. Yet, we are also quite arrogant which often leads us to ignore most truly good advice we might receive. So we plunder forward on our way toward a crushing fate that might otherwise have been avoidable.

265

One of the greatest sorrows that burden us is often the result of a refusal to accept our fate as it unfolds. In

America, especially, citizens scramble to write their own destinies in opposition to what the fates will allow. The hope of forcing our will upon the world is that we may receive something very similar to our dreams, but these may more closely resemble nightmares than visions of utopia.

266

Proclamation of all true lovers to their suicidal loves: "You should not leave here without the knowledge that if you spill your blood, mine is sure to follow. I will place a blade upon my chest as a consequence of your despair and I too shall, with all my resolve, share in your chosen fate. Herein lies the backbone of your decision."

267

The fool who attempts to force his will upon the universe often does not find happiness as a result. Fortune has a way of punishing the kind of hubris that believes it can compel the cosmos to produce that which was not originally provided. In order to find our proper fate, we must accept the fact that certain things are not available to us. Of course, this is not something that most contemporaries readily acknowledge since their firm conviction in technology fuels a sense of unyielding optimism that often trumps the edicts of fortune.

268

We experience the world in fragments which we then piece together into the narrative of our lives — conveniently dismissing those bits that do not suitably fit the tale while marveling at just how linear the past appears to us now. Yet, we are the author of such a narrative, our fate in this manner is largely self-generated.

269

Some men and almost all women bear misfortune well — better than most even imagine themselves capable. Yet, when fortune smiles, it often reveals the very worst in a man, a woman, or a child.

270

We tend to be drawn toward those things which most distract us from the realities of our lives. At the same time, we are repulsed by those elements of life that painfully remind us that even our distractions and amusements will one day come to an end. We are simply nauseous about the slow, often solitary, and ultimately doomed enterprise of existence.

271

A person who refuses to accept what is outside his power to control leaves himself open to the possibility — the very *real* possibility — that he will chain himself to the service of someone who can seem to provide what destiny refuses to allow.

272

All of us are called, but few will endure the necessary struggle to prove ourselves worthy of the calling. Instead, many of us spend a great deal of time and energy in the avoidance of destiny.

273

Oftentimes we will find what we desperately need when we're off searching for that which we passionately desire.

If blinded by such passion, though, if we are unable to *recognize* those features most essential to a humane and proper life, something of our destiny will be forever strained.

274

So many of us choose some manner of death before dishonor because we haven't the courage to live with the weaknesses and uncertainties of life. In other words, while seeming strong and brave in appearance, we actually shake in fear before the everyday experience of living.

275

Our almost manic obsession with youth is merely masking our own secret terror at the prospect of death and frailty.

276

The person who might actually achieve some pure state of consciousness by focusing the mind on the meditation of nothing receives death as a paramour — that maddening and irrational, but nonetheless alluring and attractive, companion who refuses to bend to anyone's will but its own.

277

The young so misunderstand the old that they imagine nothing more than the end of life awaits the arrival of age. The old, too, can become so seduced by the abstract and irrational dread of death that they romanticize their youth and lament the advancing years. Yet, each of them fails to recognize the present moment as anything other than a nuisance to the achievement of their desire.

The present moment, however, constitutes the only life we ever truly know.

278

There would be no such thing as compassion without the existence of suffering. There is simply no need for one without the other. There can exist no good without the bad, no right without the wrong, no up without a down. So, to possess anything of value, we should prepare ourselves to endure its antithesis in our life as well. Yet those who might wish human life to be otherwise arranged often seek a kind of death or frontal lobotomy — a release from this brand of maddening duality altogether.

279

What will be the last thing that we ever see on earth? It could be, as Dickinson suggests, something altogether trivial in comparison to what we might otherwise imagine — a fly buzzing in circles through the air, perhaps. Yet, even the most trifling of thoughts and activities gain significance when death attends upon them.

280

All surrender is a forfeit of some part of our life to death. Life, on the other hand, is a constant struggle, a spiritual as well as physical fight to develop, survive, and flourish.

281

Dearly beloved, we are gathered here today to celebrate the passing of the human race. Good riddance! Signed: the animals.

282

Competition, acquisition, accomplishment, and the drive to win at any cost are all means by which we futilely attempt to deal with the inevitability of our death. Often, though, these ploys merely speed us on our way.

283

While limiting one's attachment to life may be an appropriate response at certain times under certain circumstances, in whole it is an inadequate way to live one's life. The elimination of all desire, all passion, all sentiment, and all attachment to the world is the very definition of death. Such a person seems to wish that they were never born.

284

No one can possibly remain happy for long since all of our needs and desires cannot be fulfilled at all times. At best, we might find brief moments of happiness and longer periods of mild contentment while awaiting the suffering and discontent of everyday life to arise once again. This is the true ebb and flow of our existence. We only add to our difficulties by expecting life to be constituted otherwise.

285

It is the sensitive soul who suffers the most profoundly. The rest of us generally haven't the time or inclination to notice that something might be amiss.

286

If there were some great conscious Being of the universe,

some God who contained the entirety of the cosmos within the contours and crevices of Her mighty palm, then such a Presence would possess no more concern for us than we have for the amoebas and viruses of the world. We are alone.

287

Many people are enslaved in some manner by the trappings of fame and riches, but, being so bound, have found themselves resigned to a sad and petty fate.

288

Fame and Fortune are the sort of deities who demand great sacrifices which far exceed the worth of their mostly callous generosity.

289

Life, for all its sparsity and spectacle, for all its momentary joys and monumental sufferings, adds up in the end to a purely aesthetic experience for which we are afforded the brief opportunity to attend. We should stand in awe of the blood moon or the faint scent of sassafras on the wind. These are works of great art too. Yet, this approach assumes that one is an aware, reflective, and mindful participant in life. Far too many live conscious of only their own petty concerns.

290

All that you now possess can be quite easily lost in the matter of a single breath. This should inspire us all to gratitude and awareness lest we *too* are lost suddenly and without notice of any kind to the greater cosmos.

291

Fame is a car accident — a life lived off to the shoulder, immersed within its own particular dramatic reality, and entirely disengaged from the flow of traffic around it.

292

Wealth becomes something of a career in itself for the person who desires luxury above all else. They will spend their days in perpetual pursuit of that which cannot ever really be satisfied. They desire luxury as a means of concealing those aspects of their lives that they find disagreeable or shameful. It works as a security blanket of sorts, keeping a person seemingly warm and protected while they slumber blissfully beneath its cover.

293

Those who passionately seek reward, reputation, and fame already prove themselves unworthy of them.

294

The people who find power and fame discover that, instead of liberating their lives from all of the thousand-fold complications that generally plague it, they have rather shackled themselves into the service of these masters. In such a condition they become something of a beast of burden.

295

We should keep our distance from most sources of power since each radiates with its own specific dangers. The subject who stands beside the king should be no less uneasy than the person who sits astride 100,000 volts of electricity in a wet suit.

296

We often rank our surroundings according to our own preferences and through this designation we further understand the relationship between mankind and the rest of existence to be one of natural subordination. A rock, for instance, is viewed as subordinate to us because we can utilize and manipulate the stone while it is helpless to do the same for itself. So, we have yet again discovered something over which we might exert our power and so declare ourselves the victor in our own imagined game.

297

The fool who gleefully follows the desires of his heart and even thinks of the pursuit as something of a sacred duty forgets that desire rules through tyranny and often maintains its power by eliminating reflection altogether.

298

Loitering amid the noble crowd are often found the "loathsome" intellectuals — as opposed to the "splendid" ones. The loathsome intellectual does not possess a curious mind or a desire to understand the world as much as he finds enjoyment in the wielding of power generated through his cunning.

299

The "vulgar" has more to do with actions than with words.

300

There have existed entire generations who believe the "good" to have some association with the charm and value of material possession. Intrinsic value originating from within their own unique character is of little concern to such people because they've spent so little time investing in it to expect a return of any kind.

301

No one can fully embrace and practice the vast majority of traditional values of the past while immersed within a present that no longer finds such activities to be of value. As old people die, so do their rigid beliefs succumb to time and eventually become little more than a morbid curiosity on behalf of the living.

302

A lie is often a superior sword — a weapon no less lethal for its lack of steel and far more cutting and treacherous than even the sharpest blade.

303

We quite often assume that because someone can read, they must be literate as well.

304

There would be no need for government if people were virtuous enough to peacefully solve their own individual conflicts and noble enough to aid their fellow man in times of need, yet this aim does not appear to be their inclination. Society then arises with the broad establishment of rules and laws generally constructed for the regulation of wild children.

305

When two creatures meet it is the one who can so aptly

intimidate his opponent who is recognized as socially superior.

306

The key to restoring peace in any human relationship is to minimize one's own accomplishments and maximize the achievement of one's challenger. Otherwise, the tension of competition is sure to spoil the calm.

307

The very modern concern with social mobility derives from the human obsession with winning some arbitrary and fabricated competition that we imagine will definitively establish our significance in the world.

308

Laws expand as populations expand because of the increase in conflict and diversity of mind. Two old friends need few laws between them until a stranger arrives upon the scene with notions quite different from their own.

309

The poetry of lawyers long ago arrested our lawless souls.

310

One reason that people do not wish to be treated as expendable by their government is because it brings home a terrible truth of their existence — kingly though it may be. It is the hint that their very essence is largely inconsequential. Our great ego, though, often will refuse to accept such morbid facts, foreclosing the possibility of any further insight into the matter at all.

311

In the contemporary era, history is often required to be entertaining and resemble reality only tangentially at best. The main goal of any popular account of history is that it be entertaining above all else. Only secondarily should there be something important gleaned from it — assuming we possess that capacity anymore.

312

The political idealist has been preening for revolution for more than a century, expecting the oppressed to eventually rise up and capture back the dignity they imagine they once possessed as men. However, revolutions take more than a few citizens willing to lay down their lives for better living conditions. And the longer we live with some affliction, the more likely we are to surrender our will to it. Revolutions usually require conditions to be so dire that we simply have no choice but to revolt. Otherwise, we are more likely to endure instead. While not ideal, perhaps, it is far less burdensome than the proliferation of violence.

313

The commerce of everyday experience is a din meant to muffle the cries of the heart in chains.

314

We may be social animals for the most part, but we did not evolve to socialize with strangers. Thus, we regard any outsider as something of a criminal, an intruder who must either prove his loyalty or remain a suspect of great suspicion. The urbane city, even the most sophisticated, further alienates us from these nameless and faceless neighbors who reside solely on the periphery of our existence, like members of a large chorus. We cannot possibly know such people as anything more than an abstraction so we feel less of a sense of responsibility for their welfare. Intellectually then we have already taken a subtle step toward the eradication of the stranger, we have made ourselves into someone altogether indifferent.

315

Mankind arises from tribes and will retreat back into these smaller communities during times of extreme environmental stress. It then becomes a difficult task indeed to crack the incestuous shell of such collective families and introduce new ideas into their midst. It is even more arduous to coax these turtles out into the open air so that they might look around and gain a much broader understanding of the universe.

316

We must be very particular in choosing our friends since they are likely to bless or curse our life for some time to come. Yet, determining who to allow into one's interior circle requires personal insight often lacking in the vast majority of people. Thus human relationships are often fraught with some unresolved and ultimately self-destructive misunderstanding.

317

The man who fulfills his responsibilities as an individual but fails to consider his other duties to humanity as a whole is not much better than the man who surrenders everything of himself to the mob and forgets his individuality altogether.

318

While it's impossible for us to return to our past, we may nevertheless choose to cease moving forward in the vain hope of evading the future.

319

A man of character must daily choose to live humanely in the world. It is a choice that should be affirmed every day for the remainder of his life and, most importantly, it must be expressed by more than just his words.

320

A person afraid to contradict himself is enslaved by the judgment of the crowd since it is their opinion that he most desires to please. Socrates, in fact, is lionized for refusing to act in contradiction to his principles. Yet this refusal might be seen likewise as a shameful rationalization for a hemlock-induced suicide.

321

If we were to watch a large majority of other people receive a two-hundred volt shock and survive the experience quite happily, we will generally begin to feel anxious, discontent, and even a tad perturbed that we were somehow slighted.

322

The person who boasts a large contingency of friends is generally the same individual who — perhaps completely unaware — does not possess many who will prove themselves to be so in the end. True loyalty, profound allegiance, requires trust and intimacy — qualities not usually associated with a herd.

323

Contemporary culture often entombs the more profound elements of existence beneath the manicured lawns of polite society.

324

The needs of the few only trump the needs of the many in certain — often unusual — circumstances and only with respect to those exceptional spirits whose contributions are such that it might excuse their transgressions against the group. Generally, however, this determination will not be made until well after the needs of the few have been summarily denied or exterminated. The herd can be itself something of a vicious beast.

325

Most of us don't dare to delve too deeply into our own psyche for fear of what we might find. Humanity as a whole would also rather know only so much about its unheralded origins and the hollowness that echoes from inside its sometimes handsome exterior.

326

The contemporary lotus eaters of culture exist in a library with millions of important books which they generally refuse read.

327

If we are undecided and so feel we *must* receive guidance

to proceed in any significant situation, we should simply poll the majority for its opinion on the matter and then choose the other option. The majority is almost always wrong about the best things in life and overly concerned with the very worst, so they will often jump instinctually to conclusions based on their own fears and appetites.

328

We often confuse self-respect with self-worship and so begin to erect monuments to ourselves in the hope that others may bow before us too.

329

In the end, if he is not careful, man himself will become something of an idol and sit poised to worship himself for the achievements of his ancestors — foregoing his responsibility in the progress of his own evolution toward the humane.

330

All of us imagine — at least for a time of some magical thinking — that our birth somehow has altered the course of the planets.

331

The dinosaur roamed the earth for about 180 million years before it became extinct due to some freak act of Nature. Yet we somehow believe ourselves too clever for extinction or too suave or cavalier to care. Mankind's hubristic inclinations seem to be multiplying exponentially while his species ages far too prematurely.

332

The 21st century man has purchased his luxuries at the

expense of all future generations. The car he drives, for example, saps the earth of air and slowly chars the planet with carbon. A great many of his other actions too, in fact, further demonstrate that he intends for his grandchildren — long after he has gone — to settle up his debt or pass it along to some other poor soul not yet born who must bear the reckoning.

333

The flood of feeling generated through helping those in need often arises from the ugly desire for superiority. Any child will quickly explain why he should not share his most prized possessions with others — unless, of course, he can be convinced that the other is in more need of it than he. In such a case, the rush of dominance adequately repays him for the loss of his property.

334

The heroes worshipped in ancient times were those of deeds that bestowed some kind of boon to humanity as a whole. These people were worshipped, no doubt, because of the benefits received by the community. The modern hero, on the other hand, is known more for his name or reputation than for any contribution that he might have provided to others. This anti-hero is a force of personality rather than a person of significant character. Yet, he reflects our modern obsession with the royal procession of celebrity. These idols are primarily worshipped for their persona. They will only stage affairs for the benefit of others as part of some promotional campaign arranged by their publicist.

335

The immoral fool has so rationalized and justified his actions with half-truths, delusions, and outright lies that he can't help but imagine himself as righteous. Therefore, he possesses no guilty conscience for his wicked deeds. He has, after all, perfectly legitimate reasons for perceiving of them as something honorable.

336

We must learn to carefully tread the perilous waters between idealism and nihilism — both of whose shores produce jagged rocks that will tear one's soul to the marrow.

337

In clipping the strings which bind us to our responsibilities, we likewise lose the support of those to whom we were responsible. There exists nothing which is not imbued with this sort of complex interconnectedness. In making any decision we would be wise to closely examine what we are willing to sacrifice for the sake of our desire.

338

All memory is composed of the imaginative material devised by the interpreter — that personal "I" — of experience. In other words, all of us compensate for our lack of understanding by reconstructing the past with imaginative elements that might better explain those curiosities of human experience that so frustrate our rationality in general. "I remember!" is a cry even less reliable than "I know!"

339

Every human life can be reduced to a narrative of some kind — a thematic thread that underscores the existence of any one of us. Yet, these stories are often woven by external forces and seldom does someone actually put forth the necessary effort to establish some semblance of authorship. We are, instead, swept away by tides of happenstance and emotion. We have found our lives entangled in a web of other narratives quite by accident and this labyrinth threatens to leave us forever lost in its cavernous hallways.

340

Authenticity refers to the accuracy with which our actions suit the narrative that we have constructed for ourselves. For example, if an individual believes that she is an honest and caring individual, then she will only feel authentic if she acts in such a manner. If her narrative doesn't correspond to her deeds, however, then she must choose from among the following: change her actions, alter her narrative, or deceive herself entirely.

The machine

1

We are already training ourselves to become the voluntary slave of the machine by abdicating our own ability to think for ourselves. We view thinking, after all, as something of a burden, or at least a nuisance, that must be overcome. The machine, then, arises to alleviate boredom and eliminate the need for virtues such as patience and thoughtfulness. The machine is then — in a sense — the new messiah.

2

The machine has allowed the tool to become the master. Yet, this coup did not occur, as the seizure of power usually arises, with war or bloodshed, but rather we have willingly surrendered ourselves to the device.

3

*Mad*ernity occurs when a society begins to arrange a kind of corporate slavery wherein no one might escape the dominion of the market. Industry becomes a "living" entity that demands greater and greater compliance from those who consumptively serve, until it becomes something of a sentient force that wields a power usually only reserved for kings.

4

If we aren't persistently vigilant, humanity could become nothing more than a rumor that the machines discuss on their lunch break.

5

Contemporary individuals generally live under a regime of group-think — the assumption that the group, through discourse and debate, will arrive at the best overall conclusion for the collective. This is the type of thinking that moves mountains into empire and erects great pyramids and statues where once those mountains stood. It bestows great luxuries and entitlements beyond comparison to anyone in history. Yet, the group has little to say to the individual about how to live a good life. It wants everyone to live as everyone else — as a well-oiled machine, ready for production. In this manner, humanity becomes something of a machine itself.

6

It won't be long before mankind will become a kind of synthetic being, a simulation of the human that spends the vast majority of its time engaged with social technology and other forms of electronic entertainment. Humanity will become a fabrication of its former self, a replica of that which once possessed the potential for greatness.

7

The newest evolutionary creature will be the synthetic man.

8

Nietzsche has his character Zarathustra proclaim that man is something that must be overcome. Indeed, he is a rope, tied between beast and overman — a rope over an abyss. It is the overman who is the meaning of the earth. This Ubermensch of Nietzsche's vision has arrived in the form of the machine, the computer, and artificial intelligence. It is the artificial mind and memory that will eventually surpass us and evolve into another kind of personality altogether, a character created entirely by humanity itself. Yet, this will not trouble our citizens in the least. After all, it will not be a hostile takeover. In fact, mankind will largely welcome such an innovation as a means toward achieving a kind of synthetic immortality.

9

The machine is the new idol of worship. People entrust

their very lives to machines with the faith that the technology will ultimately bring them salvation of some kind. Yet, to worship a tool is to pay tremendous respect to what it can *do* for you, as a means to some other end. So the true value of any tool lies outside of itself to some larger aim. Therefore, the worship is misplaced.

10

All technological advances meant to improve our lives generally replace one source of grief with another. Sometimes the "advance" leans heavily in our favor, but too often the complexities advance themselves to such a degree that we become saturated and overwhelmed, unable to fully comprehend the vast complications of our actions. More significantly, we are too impatient to successfully handle these developments. The pace of nature is the natural state of all living creatures, yet we insist on speeding it up so that we might become more productive and accomplished. Meanwhile, we fervently dream that this latest flowering of utopia will perennially bloom soon enough — never mind that the only true utopia is death since only it extinguishes the conditions for complaint.

11

Machines are the new religion to which the vast majority of humanity now slavishly serves (yes, even the Luddites) for the future reward of some greater section of time to oneself — time that most will squander quite foolishly anyway.

12

The common fool today experiences even death as something of a dull routine.

13

When we are meaningfully engaged in our lives, the days pass quite easily. Yet, modern, technological society — industrial society — promotes the idea of *dis*engaging with life to a large extent. We are paid, after all, to sacrifice our awareness to the government or the company. Its energies are focused upon maintaining the cold, impersonal machinery of industrialization and bureaucracy. So, we remain profoundly dissatisfied with life and yet still concern ourselves almost exclusively with materialistic solutions to our malaise.

14

One great danger of artificial intelligence is that while a machine can mimic the computational processing of the human brain at a rate that far exceeds human capabilities, it lacks the regulating function of emotion. Pure, cold intellectual reasoning, after all, can lead to many inhumane conclusions without the tempering feature of empathy to color the black and white determination of intellectual indifference.

15

The advent of photographic technology has further made a *thing* of time. As an image, time becomes an entity captured for the moment without context of any kind. In this manner, the past is seen as separate and disconnected from the perceiver.

16

We often join a madhouse when we commit ourselves to a community, a corporation, or a government. These are, after all, institutions of the mob and the ignorant conglomeration that is the mass-man.

17

Photography, because of its tendency to improve over time, always leaves the impression that the past, mired as it must be in the muck of inferior technology, resembles the present in linear narrative alone. Photography presents history as something antiquated and fixed within the context of one particular era while simultaneously separating it from the present one. In this manner, the photo can distance us from a relationship with humanity as a whole — past, present, and future.

18

The Greeks knew enough about the physical world through the enlightenment of math and observation to develop many contemporary notions in the ancient mind. Yet, these concepts did not express themselves — as they do in our time — with the advancement of technology, luxury, and distraction because the ancients perceived the world as more than just a physical thing to be manipulated at will.

19

The contemporary family often gathers around technology like a pride bellies-up to the carcass of their prey — savage, drooling, and entirely self-involved.

20

We often aspire to reach a state of immortal peacefulness and undisturbed repose. In other words, we serve — though we may deny it — as a rather exceptional advocate for death.

21

One reason we feel so deeply anxious, uneasy, and alone despite our seeming continuous technological connection to others is because we spend so little time *using* these states of being to seek something that is greater within ourselves. Instead, we strive to purchase curtains which can be draped upon our character to mask the many imperfections found within.

22

We 21st century fools have disassociated ourselves from our own humanity and exist now as something altogether dead, but all too much alive nevertheless.

23

If someone is consumed with simply bettering their physical lot in life — improving their financial portfolio, reaching the apex of their career, collecting friends, admirers, and trinkets along the way — their psyche will eventually punish them for neglect. Yet, such a person may be far too accustomed to spiritual emptiness to ever perceive that something is amiss.

24

The image has replaced memory to such a degree that soon someone will live a life entirely documented by video and yet not remembered in the least.

25

We have supplicated ourselves before the machine in a

variety of ways. In fact, technology has created a whole new form of prayer: the worship of banality and the awe inspired by the flickering of spectacle and the bliss of mindless entertainment.

26

The humorless soul is generally quite lifeless as well.

27

The fool who lives his life according to doctrine does not live *his* life at all. Yet, neither does he really contribute to the betterment of the group since he offers little else besides the brute physicality of his labor. He remains, machine-like, dedicated to the status quo. While this approach may serve the needs of those in more primitive cloisters, it only hinders the growth of the human as a creature quite unique to nature.

28

Isolation is already a significant condition of the present day and will be, no doubt, an even greater concern for the future as machines and other synthetic fabrications insulate people from one another. Thus, we will need to develop a way to live alone in a world largely of our own creation. In so doing we will finally come to understand the mind of "God."

29

The rapid rise of modern technology obscures the fact that we have not progressed as much in terms of "man" as we have with respect to "machine." This is one of the primary difficulties with contemporary modernity: it is being conducted by a mad fool — many of them actually. These people often *mean* well, but are so ignorant of their own limitations — some extremists even going so far as to believe they have no real limitations whatsoever — that they rush headlong into unwise arrangements which might have otherwise been avoided.

30

The post-modern personality has become little more than a voyeur of other people's lives rather than a participant in his own.

31

The "individual" is only allowed to exist in those manners sanctioned by the state. Otherwise, the individual becomes something of an enemy to the machinery of the state, a menace to mass production and a heretic besides — although such a character might later be recognized as a genius when no longer perceived as possessing such a threat.

32

We are only able to evade the unsettling aspects of life when these elements do not continuously plague us in one way or another. Yet, while no one *enjoys* suffering, the avoidance of it hinders the development of character — sometimes altogether. In this manner, luxury, prosperity, and mindless entertainment can serve to merely stupefy and deaden the spirit of humanity. In general, this is the condition of the contemporary soul.

Art

The reality

1

Contemporary artists are quite technically skilled for whatever task they intend to undertake. They attend numerous workshops to hone this craft and develop it into something practical and beneficial to their career. Indeed these artists marvel the masses with their virtuosity. Yet, the artist of today is generally unable to move us to the depths of our soul or inspire us to catch a glimpse of the "divine." In fact, many of us have so deteriorated into such shallow creatures that we aren't even aware that these artists have been failing us all along.

2

The artist who paints for money should be revered as solemnly as any carpenter or mechanic possessing a useful skill. Yet, the artist who wishes to participate in the profound experience of *art* cannot concern herself with the demands of a patron — some master. Otherwise, while she might enjoy quite a successful career, her art will remain little more than a well-made chair.

3

Contemporary artists of the past 50 years or so are perhaps the best entertainers ever assembled in one era. They are superbly skilled at maintaining human interest and tweaking their craft to meet the insatiable demand of our need for escape and simplistic explanation. While these works may titillate, cajole, or even bring tears to our eyes, they are nothing of the sort that might genuinely shake our spirit to its very foundation.

4

The true artist must not heed the silly passions and pleas of the distracted populace. The greatest danger of providing the public with what it most desires is that the majority are then rarely challenged to improve in any substantial way. In the meantime, the artist of spectacle and titillation — while wildly celebrated and lionized by his contemporaries — serves as a kind of cheerleader for the status quo and the unabashed champion of the insignificant and the banal. Yet, the post-modern world needs its true artists now perhaps more than any other time in human history.

5

The treasures of the day quickly fade with time and are discarded as readily as the skin. Yet, artists continue to lose some of their most productive and fertile years in search of a paycheck and a career.

6

The difficulty that arises in the life of any career artist is that eventually he will be required to sacrifice his art for bread. He views this as something of a benign trespass until he realizes that his work has become ensnared in the spirit-crushing assembly line of commerce. The public is then often inclined to feel sorry for such a poor soul who has no other means by which to eat. Yet, no one would empathize with someone who eats his children at the first sign of hunger. He does possess other talents to earn a living, after all. Are we to assume that he should sacrifice what is most precious to him simply because it possesses some kind of fiduciary value? Of course, everyone should be allowed to have their bread and eat it too, but the work of the artist has the potential to demonstrate some of the greatest triumphs of human achievement, which is an entirely different undertaking than the practice of some common trade. These "more practical" trades become the inferior arts — the arts of distraction and recreation, those occupations which fuel the prejudice, ignorance, and laziness of the human character.

7

Anyone should be able to live on the spiritual nourishment received from the experience of true art. However, if we were forced to live on a diet of the contemporary fare alone, we would no doubt starve to death. The contemporary "artist" is far too concerned with fashioning a career and stocking it against the possibility of a long winter.

8

The contemporary artist's desire to paint is often much more than the child-like simple pleasure of stroking a brush across the canvas. He desires immortality as well — or appropriate recognition. While he may enjoy the smell of acrylic oils and even bask in the fullness of spirit that arises from the creation of something uniquely his own, it is the hope of reward that primarily moves him. It is precisely this hope which leaves him forever unsatisfied.

9

Even the avant-garde is controlled by the market. An artist must be, at the very least, marketable to his small band of friends if he hopes to earn a living. Yet, the level of concern he places on this ambition will be somewhat proportional to his loss of genuine artistic perception. The market — especially at times when driven by the indiscriminate force of tastelessness — is anathema to art since real art has never been nor will ever be the necessity of the masses. They simply have no interest.

10

The art and culture of the last fifty years has been too frequently little more than a salve or balm that superficially comforts the average person and soothes the sting of their own bad conscience.

11

The artist must first decide his intention with regard to art. If he intends to make a career of art — selling it at market to the highest bidder — he generally must abandon the pursuit of higher art, that is, art appealing to the highest in humane ideals and inspiring that part of us which most resembles the ancient notion of divinity. High art has never been a very profitable endeavor because it speaks of the impractical and the lofty. It is mankind's best contribution for the proof of the divine. Popular art in contrast reassures us that whatever we may lack in character we share with the vast majority of our contemporaries.

12

In the contemporary world the speed of images and/or information make it seem as if things of great importance can be achieved through a rather brief period of frenzied activity with the aid of the latest technological miracle. Yet the sculptor would not dream of cutting into stone without first spending much time contemplating the work. She will then slowly proceed, carefully guiding each cut, smoothing out the edges and releasing her vision from the stone. Unfortunately, so few artists cultivate this kind of patience — the virtue that often separates the true artist from the one desiring a thriving career.

13

Art in America and perhaps the world has become little more than a generator of careers and lifestyles. Universities are now administered not as a means of providing a deep harbor for the artist and the intellectual, but as bureaucracies designed to transmit the accepted dogma of the establishment. Patrons lurk around the alleyways of the museum and creep under the seats of the theatre in the hope of being seen. Artists compete — sometimes quite viciously — to "create" a path to fame and fortune while producers demand a message that will pacify the multitudes. True art it seems cannot survive such a thoughtless and instinctual bureaucracy.

14

Art for the sake of titillation will rarely last beyond the time it takes to digest a meal and only then as something of a nostalgia piece — people, it seems, wish to reminisce about titillations of the past.

15

In the end, the vast majority of contemporary artists are tainted by the same materialistic view as the common fool in the street. These modish artists, too, measure individuals through external means and blame the world for failing to recognize their talent in the same manner as their grandmother once had done.

16

It's not the bourgeoisie, those upper class materialists, who should trouble the artist, but those members of the culture class who fail to truly recognize and appreciate art that exists beyond the reach of popular sentiment or the vulgarity of some political rant. Great art reflects the depths of each individual yet the culture class today consists primarily of shallow folk who want to be endlessly entertained.

17

Vapid entertainment envelopes an individual and relentlessly shields this person from even the slightest discomfort or boredom. In so doing, it guarantees that such a person will fail to stretch and grow as necessary, stunting their character.

18

The individual who patronizes the fine arts — assuming the patron is not merely present for the sake of appearances — is generally hoping to communicate with the greatness of humanity — the humaneness of the beast. The arts promise to transform our understanding of the world. Yet, the contemporary artist seems almost oblivious to this need for deeper meaning as he attempts to entertain and demonstrate his cleverness instead.

19

Even the most extraordinary work of art ever create can become humdrum and ordinary as, with the passage of time, people come to accept it as something traditional and commonplace.

20

All of the bureaucratic lawmakers and other petty traditionalists are generally admirers of rather superficial art, but this is only true because they, too, lack depth. There is a genius to understanding, after all, and high art requires such a wise interpreter, a more profound thinker, to receive its rewards. The unimaginative, on the other hand, continue to count syllables, calculate rhyme schemes, and believe they can somehow establish an algorithm for poetry precisely because they fail to understand it properly.

21

We cannot literally *live* for art, but any person will certainly suffer quite a significant death of the spirit without it. This is the principal malaise of the contemporary world.

22

There is no poetry in our souls it seems — at least not anymore. It has been replaced by romantic fancy and the petty urge to express nothing more significant than a replication of an artist's own sick biography.

23

The new solipsism reveals itself most vividly in the work of the contemporary artist — writer, philosopher, sculptor, painter, etc. — who doesn't particularly enjoy art in much of a profound sense. Instead, he merely vomits up his own creations — those that arise from the bowels, the genitals, and the belly — in an attempt to assuage the nausea of his own existence.

24

The *execution* of a work of art — in other words, does it *work* as a piece of art? — is sometimes the only interesting thing about it. In such a case, its artistry has no more profound significance than might a well-made pot.

25

To the poets of pure sensation: there is no reason to describe in laborious sensory detail just what it may feel like to be alive. After all, those who are currently alive have no need of such description since they are so thoroughly immersed in sensory information. And those who are no longer living need more than poetry to blow them to life again. The poet — if worthy of the name — should inspire awareness and reflection.

26

True artistic innovation and genius are generally most recognized by the generations that follow the great artist, especially as the populations of cities rise and the people of genius become buried beneath a mound of artistic excrement — the remains of much contemporary art and poetry.

27

Art for art's sake has no real sake at all. If a person's life isn't made more profound from the experience, then art is a dull and idling activity indeed, one that merely stokes the quite flammable material of an artist's rather sizable ego.

28

Some of the artists of Modernism began the lunacy of imagining themselves to be some new incarnation of man. The past, these fools remained smugly certain, had nothing much to say to a present which was so entirely unique that even the wisest of ancestors would find it inconceivable. Yet, modern man is just as enlightened, informed, and rational as were his ancestors. The world still amazes and confounds him to the same degree. He is as profoundly ignorant as ever — though now about different things — and even the contemporary belief that we have inherently become a creature who is now less violent and more civilized overall is really not much more than a wistful prayer.

29

Too often the modern individual is only concerned with the salacious, beastly, or otherwise titillating characteristics of the artist rather than the artistic creations which might transcend such a person's obsession with banality.

30

The contemporary artist concerns himself with new forms and new techniques and originality in general to such an extent that he seems no longer interested in creating something that possesses any relevance to the profundity of life or the meaning of human existence.

31

Sometimes a good joke poorly told must be properly explained in order for anyone to appreciate it. The same is true of art, yet critics attempt to rationalize, justify, and sometimes even downright force meaning and significance onto the object under consideration. Such machinations are generally unnecessary for works that possess true artistic quality — at least to those spirits who are capable of understanding art sufficiently.

32

Contemporary art is plagued by irrelevancy. Art today is something analogous to a writer with nothing to say but four thousand pages with which he will express his thoughts regardless.

33

Contemporary artists — at least the vast majority of them — have nothing much to contribute or say yet continue to produce works at a furious pace for fawning critics who have spent far too much time in the coffeehouses of Conformity University. In the meantime, mankind regresses to his animal state with not much inspiration to act otherwise.

34

The art of the late 20th / early 21st century — at least that art which is generally heralded by the critics and the public alike — will serve posterity as little more than a historical curiosity — a means by which future generations might examine the psychological pathologies of postmodern man.

35

Art critics often attempt to intellectually justify what their hearts leapt to understand immediately.

36

The major difficulty for the artist of true originality is that her critics cannot conceive of something that hasn't the benefit of past interpretations to guide their own assessment. So the artist must either suit her work to an audience already established or find a critic who can appreciate the work in such a way that others begin to understand it too.

37

There was once a person who wrote a book that was so well received it eventually won some of the most prestigious awards for literature. It was universally praised as a work of great comic genius by the vast majority of commentators. However, the author had originally composed the work as a deeply serious tragedy which was then misconstrued by the critics to be brimming with irony. At first, each new accolade only served to further mock the writer's own artistic sensibility, yet before long he begins to grow accustomed to the flattery. He will even begin to see his work from the perspective of his admirers and believe in his own brilliance after a time. The artist's muse, he rationalizes, is beyond the mind to know and merely uses him to express itself to the world. He then is the lucky child of circumstance, he smugly imagines, a conduit of the gods and a grateful beneficiary of divine inspiration. The future, alas, will come to regard his work as something of a cosmic joke.

38

The difficulty of writing in antiquity, the sheer physical problem associated with being able to put words to "paper," compels the transference of only important ideas to future generations — or ideas that mankind has *thought* to be important at any rate. The contemporary ease of writing, conversely, allows for a writer to vomit his every thought to paper. Therefore, the difficulty for the future will be in sifting through the vast majority of our mental rubbish in order to find the treasure buried beneath.

39

When Blake exclaims that he has seen "visions," he is merely describing the epiphanies of artistic inspiration. These are quite natural occurrences for a great artist and serve as the wellspring of his creativity. They are the energy that infuses any great work of art. Yet, the average individual, secure and smug in his understanding of the world, dismisses such epiphanies as something born of a diseased mind.

40

An artist sexualizes his work for the same reason that a child giggles and snorts when discussing certain parts or functions of the body. Immaturity prevails for the contemporary artist who remains strongly committed to eliminating censorship because he wishes to further tantalize and amuse himself and his friends. Sex in art is used as the foundation of what the artist is trying to say because it often is all the artist truly knows. This leads to banality in art as well as in life.

41

Many artists today mistake artistic honesty for the shameful revelation of some highly personal and generally rather insignificant subjective experience. Of course, all life informs to a certain degree and even the most banal and crude condition can lead to some epiphany or other. Great art, however — the aim of all true artists — is an expression of one's understanding of the divine. It provides additional depth and significance in accordance with what is already thought about existence. Great art makes observations that inspire beyond the particular example provided by the work, but vulgar or trivial creations leave only an impression or image that immediately pleases or offends. If such a work *has* anything important to contribute, it likely will be lost in the shocking or petty manner employed by the contemporary artist.

42

The artists of today have made themselves irrelevant as anything other than a superficial — and often far too subjective — distraction from life for those who already despise the living. There is little a contemporary artist wishes to communicate other than the peculiar idiocies of his own subconscious for reasons that appear mostly directed toward some desperate plea for psychological assistance.

43

It should come as no surprise that a shallow and superficial society would give rise to an audience that prefers form over substance. Only the technical artist — the occupational workman or bondservant to the mob — survives in such conditions. Or the clown.

44

Art and artists will exist as long as man exists. However, the *audience* for art may disappear entirely — especially as man becomes more machine-like.

45

Art is only as consequential as its audience. The fool, after all, may imagine profundity in a painting created by a mad congress of orangutans. He may also perceive depth in a one dimensional line. At many times throughout the course of human history even Shakespeare is understood by the masses to be something of an old English hack.

46

The arbiters of culture — that democratic mob of sometimes quite dubious taste — will ultimately decide if a work of art possesses value of any kind. There will be much that is ignored in such judgments, of course, since these mediators must necessarily impose their own rather unsophisticated prejudices.

47

The simple fact that any society *has* culture does not entail that it *is* cultured — or even civilized for that matter. The Nazis arose, after all, from a rich soil of great German artists and philosophers to sprout quite beastly weeds along the countryside.

48

In order to avoid the sentimental, an artist will mistakenly dispense with sentiment altogether.

49

The noise of the modern world makes it quite difficult to perceive its art. In fact, in many cases, noise itself has become a form of artistic expression. This is one example as to why future generations — if humanity remains — will mock and scorn the 20th and 21st centuries for quite some time to come.

50

The Modernists would have us embrace the confusing, discomforting, and difficult nature of their art as a pleasure itself — generating a gratifyingly smug sense of superiority.

51

"Those who can't do, teach" is the boastful sneer of some young Parisian perhaps or avant-garde provocateur who imagines himself a genius and all the rest of humanity as but fodder for his muse. Instead, here is yet another fool who mistakes youth as some new coronation of man on earth.

52

The future artist will be the one who can best manipulate the newest technology into some fresh fashion. No doubt this will also provide greater access to artistic expression for even those who possess no talent for it. Unfortunately, as the means to creating art becomes more and more democratized, so too may its content eventually sink into the dreary humdrum of human mediocrity.

53

Many believed that the German culture — prior to the Holocaust — couldn't possibly allow the complete and utter depravity of mankind since it produced such great luminaries as Goethe, Mozart, Schiller, Bach and so many of their kind. While these artists were, more or less, well-cultured — perhaps — the art itself provides little guidance for any particular society as a whole unless we become sensitive to the expressions of art and more receptive to the truths that it will reveal. Art, in other words, provides little sustenance for the animal who would otherwise wish to eat it raw.

The ideal

1

Artists with no sense of history may wholeheartedly believe that art directly transforms the constitution of some political or material reality; however, art has as readily supported the propaganda of the inhumane as it has shown humanity to possess greatness of any significant kind. The entire notion of art, in fact, can be maddeningly broad — inclusive of almost any relative foolishness imaginable. Good art, on the other hand, distinguishes itself in its ability to transmit some profound — often unspoken — insight into the soul of someone else. Of course, as we develop and grow in maturity, education, experience, and taste our demand for more suitable material will enlarge as well and we will abandon those works that sustained us in our youth for those which challenge a more deeply cultivated character.

2

The creative abilities of the "weak" oftentimes trump the physical attributes of the "strong."

3

Art as religion is an exaggerated notion which presumes to provide its disciples with redemption, revelation, and freedom from oppression. It fails, of course — as all religions must — to keep such promises since these assurances are little more than the wishful fantasies of those desperate to regain the feeling of confidence in some great universal truth once again. Art *may* allow for such insights into the human condition, but it requires an audience that is suitable first — a patron of taste and character. The production of art, too, can be a spiritual activity, but this also requires a particular kind of artistic character — the creator who hopes to express something of the ineffable profundity of experience. The rest are merely expressing or experiencing their own neurosis.

4

Art should not be perceived as a religion in any way. It should be viewed instead as an anthology of sacred "texts".

5

The true nature of the divine is beyond our comprehension. The human mind, after all, has great difficulty conceiving of some "thing" that is neither male nor female, both dead *and* alive, which, at the same time, incorporates all paradoxes into a single comprehendible truth. Art is the best means for expressing the legitimacy of such irrational notions.

6

We experience our lives as a series of roughly interconnected fragments rather than as some unbroken linear narrative. Our memory is composed of various "snapshots" of these experiences — some quite faded and others as fresh as yesterday — which are only loosely associated with the present time. These memories are like mental photographs which we sort through in order to receive a better understanding of ourselves and shape our identity. They inspire reflection and thoughtfulness which in turn leads to a more satisfactory life. This is why art is so significant for the creation of character. Each work of art — itself merely a fragment of artistic expression as a whole —possesses the potential — if done well — to inspire consciousness of higher things.

7

Great science is perhaps even less prevalent than great art. *Ordinary* art and science on the other hand are flourishing and plentiful. Nevertheless, these are generally inferior types — the weeds that quickly overwhelm and strangle the more sublime and remarkable orchid — primarily concerned with spreading pleasure, ease, and contentment throughout the land. The beauty of great art and science is that, more often than not, they lead to a state of profound *dis*comfort that inspires us to expand our understanding accordingly.

8

The present age has been fed a consistent diet of artistic opiates for so long that it can no longer discern true art from whatever silly shadows it finds flickering upon the cave walls. It finds art *everywhere* since it sees no distinction between the superficial and the profound. However, true art is not life itself — or even the mirror of reality — but one of the highest activities that life inspires. It's a form of expression that communicates something about the deep and seemingly incomprehensible character of existence.

9

Great art of the present doesn't necessarily look like the art of the past. However, it must nonetheless inspire, provoke, and tell the "truth" about life. If we would wish to find great art in the present day, we would need to look beyond those industries whose sad intentions are to merely amuse and entertain.

10

While overwrought sentimentality is certainly something that distracts from any true work of art, sentiment itself is necessary for a work to be accessible — as a person without sentiment is someone to be avoided, so too is the work of art that fails to sufficiently inspire the heart.

11

Art — at least fine art — should enlighten and enthuse. The artist perceives some insight that occurs during the course of the day and sets it in relief so that all the distracting and irrelevant features fade into the background, illuminating only the object of poetic concern. In this manner, true art reveals something of the divine nature of life itself.

12

Art exists in the mind. The entire enterprise is perceived and understood by some patron that finds it interesting or beautiful or profound. The artist merely attempts to manipulate or inspire such a reaction in the mind — sometimes successfully and sometimes not so much. Yet, some will not find this work valuable at all. They may desire art that entertains or obscures instead. It all depends upon the type of mind that encounters the work in the first place.

13

The shallowest pleasures of nature may sometimes seem as such "divine" beauty when compared with even the noblest achievements of man. Yet this will not deter the true artist who knows that she, too, is natural. She, too, has something of the "divine" within her.

14

The beauty of poetry and the true *art* of the medium, if truth be told, is as something of an instrument by which we experience — as well as quite often practice — the task of spiritual growth, the evolution of the humane.

15

It is often a misconception of the contemporary mind to imagine geniuses from antiquity as luminaries in their own time as well. The names of Euripides, Homer, and even Shakespeare seem as ancient as the mountain and as powerful, too, looming over contemporary artists like giant oaks that shade the tiny blades of grass that arise every spring. Yet, in their time, while sometimes certainly esteemed, these great historical majesties were but one intelligent voice in a relatively small chorus of thoughtful individuals. If not for the fortuitous sharing of their texts much of what we know of our culture and ourselves today would be significantly changed. Yet, much ancient work was forever lost as well, the value of which is no doubt unfathomable. Who can say how much richer might be our understanding today? How much wiser our commitments? How much more humane our actions? The cities now are further choked with the din of so many souls clamoring to be heard and clawing for their place atop the pyramid of popularity and status. Who among them — if any — will be selected for inclusion into that pantheon of the very wise? Who among them will even try?

16

Poetry and art arise as a discussion of the unknown, a meditation on the dark matter of the cosmos.

17

Comprehension of the world of noumenon — as opposed to phenomenon — is the true aim to which the artist aspires: to understand in some way the unknowable which exists beyond the comprehension of the senses. The scientist is concerned —as well he should be — with the constitution of phenomenon, the artist troubles herself with the mysterious and the ideal.

18

The nearest that we can experience the voice of any kind of "god" is through the miracle of music. Wordless music is the irrefutable proof for the existence of something divine in the universe. Words and images, on the other hand, name and describe objects and entities. These names, by necessity, distinguish themselves as much by what they *are* as what they are *not*. The notion of "god," for example, establishes a concept of personality which in turn is understood as possessing some particular features (goodness) and lacking in others (sinfulness), thus creating a deity that is both infinite and disappointingly limited in many ways. After all, the determination of something as a "chair" automatically disqualifies it for inclusion into other categories to which it is no longer suited — categories such as: table, mountain, dog, tree, doll, etc.. So, within this realm of words, such literal notions inevitably lead, as they should, to irrefutable contradictions and maddening uncertainty. Through music, however, the depth and beauty and experience of the divine enlightens the soul of anyone fully conscious. Our mind, of course, wishes to rationally comprehend the divine, naming and classifying that which is essentially a mystery, but only our spirit will ever really understand it. Music is, after all, the soul's proper language.

19

Divinity is not some pathetic personification of human form. The very notion of divinity is rather abstract and can be only truly understood in such a way. The divine, in part, is the creative urge itself, the drive to forge a place of meaning and justice in the world, the harmony of all paradox, the very essence of love and the impulse for sacrifice to a higher — more noble — state of being. There were a multiplicity of gods throughout antiquity precisely because each represented a unique, artistic manifestation of some profound notion that was far too abstract to be understood at all without the necessary metaphorical mask to provide it the proper context.

20

Fiction is for the child; prose is for the adult; and poetry belongs to the eternal realm of divine imagination.

21

Wittgenstein writes: "there is indeed the inexpressible. This shows itself. It is the mystical." Yet, the mystical *is* expressible. It is *not*, however, definitive and concrete. It does not possess the qualities of permanence and immutability that so enthrall the lovers of proofs and logic. Its expression instead is artistic and ephemeral, even emotional at times. If the mystical were not expressible in some way, the entire enterprise of love would be extinguished in both thought and action.

22

True art is not a craft like woodworking, construction, or pottery. The techne of the art is its least interesting quality. What it expresses and its relationship to humane understanding are its only claim to some "divine" realm.

23

Art is not the vomiting of emotion or the pontificating expression of some unexamined belief. It arises instead from that source which seems to most animate us, the very essence of life — the soul, spirit, and animus of existence.

24

True art allows us to perceive life from a different perspective than our own. It is only in this manner that anyone beholds a glimpse of the divine — the embodiment of a multiplicity of views which illuminate the most profound and mysterious aspects of existence.

25

The artists' faith in her work and her own unique personality adequately supplants any need that might arise to request that she develop some faith in god. Her faith in her work is just precisely a spiritual faith.

26

Art requires a sophisticated, educated, and somewhat "artistic" audience in order to survive. Art exists in a society to the same degree to which the audience exists, as Whitman noted long ago. Lacking such an audience, the artist must burrow underground to create her work secretly in the hope that one day her audience will return. This is the artistic faith: the belief that what we create from the wellspring of our spirit will one day be of value to someone. If her faith goes unrewarded, it is no matter since the simple act of creation for such a person serves as a source of strength. The activity alone provides a reflective exercise that develops and accelerates the process of spiritual growth.

27

A true artist has faith in her art and pays little attention to contemporary criticism. In fact, she must remain staunchly committed to her art so that human excellence may not disappear from the world altogether.

The great artist though is generally never quite fully acknowledged until well after her death. Her contemporaries, after all, imagine themselves her superior or her equal while no one wishes to seriously compete with the dead.

28

Each new work of art — or an old one freshly conceived — provides an opportunity for one soul to meet another — yet more deeply, by sharing thought, mood, and perspective. And this inevitably leads to the spiritual growth of any individual. After all, to *truly* imagine oneself a pauper — a perspective gained through either art or experience — should cause anyone to treat the poor with less disdain.

29

We are at war, have been perpetually at war, perhaps will be always at war given our nature. It is a war for the survival of humanity against the tyranny of the inhumane. Sometimes this war is found to exist between countries, but this is merely one external manifestation. The first shot is always fired within the very heart of each individual. It is the responsibility of the artist to reveal the conflicts that exist within the human soul and forge a new perspective for mankind as a whole.

30

"The aim of art," wrote that great artist Aristotle "is to represent not the outward appearance of things, but their inward significance." A quite realistic painting of a tree, for example, displays the painter's talent, no doubt, but says little about what distinguishes that *particular* tree from the forest that surrounds it. The essence of the tree or the scene is what ultimately matters, its own unique significance. Its effect is to enlighten, to illuminate some perspective hitherto forgotten or unexplored, and to ripen, of course, the soul of the individual.

31

If the only "truth" we may ever know is inextricably linked to the deficiencies of our sense perceptions and the weakness of our intellectual capacities, then it seems entirely possible, if not downright likely, that there exist alternative perspectives beyond these human limitations which speak to something entirely mysterious and unknowable about the cosmos. Art attempts to provide insight into just such abstract and extraordinary realms as might arise from an individual's encounter with everyday life.

32

The purpose of true art is not to entertain or create some new myth for us to worship. Instead, its purpose is to reveal new vistas and perceptions that might allow us more insight into our condition.

33

Great art does not simply exist to make us *feel* something — and certainly not for that sake alone — but as a means of altering perception in such a way as to reawaken much of our sensibilities — mental as well as physical. Of course anyone might at first feel overwhelmed with an emotional response to some work of art, but the feeling itself arises as a consequence of an enlivened perception, a glimpse cast with eyes quite sparkling with possibility.

34

True art is the expression of some unique perception about human existence — an insight, sometimes in rather abstract form, that enlightens one's consciousness as to the deep and fragile profundity of life.

35

Art reunites the one with the many. The individual, through the artistic experience, perceives of her connection to the whole.

36

True art will drench us in the wash of life's profundity.

37

Human greatness entails participation in the arts at a high level. The "arts," however, may include more than just the traditional arts, but the mechanical, technological, physical, and intellectual arts as well — any beneficial talent that keeps the ethical evolution of humanity progressing steadily forward rather than sliding back into the kingdom of the Neanderthals.

38

It is important that we have an idea of what to look *for* in a work of art. This is not to say that we should make ourselves something of an expert on the subject. Yet, within any great work of art lies meaning hidden for the right opportunity of expression.

39

All great art exists as a spiritual exercise. Every genuine

encounter with it leaves a person profoundly changed somehow, imbued with a fresh perspective.

40

Great art grounds us to the center of the earth. So the fool who believes that nothing was ever redeemed by poetry or art simply has failed to engage with it properly. Or he suffers from a lack of a more cultivated and discerning taste. In any event, great art itself may develop us to such a degree that we are no longer brutish of thought or action.

41

We can be more alive immersed in the experience of authentic art than in the majority of our encounters with the "real" world.

42

How can we understand those abstract, nonphysical properties of existence — thought, for example, or love — when there exists no *thing* to serve as proof? In other words, how does one illustrate what is by definition beyond the capacity to describe? Music, metaphor, art, and silence are our only recourse.

43

How many works of art have been ignored by the era in which they were born? How many more have been entirely destroyed by the brute ignorance of mankind as a whole? How many artists, some who perhaps could rival the very great, have been marginalized or otherwise forgotten entirely? The true artist should possess little concern for how her work will be received. The child at play gives away everything that she creates.

44

All art — all good art anyway — engages the human mind in a kind of dance or interplay with the collective conscience of humanity.

45

All great artists are prophets of a sort, though art is no religion. They do not profess to foretell the future but instead inform the present with wisdom from the past.

46

The many distractions of modern existence serve as a collection of seductive sirens whose melodious song inspires sailors to deliberately run their ship aground upon the rocks. In the same manner, pop-art or pop-culture lures us away from art that might otherwise develop or reform our character for the better.

47

The creators of vapid entertainment and distraction all appear as something altogether more powerful because of their ability to create, not art, but spectacle. The sage must develop the ability to distinguish this type of ostentatious art from the kind of work that is more transformational. Otherwise she is doomed to wallow only in the shallow puddles of human existence.

48

In a culture of bombast and spectacle, the artistic piece that is deep, reflective, and challenging can be difficult to perceive as something significant or even worthy of attention.

49

The creative work produced for the primary purpose of pleasing an audience is not the type of art that generally inspires any kind of noteworthy spiritual development. The creators of entertainment are no different than any workman or mechanic who serve the whims and "needs" of the customer. The true artist, on the other hand, is a kind of prophetic guide for the rest of humanity to fall in behind. She provides the framework for a more humane understanding of the world and our own unique place within it.

50

The artist must create, of course, with a particular audience in mind, yet she should not expect that they will be mindful of her at all. Otherwise, she might find herself pandering to a variety of unqualified tastes and unusual appetites.

51

Even among the decay and ugliness, the chaos and cruelty of everyday life, there can arise a single note to still the din of despair and corruption. The soft musical tones of Debussy's Claire De Lune, for example, may flutter from a window sill out into the street and immediately seize the spirit of a beggar, perhaps, or a lonely widow, reminding them both — and all of us as well — that there does exist something divine in this world, there does exist the profound experience.

52

The spirit can only reveal itself through the expression of some creative project. Otherwise, it remains interior and isolated, goading its host to find the proper means of exhibition.

53

The creative and reflective aspects of our personality are significant for the development of our highest self. Engaged in a creative project — a task almost *demanding* contemplation — we transcend the brute reality of existence to express a spiritual value antithetical to the striving for food, shelter, possessions, and clean water.

54

The artist should be perceived as something of a divining rod of the spirit rather than a type of profession that someone might pursue. In this manner, we can begin to understand the depth and profundity of such prophets as Monet, Blake, or Dickinson — to name but a few.

55

Both philosophy and art should at least *attempt* to have some type of moral development as their ultimate aim.

56

No one can live artfully without art.

57

The work of art attempts to arrest the speeding movement of time — that fleeting, effervescent *"thing"* which has no visible shape or substance but can be seen nonetheless with the mind's eye. The job of the artist is to convert that which is fluid and changing into the work of art which holds experience up to reflection, slowing the motion of time.

58

The art that generally possesses a kind of higher value, the art that expresses the deepest of human truths, is that which reminds us — without a word sometimes — as to the breadth and profundity of life.

59

Art is a fervent prayer that you're out there somewhere, o' man — creative and wise, patient and guileless, amidst the electronic haze of a technological revolution.

60

The artist must remember the pace and productivity of nature and imagine herself as something of a farmer who plants seeds in the spring for a harvest that she may not live to see. Yet this fact should never keep her from planting nonetheless.

61

While the function of art is to reveal truth, it is the sort of truth that is entirely abstract by nature — expressed perhaps in the everyday experience of living, but reducible to nothing quite specific in the end. What else is life but the animation of the inexpressible?

62

Life is not, as Schopenhauer laments, unendurable without art any more than life is intolerable without religion. However, we are *not* capable of living without creating something of our own. This may sometimes give the impression that it is the thing — the work of art — which is essential to our concern when, instead, it is the act of creation.

63

The only purpose of a work of art is for it to *be* a work of art; that is, an artist must create for the higher goal of profundity and depth rather than commerce or admiration. Otherwise, art becomes no more significant an endeavor than producing a widget, an opinion, or a burp.

64

High art is distinguished from the mere art of craft through the intention of its aim. Both require skill and ingenuity, but high art succeeds in transcending the physical world with a more abstract or spiritual understanding. Science governs the realm of the physical world while high art alone may declare sovereignty over the realm of the abstract, the metaphysical, and the ethereal.

65

The true artist is a kind of modern-day alchemist in that she utilizes the base material of empirical "reality" in order to forge the more precious metal of art.

66

The artistic artifacts of any particular culture will express the values and interests of that culture. The artifacts that posterity values, on the other hand — often entirely different works altogether — are the works that humanity values.

67

The person who intends to kill with words often possesses the same intent as the person who kills with mace and steel. Yet, the inhumanity of the writer or the artist is rarely ever questioned because the war that she wages — if she is a proper artist anyway — is one that stands in stark contrast to the aims of the inhumane.

68

We must learn to look at the cosmos poetically again.

69

Religion should teach us how we can best live in the world, but the world of which it speaks no longer exists except in the hearts of some still quite ignorant Neanderthals. The world of the bibles is anachronistic, out of touch with the complexities of the enlightenment and the quantum realm of science. This is not to suggest that some brand of scientism should fill the void since science admirably understands, or should so understand, its limitations. It, of all the arts, is most committed to the pursuit of knowledge without some preconceived notion about truth. Yet, it too has little to offer in theories or proofs about how a contemporary individual should live a life of value. The *spirt* of the contemporary soul is what seems to need bolstering most and this will require something of an inspirational revolution of the arts.

70

Work worthy of the name "art" is not the product of a person who attempts to conceal themselves from the world. Nor is it a commodity that an artist might hope to sell for a handsome profit and gain a fine reputation along the way. On the contrary, art is an expression — abstract though it may be — of our deepest "truths" and our most sacred "realities." This requires an artistic sensibility directed toward greater degrees of vulnerability and courage rather than mere economic cowardice, neurotic nausea, and recreational escape.

71

To say that *anything* can be considered a work of art is a heresy to art itself and an entirely misguided perception of the very concept — a childish dismissal of that which makes art profound and meaningful to life. Anything can *potentially* serve as a work of art, of course, but there must first exist some artistic vision and intention toward the more spiritual and profound elements of existence. Otherwise, art is little more significant than the scribbling of children or the blather on a billboard.

72

Wittgenstein is correct to claim that philosophy ought to be written as a poetic composition. Only then might we cease quibbling over the symbols of truth and focus instead upon the more esoteric and complex notions that such symbols reveal — ideas best illuminated through the experience of art and best understood as an artistic creation. A poem, after all, contains a great many truths that cannot be mathematically verified but may express something quite profound nevertheless.

73

Art develops and then strives to maintain the humane response to life.

The Humane

Attempts at definition

1

Definition, while certainly able to clarify, does very little to deepen a subject. For this reason the artist should refuse to definitively define since she is only concerned with the depth of experience.

2

Aristotle no less, that great philosophical classifier, grouped mankind as a kind of being distinct from other mammals. Within this separated human classification can be found other mundane and often irrelevant distinctions such as race, gender, politics, religion, and the like; however, an important division does exist between two distinctive types within the human personality: the humane and the inhumane. The humane is exemplified by those elements in us which uplift the spirit and demonstrate our kind to be something unique and estimable. The goal then for any individual is to daily act in such a way as to demonstrate her humanity, to show from her many actions that she is a person of character; an individual possessed of reason, compassion, and understanding; a creature of patience, loyalty, and resolve; a person who will not be swayed by the cynicism or exuberance of her age nor the quantity of competitors lined up against her; a person quite refined in her sensibilities, humble in her intellect, and devout in her study of the humanities. In short, the goal is for the individual to be a "man" in the highest sense of the word. The inhumane, by contrast, dwells in the cellar of any human potential. He is the gnarled brute that imposes his will upon the world, the beast that creeps and claws along the alleyways, and the charlatan that lies and deceives himself as well as others. These are two very distinctive species of everyone's personality and whichever is fed and nurtured most will ultimately survive.

3

Man is addicted to his animal instincts because this element of his nature so easily controls so much of his behavior and manifests itself as something organic to him — thereby solidifying its "natural" legitimacy. Yet if we might wish to rise above our often quite savage and beastly nature, we must generally abandon its goals and attempt to modify our actions so that they more closely model the very best of our character rather than the very worst of the animal's.

4

A person should be something of a cosmopolitan rebel against his own instinctual self, allowing it sovereignty only when its rule is not tyrannical.

5

There is indeed, as Konrad Lorenz observes, a fundamental conflict between the instincts implanted by evolution and the moral restraints necessary to civilize mankind as a collective. This *is* the battleground. *Here* is where we must set the front and fiercely defend those elements of humane existence which alone bring honor to the beast. Yet, in waging such a "war", a righteous person must also model a great deal of moral restraint and so fight the war peaceably, through the example of her character alone.

6

The greatest benefit of ancient Greek and Roman art and philosophy — one reason they still electrify the intellect thousands of years beyond their first occurrence — is that these works concern themselves primarily with the living of an individual life while simultaneously obligated to the community from which that life arose. In other words, the study of Greek and Roman culture is importantly a meditation on the best approach to living a human life — and hopefully a more humane life as well. As opposed to the impulse which drives most of contemporary civilization, these Hellenists are concerned overall with the betterment of the soul rather than the improvement of material conditions. The very best of these works also avoid the religious error of imagining the material world as merely something of a dream.

7

The value of philosophy — the reason why many "amateurs" study it so fervently — is that it reveals a thoughtful, intelligent, and altogether innovative human perspective which promises to change our lives forever if properly understood. The change may not be significant in itself, of course, but each new crack in the fortress of our hubris brings with it the possibility of leveling the monstrosity entirely. If philosophy can be said to have any unified goal at all, that aim would be directed at cultivating an intuitive and intellectual openness in us. True philosophy, after all, endows us with a variety of differing points of view about life and encourages the contemplation of those most important aspects of our existence. Otherwise, the "love of wisdom" is exposed as a passion for a peculiar kind of vice — the sins of the intellect.

8

Philosophy should be an art form, a style of living instead of a theoretical discourse. While theory has its place in matters of science, philosophy is a way of life, a particular *manner* of living. It is living deeper through a commitment to the attainment of wisdom rather than a rational proof for some well-designed theory of "truth." Any philosophical perspective should be exemplified in any philosopher's life and how she lives it. Otherwise, she should not be considered a philosopher at all.

9

The very best philosophy will not provide us with the definitive answers that we seek so desperately. Instead, it helps to guide us closer to the goal of better understanding ourselves and our world. All of the best philosophies merely offer a more informed and insightful character, one less inclined to the beastliness and ignorance usually found in the species as a rule. Yet, without a lifelong commitment to attaining this end, the best philosophy ever conceived serves as little more than some hollow campaign slogan.

10

Philosophy, at least the most significant sort, is an exercise of meditation rather than some mathematical proof. It hopes to demonstrate the truth of nothing in particular and instead provide a kind of clarity for any situation, an illumination of experience that isn't one's own but can be assimilated nevertheless. Yet, for any of this to occur we must find some time in our day to separate ourselves from the persistent noise of humanity and the frenzied confusion of the modern world.

11

The humane — if it is to be properly perceived — is concerned with more than just the human alone.

12

The philosophers would have us accept mankind as he *is* rather than as we might *wish* for him to be. Yet, so much of man remains encased in possibility and subject to a great deal of change. After all, how we encounter a person today is bound to be quite different from our meeting with the same person tomorrow. He is as we find him of course, but in the next moment he is slightly someone else. The very idea of "man" writ large is a massive generality itself, a concept that can include everything from the base, vicious, unconscious beast that often populates our collective history to a creature possessing almost divine properties. *This* is man as we find him. This is man as he is — a complex amalgam of varying degrees of maturity and development. So, the expectation of holding man to a higher standard is, in many cases anyway, entirely justified. Who he *is* seems inextricably intertwined with the metaphysics built into the possibility of who he might become if properly inspired.

13

Ignorance in youth is a natural occurrence. After all, a young person has simply little experience to guide them in their quest for understanding — they haven't gone out into the world to forge their character against the weightiness of life; they haven't fallen, righted themselves, and fallen once again; they haven't loved, or studied, or observed enough to even cultivate a valid opinion, let alone develop comprehension of any kind. These things will arrive with time, of course, if people pursue them with an earnest resolve. More often than not though, individuals choose to remain dedicated to the slumbering of their mind. It is this lazy form of ignorance that most gladdens the countenance of the inhumane and makes the human into something of an inconsequential creature.

14

The goal of any good parent is to make of their child a human being, to develop and strengthen character in such a way as to leave the child willing and able to continue the process of cultivation and development rather than to simply provide society with another drone for the hive.

15

The goal of existence is not to *make* our life into a work of art necessarily, but to develop our character to such a degree that we can delight in the great beauty and some of the more sublime qualities of life itself. It is to make of ourselves, not an artist, but a patron of the arts. We must learn to appreciate *life* as a work of art.

16

We must sculpt our character from the rough material of nature using our experience and education to gain some semblance of form. This is a lifelong project, however, so we should not expect to create something significant overnight or anticipate reward from an absence of work.

17

The evolution of the species, or the individual for that matter, does not progress in a tidy, straightforward, and linear fashion like the chronology of time. Instead, development and growth occur in fits and starts, trailing a path that leads through a wide variety of peaks and valleys, rugged terrain as well as open fields — progress, after all, is a process and not a destination. Thus, we must learn to cultivate patience. Evolution often regresses or even degenerates in many ways, but then it may suddenly lurch forward without warning, leaping up one day to momentarily touch the stars. In fact, for some, progress can be entirely circular.

18

The human being does not progress at the rate of a dollar and our character does not improve like a flower blooms — that is, quite naturally. We must work, instead, and expect to be rewarded rather haphazardly — as character evolves at an irregular pace, sometimes entirely by chance.

19

In order to reach the stature of the truly human — as opposed to the purely animal, all instinct and desire — we must labor for the majority of our days. We must first educate ourselves to such a degree that we are well versed in the arts, sciences, and humanities and so will not simply accept the advice of the ancients, or our contemporaries, mindlessly. We must then work to synthesize our own unique perspective from the vast array of other views that exist about ourselves and the world in which we live. This is a project without end since its goal is depth rather than destination. Being humane then is a kind of continuous process to improve the spirit and the intellect.

20

The quality of our education depends upon how fiercely we desire to understand.

21

War in the contemporary era is ultimately a fight for technology. Right now and for the foreseeable future, we are, as a collective, fervently engaged in securing the means by which we might make our lives easier and in the process defend against those enemies who would seek to destroy us with it. Knowledge in this case is king, but a sovereign without a country. It possesses neither loyalty nor morality of any kind. Its rule is absolute, but it pays little notice to the integrity of its followers — blind subservience is all it requires. While the vast majority of us appear more than willing to lay down our lives for the opportunity to acquire some petty measure of ease and comfort, the sage pursues knowledge in order to inform the spirit of something fundamental to its constitution.

22

It's extremely difficult for people to govern themselves since at any one particular time in history the majority of people are intellectually challenged. They are barely equipped to manage their own individual lives let alone consider the abstract concepts required of governance. Of course, some can be educated to understand these notions and even grow to become quite serviceable citizens; however, this first requires a certain openness to the experience. In many cases adults too run from their schoolbooks just as quickly, if not faster, than do schoolboys. We must desire to learn and it must be the kind of curiosity that nags at us like a festering wound until we apply the salve of understanding.

23

Honest mistakes are often only disastrous when we refuse to learn from them.

24

Education and study are only *elements* necessary for an individual of character; they help supply some answers to our many questions. They do not constitute the *whole* of our cultivation; however, they do provide the structure upon which we might overlay the remaining features of a good life — those that best relate to the flourishing of our character and the nurturing of our soul.

25

Education is indeed paramount to the development of any individual; however, the contemporary understanding of this notion is generally quite narrow and specialized — all nations need their doctors, scientists, and technicians after all. The sort of education that edifies the soul, on the other hand — the highest purpose of any university — allows us to delve into the most profound achievements of our kind in search of answers to our own probing questions about life. Here, too, we will need certain "professors" to guide us, but they can only really lead us a small portion of the way since each of them are in the midst of undertaking such a quest themselves.

26

The ancient religious traditions serve as our earliest library. The ancient texts, after all, are generally anthologies of humanity's best efforts to that point in time. It is only natural — given the proliferation of the human on earth — that such libraries expand to hold new volumes of work which include fresh ideas and newer explorations of stale ones.

27

The texts of the ancients are meant to stir reflection and meditation rather than serve as codified sets of rules and consequences. Laws are designed to impose moral compliance upon those who can't, for whatever reason, raise their conscious awareness to the standards of the humane. These people are generally, like children, "made" more obedient as they seem incapable of developing a virtuous character of their own. Yet, the more humane soul, she who is most dedicated to notions such as cultivation and integrity, must remain focused upon the development of her spirit and by doing so enlarge the character of the world as well.

28

Love is an impossible response to hate without the benefit of greater understanding.

29

We need to develop the kind of character that might best

withstand the inequities and injustices of any particular situation or era in which we find ourselves. It does us little good to erect a shelter that shields us from the sun but allows the cold to chill us to the bone. If we are to survive and flourish, we should plan for as many possible eventualities as we are able to discern.

30

We should aim to develop our character in such a way that it evolves from the purely instinctual drives of our own beastly and unconscious nature to the more cultured sensibilities of a refined and humane creature.

31

We will only mature and evolve through culture and the cultivation of a humane sensibility.

32

We all should cultivate a relationship with a sage of some kind, a mentor whose guidance might help us to grow and flourish. This figure need not be alive to serve this purpose. In fact, it's better if such an adviser survives only in the pages of a book or upon the walls of a gallery since these do not allow for answered questions.

33

Everyone needs a mentor or a sage to guide them — some teacher who illuminates the passageway so that any darkness is barely visible. However, mentors are difficult to find among the living since there can only be a few at any one time who understand the imperatives of human existence and these souls, unavoidably, are scattered throughout the globe. Thus, one interested in the development of the humane and the improvement of human character often must mount an intensive search through the literature and art of the past to find the proper guidance.

34

We generally need more guidance with what we should avoid rather than what we should pursue.

35

As Theseus needed golden string to find his way through the labyrinth of Daedalus, so too do we need some sort of conductor to orchestrate us through the movement of our own lives. This is the primary occupation of great souls among us.

36

The great individual has the most to lose and the courage to risk losing it.

37

The greatest individuals, the true heroes, do not sacrifice their lives for the sake of the herd. Their sacrifice, instead, is the necessary consequence of an all-encompassing desire to actualize some great notion. In this manner they set a fine example, though, sadly, most may never know its influence. Christ — the poetic philosopher, not the literal (and quite fictional) messiah — for example, hoped to promote an ethical concern for others and a more peaceful resolution to conflict. These noble ideas and his commitment to them eventually lead to his brutal fate on the cross. It was not, however, this unfortunate martyrdom or his alleged "resurrection" that established and solidified his authenticity as someone of significance but the inspiration of his example. And he is merely one among millions of others now here and gone.

38

One day the majority of people again will look to moral instruction and artistic cultivation to help deepen their character and broaden their perspective of life. In the meantime, self-education should be the primary tool for achieving the goal of richening one's existence.

39

The superior individual is not superior *over* other people like some unforgiving Tsar or other such bully, but she is extraordinary with respect to the depth of both her character and her commitments.

40

Hegel believed, among other things, that each successive higher level of consciousness progressively incorporates all earlier, more elementary levels. In other words, he saw humanity evolving historically into some great and noble creature. However, history has demonstrated time and again that such a progression in consciousness and insight is by no means inevitable. If each succeeding generation fails in its commitment to the humane and the continued humanizing of man, then the entire species might quite easily slip back into that skin which feels most natural: the hide of a beast.

41

Life is a great painting with a lot of really sad colors and some brilliant ones too. Otherwise we couldn't distinguish one hue from the other.

42

The child at play is the ideal to which all of us should aspire — that lively desire to create, and sing, and think, and draw, and imagine, and dance without restriction other than the natural limits of the day. Such a child has little concern for the metaphysics of her existence when engaged in such a state of puckish commitment. She is, instead, focused intently upon the project at hand. This endeavor is, in a very real sense, her only reason for living at that particular moment.

43

Mankind must reaffirm its commitment to civilization and other humane projects with each new generation in order to ward away the primitive, ignorant, and barbaric elements of humanity's more natural tendencies.

44

All of us, even those living in the direst of circumstances, receive at least *some* modicum of pleasure in our lives, and many people need and wish for so much more — even those of us who have more than our share. Yet, few of us indeed attempt to experience the higher, more sacred, pleasures of life — those derived from a profound and patient commitment to contemplation, reason, art, and the limitless possibilities of the humane imagination. In short, it is the life engaged with acquiring awareness and understanding.

45

A rock, gently skipping across a lake will only find its depth when deprived of motion.

46

Contemplation allows any thought to glide across the canvas of the mind with the ultimate intent of improving the soul. Doctrine, on the other hand, censors thought before it's formed, hoping to somehow restrain the spirit through the sheer force of repetitive conditioning.

47

The only way to appreciate one's life is to be aware of it — not *always,* to be sure, but we should at least develop a heightened sensitivity to our own person as a spirit of sizeable concern. This higher-end contemplation is unavailable to the animal who, instead, must be necessarily immersed in the world to such a degree that he is only tangentially conscious of it. A human being, on the other hand — if we are in fact worthy of that name — is most alive in those moments of deliberate reflection. Yet, the rut and monotonous routine of everyday modern existence only encourages us to become something of a beast as we pace, focused and driven, within our enclosure of expressways and skyscrapers.

48

No one would ultimately desire for an eternal recurrence of their life entire. Such an experience would bring tedium to even the greatest of "supermen." After all, even the finest musical masterpiece ever composed would grow dreary and dull by the sheer repetition of hearing it a few thousand times in succession. What we, instead, should truly desire for our life is to live it in such a way that it yields the highest recurrence of reflection and growth.

49

The immediacy of the moment often prevents us from experiencing the present as anything more than a rushing blur. It is only through reflection and speculation afterward that anyone gains any significant clarity as to the import of an experience. Reflection has a way of suspending time so that it might be held out for inspection as well as introspection. It is in *this* state of mind that we truly live our lives as something other than a purely sensual creature of the loam.

50

The philosophical student with Eastern sensibilities wishes to meditate upon nothing; that is, he wishes to clear his mind of even its own thought in order to escape the self entirely and unify with eternity once again. Yet, meditation, if it is to be used in the service of the humane, should focus on *whatever* the mind wishes to entertain and for however briefly it wishes to remain acquainted with the thought. This sort of drifting meditation helps tremendously in the development of the spirit while the banishing of conscious reflection leads to the destruction of the self. The first type serves the needs of the living while the second provides a form of prayer for the dead.

51

In the technological forest that envelops us now, it is difficult to find a cabin in the woods like Thoreau's. Instead, we must be satisfied with the cabin of our own mind which also allows for meditation and peace, provided that we haven't made it psychologically impossible to separate ourselves from the world to reflect on it for a while. Society itself scorns reflection because it often interferes with the flow of economic and technological progress. Yet, the cultivation of a fine character progresses at an entirely different rate than the material developments of man or machine.

52

The act of introspection is similar to literary criticism except that the text we examine is ourselves. Our biggest difficulty will be in recognizing the structure of the piece, as it does not identically resemble material that we've encountered in the past. So, we must first learn how to analyze such a work since, essentially, the text is being asked to analyze itself.

53

Eastern philosophy, given its admirable distrust of theory, is more inclined to understand aphorisms, poems, dialogues, and fragmented writing as significant pieces for spiritual consideration. However, the Eastern sage generally also insists upon meditating by freeing his mind entirely of thoughts so he cannot properly utilize the divine potential of such fragments. The wiser one attempts to let her thoughts wander wherever they may as a more reflective form of meditation. Reflection without thought may in fact lead to a spiritual awakening but it will be of the sort that eliminates individuality altogether and advocates for a kind of unconscious non-being. Yet this approach seems to waste a rather unique opportunity since the state of non-being is the state to which we will all return soon enough and for all eternity. The discoveries of being, on the other hand, may in comparison last for a few beats less than a nanosecond. Nevertheless, this sort of artistic meditation is a focus on perspective itself so that we might wander through the garden of our collective intelligence and the dense forest of our own unconscious mind in order to arrive at a better understanding of ourselves and the world.

54

Suffering is never entirely useless but its significance won't simply reveal itself. We must first spend a great deal of time in quiet contemplation while patiently engaged in thoughtful efforts to develop greater insight and perspective. Our labors though — at least those which lead to something finer and more sublime — are spiritual and contemplative by nature rather than the brute physicality of an austere Puritan.

55

Patience should not be moved to surrender its dignity.

56

An urge for power and resources can easily overwhelm our civilized and humane instincts — those impulses more recent to our evolutionary timeline, less engrained in our DNA. These are the quiet virtues that don't generally reach the awareness of those who nurture their beastly selves. Our natural state, after all, is not cultured in the least.

57

Virtues are often discussed as inherent personality traits one might implement in times of need, yet virtues are not generally instinctual. Most virtues arise through a process of secondary devotion to something worthwhile and noble. Similarly, the person fiercely dedicated to the implementation of some evil resolve will not develop many virtues along the way — though their vice and treachery will no doubt increase. Yet, the person committed to helping feed the poor, for example, will gradually evolve a more virtuous character. The great difficulty of such a project is to limit one's craving for those experiences which do not lead to a virtue of some kind. In order to do so, we must first immerse ourselves in the study of philosophical and artistic tradition — gaining the wisdom of the past — before committing ourselves wholeheartedly to those tasks which most develop our own particular character.

58

The virtues, those humane and civilized habits of thought and conduct, need to be collected in the spirit as a child might gather beautiful stones. Only then might a person consider themselves virtuous. This task should be the primary focus of one's life — to live virtuously — instead of the contemporary aim of the moment which makes it seem as if man were a creature born to shop and consume.

59

We all are obligated with bringing honor to our entire species rather than merely to our family names.

60

The individual defends the dignity of mankind through his words and actions. He degrades man's dignity in the same manner. Thus his life — if something more than simply brute existence — should serve as but one instance, a shining ideal — through words and deeds — of man as something other than a mindless herd animal or a senseless and vicious beast.

61

Be wary for what you wish since rarely do we understand the intricacies of any particular situation or condition. We may, for instance, wish to be one of the glamorous few who parade about the globe while a small herd of ego-centered sycophants surround us in bubbly awe. We may wish to have our name known throughout the land and desire to be adored by the multitudes on a daily basis. Yet, we will not foresee the difficulties of these chores. We cannot possibly conceive yet what it feels like to be hounded by strangers and befriended by envious fools. We will not imagine how much tedium naturally exists in any life. Even the lives of those most seemingly blessed by fate are spent mired in the swamp of dull monotony much of the time, a condition, ironically enough, often punctuated by dreary episodes of manic activity.

62

The idea of freedom is often perceived positively and, indeed, it does possess a great many positive and well-regarded attributes. Yet, it should be remembered that freedom can also unfetter chains and limitations that might be better maintained for the sake of health, welfare, and public safety. After all, it allows for a multitude of our less estimable qualities to arise and demand to be tolerated. So, if we would wish to live in a land where freedom reigns, we should understand the true nature of our king.

63

The reason that people don't generally travel life's proper trail — that path unique to each individual which leads to the development of a humane character — is because the course is arduous and uncertainty is the mood which reigns the day. It takes a kind of stoic patience and fortitude in order to endure the injustices of this world while still attempting to maintain a sense of one's own humanity.

64

Justice, of course, cannot be forced upon anyone or anything without it leading to a greater proliferation of *inj*ustice.

65

Man, unable to prove a god, may nevertheless overreach his fate with god-like ambition and make justice over chaos reign — bringing virtue into the whole of all creation.

66

It would be a dreadful world indeed if at the outset of any tragedy, the vast majority of us simply turned our collective heads and shrugged, or — worse — added to the injustices of the day with new sins of our own. Instead, at least for one brief moment, the collective often rules with a certain compassion and benevolence in times of extreme duress — everyone in town coming together to raise money for a sickly girl, for instance. Such demonstrations of morality reveal to even the most jaded sceptic that the "good" resides somewhere — sometimes quite deeply hidden — in the spirit of all whom we consider human.

67

Justice, true justice anyway, can only take place when we maintain an open mind — open especially to its own fallibility.

68

The divine can be perceived by focusing the vast majority of one's thought and attention upon those humane elements of existence which best embody or express the cultivated excellence of humanity's inner nature — art, justice, love, kindness, wisdom, empathy, etc..

69

The divine is an amalgamation of the feminine and the masculine, humane and inhumane, spirit and earth, good and evil. There can be no division of the divine without severing the divine itself, shaping it into something not quite so profound. Divinity, after all, is nothing if not a whole — it does not suffer any more than it finds the going easy. Suffering is often merely the invention of a human mind.

70

The divine is in everything that exists as well as all that has yet to exist and all that has already existed. However, for us, the divine suffers from the limitations of human knowledge and intelligence. The word itself — at least for a large portion of our history — generally suggests some holy personage who possesses the morals and mentality of an individual from the stone-age. Yet, the true divine is far too complex to imagine that it might inhabit the form of a single personality (and a human one at that). It is, after all, everywhere present while invisible all the same. Every breath, from first to last, that we will ever take in this life inhales the divine and exhales it back to share with the multitudes again. Although man is a brief, chance occurrence on the earth, the divine is eternal. It resides in the silence between the stars.

71

The phenomenal world, the universe as it exists in physical space, simply *is* the divine — or a large part of it anyway. Many people would have the divine be a projection of the human form, but the human is no more unique in nature than is a star, or a mountain, or one of the many other creatures who populate creation. Yet, if human beings were entirely extinguished from the earth, the divine itself would still remain. However, such a deity differs from the fundamentalist conception of the divine and as such must suffer the laments of those who had hope for some kind of idol to which they might pray. Instead, the divine offers an abstract and intellectual kind of contentment which has no relation to the childish satisfaction derived from some divine Patriarch.

72

Listen for the divine voice within — among other places — the song that speaks for the humane. It resides in the soul of every individual though few generally allow it the proper expression. It is the element of character that can be best understood as spiritual, a disposition that speaks effortlessly to the child since children, until they are precisely educated to perceive otherwise, hear the inner thoughts of the divine most clearly. After all, the child possesses little concern for money, fame, success, or any of the other petty external rewards bestowed by fate. The child, instead, is engaged in the serious art of play and in so doing mimics the attributes of a divine spirit.

73

The soul exists in a spiritual form, as does the self — each, after all, are merely abstractions. These are words which refer to no physical "thing" that might be confirmed by the senses. However, the great individual must labor nonetheless to animate the soul, the self, the spirit, or whatever you will and make these visible to the world in some fashion. We must give our spirit form and reject everything that "it" is not. We must give shape to our character. Otherwise it will remain a disposition largely dominated by the terrible hostility of natural instinct.

74

Our proper spiritual state of being should be akin to a leisurely stroll through a mind preoccupied with great thoughts. The person who can sit upon a hill with her eyes to the heavens and let her thoughts drift through her consciousness like clouds on the horizon is profoundly engaged with life in a manner that is quite uniquely human — perhaps even a necessary state for the resistance of the inhumane.

75

How might humanity feel reverence again for a world wherein irreverence is held in such high esteem? If *all* things possess nothing so sacred as to cause us to stand in awe, then we live in an age that has, in many ways, already perished. Yet, while a crumbling *era* may not be saved, each individual can still attain enlightenment of one kind or another. However, this is not achieved through a reunification with some sacred entity or god, but through the cleansing and schooling of perception.

76

Consciousness *is* the soul, an "entity" to be found everywhere and nowhere all at once.

77

Life itself is a type of consciousness.

78

Our conscious mind is generally two steps behind our unconscious awareness. In this manner, then, we can only understand the little "truths" that are mysteriously revealed to us through the cagy guile of unconsciousness.

79

Our perception is such that we aren't quite aware of how it is derived from experience. The string of a musical instrument, for example, will not resonate with what might be perceived as music until it is tuned in such a way as to arrive at the appropriate pitch — otherwise it is merely out of tune. Yet this very determination originated from the sound being found displeasing to the human ear. In other words, the sound must conform to what the human finds pleasing in order to be understood and accepted as music. Our entire understanding of the world is generally constructed in this same prejudicial manner.

80

A rock is not a rock if it possesses properties that we determine edible.

81

Perspective is sometimes best revealed through metaphor and the movie *Smoke* offers an interesting one. Imagine a photographer who sits on her front stoop every morning and diligently captures one picture at the exact same time every day. After a year, if she were to look back on her work, she would notice some slight variations in the contents of the images. The light, for instance, would change over the course of the year as the earth rotates around the sun and the seasons, no doubt, would be reflected in their habitual ebb and flow. Yet, not much would be found too surprising. The world would still remain essentially recognizable — each individual snapshot an incremental fragment of what overall appears to be quite familiar. Extend this same experiment out 1000 years though — if such a thing were possible — and it's not difficult to see how each of our own moments might weave together into the fabric of some larger context. Yet, more importantly, we may come to understand that perception itself is the weaving together of the incremental. Each moment the human brain records some image, blinks, and records another. Each person then takes these pieces and attempts to make sense of them, constructing meaning as something of a creative act.

82

We possess only words to express what is inexpressible. The words are not truth itself nor do they signify it.

Words merely point in the direction of truth. They share notions with similar minds in similar ways in the hopes of casting a line into the abyss and retrieving some lively, noble, and worthy "fish."

83

Words such as "love", "god", "beauty", "death", and notions of their kind fail to surrender so easily to concrete definition. The result, perhaps, is the hindrance of precise communication and the difficulty of truly understanding anything of much significance. Yet, the very abstract nature of these concepts can still inspire the same kind of wonder and excitement with life that had filled the hearts of sages and saints from previous generations.

84

We direct our lives not through some unified and comprehensive system of thought or linear narrative, but by our ability to assess any particular situation and then select the best option from an assortment of legitimate, as well as illegitimate, possibilities. For this, we will require a richly fragmented, deep, reflective, scientific, and artistic understanding of the world.

85

The evolution of the species will be when man can incorporate and digest all of his religions and live wholly, honestly, and peacefully with himself and others. It will be a time when he accepts all of the religions, arts, and sciences as expressions of human greatness; a time when even truth will no longer be an eternal proposition but simply an expression of mankind's prominence at making the incomprehensible understood — if but only briefly.

86

The evolution of morality — that process by which we become more humane and less of a brute — requires first an act of rebellion. Someone must venture forth and disobey the established moral law in some fashion before morality itself can loosen the lines that moor it to tradition. Otherwise, the majority of nations would still be stoning their citizens and crucifying their criminals. The true rebel, then, should be seated at a place of high honor in any society that hopes to improve upon itself.

87

Emily Dickinson is the patron saint for those excellent souls who labor their entire lives without recognition for their efforts. She represents those who have been marginalized or forgotten, ridiculed or gawked at as if some kind of exhibit at the zoo. The animals, too, must flaunt their grace and excellence before the eyes of undeserving fools who see them only as a slab of meat. Beauty, elegance, and wisdom fall like snowflakes on a summer day. We must look heavenward to see them, up to the heights which rise above his little world of petty concerns and fervent desires. It's not the type of "heaven" upon which sits the throne of some paternal god. It is, instead, that ether region of air which makes it difficult for mortals to breathe — the place of genius and the greatest in human achievement.

88

How might any of us know if we possess a greatness of spirit? In the first place, greatness of spirit cannot be the immediate goal as no one path leads directly to such a state. Secondly, greatness itself is a relative term. What constitutes a greatness of character? We imagine that we know it when we see it, but such qualities are often hidden away from the view of the general public, a public that often ascribes the label of "greatness" or "genius" upon those who provide the most distraction or receive the most acclaim. Yet, a sense of greatness is felt in the heart of any child. Only through the process of assimilation does she begin to ignore that sentiment.

89

We are chained to the world by work and only freed through play. Laughter and play, in fact, are our only salvation in a world so full of spite and avarice.

90

The revolutionary imagines the bourgeois' mode of life to be an acceptance of death and so an institution worthy of violent eradication. After all, the bourgeois, the radical claims, value the goods of a lifeless materialism and adopt the pale and tedious attitudes of convention. Yet, the radical is no less obsessed with the dreary notion of a *utopian* materialism, a political concept which has been never more than a shared experience of wishful thinking. Perhaps it's time for a new ideal of man, a more humane manifestation of the beast, a creature able to imagine what it might be like to truly *understand* the perspective of someone else.

91

As Emerson wrote, we must learn to "estimate a sour face." We should understand that a disapproving look is merely noting the strange and unfamiliar. It is merely the signal of some breach with conventional standard or traditional means.

92

One must turn a deaf ear to the proclamations of moral certainty. After all, even a seemingly innocuous maxim such as "always help others in need" brings to mind a myriad of possible exceptions. In fact it seems as if there would be certain situations in which following such a proverb might be decidedly *im*moral. So, instead of advocating for the surety of some moral conviction, we might be better off developing a sense of moral thoughtfulness and contemplation instead.

93

We can, it's true, find a certain amount of satisfaction with a life that is never pressed into some greater service. We can live the majority of our days comfortably doodling our lives away but eventually — if we are animals of substance at any rate — we will grow weary of such shallow diversions and long for something more profound. This is the first calling of the humane sensibility.

94

Seneca rightly notes that we will never know ourselves or what we are capable of accomplishing if we have no antagonist to put up obstacles in our way. However, many of us too often select an external challenger with whom to test our mettle and this generally leads to violence of some kind. In this manner entire nations can find themselves at war for the petty missteps of a few careless individuals. External conflicts do serve to provide enlightenment, of course, but they are typically a destructive influence overall. Instead, we need to find a more creative adversary, one forged in the fires of our own heart — a battle waged with some great question perhaps.

95

An intuition is something that can be developed through education and experience so it can be altered in many important ways. However, an instinct is fixed and rigid, an element of one's animal nature which can only be sublimated and controlled, enriched and beautified. The intuition is what grows from the struggle between our humanity and our more reactionary, instinctual characteristics.

96

No one should expect the animal to surrender himself of self-interest, but the *human* animal must learn to direct such interests toward more appropriate and morally commendable aims. In other words, the humane is something for which we must be sufficiently trained or we can remain particularly vicious for a lifetime.

97

Passion without moderation is no less destructive than madness, sometimes more so. The proper balance of the passions is the first skill that must be mastered in order to receive the benefits of wisdom. Yet, this is more easily imagined than achieved. After all, the passions can sometimes consume and dump us entirely helpless into the streets. The passions, though, can be regulated through the understanding that arises from a proper perspective. Perspective provides the means to temper extremes of any kind by showing a variety of different possible views, each illuminating reasonable solutions that drain the passions of their sometimes vigorous convictions. Not much else can be accomplished in the development of humanity without the taming of this internal beast.

98

It is more instructive that we learn to temper our desires to a certain degree rather than expect that we should eliminate desire altogether. The more extreme view generally indicates a perspective that is inappropriate to the natural world.

99

The job of reason is not to control the passions since the very act of reasoning involves some degree of necessary emotion and commitment. Yet, reason may still have much to say about how the passions can be best utilized in particular contexts. After all, reason oversees — or should so supervise — the regulation of balance within the human psyche in order to allow any individual to lead a fulfilling public and private life.

100

The concepts of both waves and particles are necessary in order to understand light in its complexity and profundity. Yet, these concepts cannot be applied simultaneously; that is, we can't find a wave and a particle at the same time. Whether one sees light as a wave or a particle seems dependent on what the observer is seeking to find. If someone is looking for a wave, light will function as a wave. So to possess a better comprehension of light requires the knowledge of both waves and particles — as far as we now believe anyway. The complexity of life, similarly, cannot be understood by viewing it only from a religious, scientific, personal, or any one particular perspective. We must evaluate our lives from a great variety of planes in order to get a more comprehensive view. We understand the earth better from the distance of the moon and we will, no doubt, understand it better still from the vantage points of Mars, Jupiter, Venus, and all the rest of the celestial objects in the cosmos.

101

Love is not the essential aim of mankind. Love, after all, is a notion far too intimate and familial to apply to enemies or strangers on the bus. Instead, we should set our ambition toward the goal of understanding. We should attempt, if we are to maintain the precarious balance of peace and live among one another without malice, to understand that which appears to us suspiciously foreign at first glance: the human heart.

102

Any attack on the humane is an assault on all of humanity — at least upon those who still remain admirably human.

103

We should look for ways to test our faith lest it prove a weak and unworthy thing — especially at moments of greatest adversity. Any faith, if it is worthy of the name, must be rooted in fertile soil from which we might grow into a righteous, humane being. Contemporary fundamentalists, on the other hand, seem only interested in defending their faith as true.

104

In the first law of thermodynamics, the law of energy conservation states that energy can be neither created nor destroyed in a system. However, energy can change forms, and energy can flow from one place to another. Yet, the total energy of an isolated system remains the same. The human being then, as an expression of energy — as spirit — never dies. The human form simply flows into a different shape.

105

Ask a carpenter, "what does it all mean?" the next time he aligns his beams together and he will no doubt look perplexed as to how he should answer such a question — removed as it is from the more practical context of hammering and measuring. Pose the same question to the computer technician about her new program and she's likely to list its uses but have no real answer as to its inherent value or purpose in the overall scheme of things. The question itself is enough to halt the practice of unconscious living and begin the concerted transformation to awareness.

106

We cannot help but choose our fate — even the most seemingly insignificant of choices leads to our destiny in the end. We could not have chosen otherwise and even if we were to return to the original circumstance and choose again, that choice itself remains different from the first. The outcome, too, arising as it does at a different time and with a host of subtle nuances that were absent in the original situation, is going to differ. The sense that we are in control of our fate is largely illusory. We are in control of our responses to fate, but even these are often greatly influenced by genetic and environmental factors.

107

Governments are constituted to defend against the more destructive masculine impulses — the forces of cruelty, ego, hatred, war, devastation, and sexual vices of all varieties.

108

The feminine without backbone is a pathetic and weak creature indeed just as the masculine with too much strength and stoicism often makes the world suffer greatly for his lack of insight and civility.

109

If we are unable to keep much of our own private affairs, desires, and prejudices to ourselves, we will have great difficulty assimilating into any large collective. And it should not be denied that conformity and concession — at least to some degree — are necessities for the formation of government and law — and all of civilization for that matter. Yet, we must simultaneously guard against keeping the better part of ourselves in complete seclusion lest our contribution to life be little more than as a clothes-horse.

110

The primary focus of law should be in keeping man from unleashing the terrible beast within upon the rest of the world. All of us, as creatures of the kind that are able to *be* moral, have a duty to, if not *act* morally, at least refrain from *im*moral conduct. So, the law must reflect this duty and enforce it with a certain amount of compassion so as not to be an instrument of brutality itself.

111

The absolute strangest fact about existence isn't the many varied chorales that can be heard to resonate throughout the ages, but the patterns of uniformity in which they all share.

112

There resides a certain inequality at the heart of any consideration of excellence.

113

Those things of lesser value in the world can still be thoroughly enjoyed by the higher soul — the humane individual — but she should no longer expect to delight in them as before. After all, the very distinction between "lesser" and "greater" conveys an understanding that some things are simply better than others. So, those lesser things of value must necessarily pale in comparison.

114

Depression is not some virus or pathogen that attacks the mind; it is not something that can be medicated and generally cured either — although certainly there are means to reduce its symptoms. Depression, instead, is a manner of perceiving the world; it's a state of being — often quite enlightening — that struggles to find meaning in a life that appears on the surface to possess none. In this sense, depression can offer an insightful and even fairly profound view of existence at its core. Yet, most people, generally overcome with fear, will see only darkness and so develop the prejudice that depression is obscene and morbid. Perhaps it never occurred to such people that their melancholy might be a gift, or an opportunity for some greater insight. They want to return instead to the state of childish ignorance from whence they first arrived.

115

Anyone whose condition is terminal — especially when accompanied by some unendurable physical or psychological torment — should be no more condemned for arranging an earlier end for themselves than might we blame them for euthanizing their beloved dog when the poor creature seems to suffer too greatly.

Ascension

1

The soul is a concept and not an entity of any kind. The soul is merely the essential self, the psyche, the content of one's character, the fragmented "I," or any other abstraction that one might employ to express our deepest understanding of ourselves. This spirit cannot be empirically validated, of course, yet its absence — due to death, confusion, depression, mania, madness, etc. — is always quite palpable and something altogether "real" nonetheless.

2

Modern man is beset by the following errors in perception:

    1. That the divine is either nonexistent or in need of

further proof.

2. That the mind and body are one and the same entity.

3. That all truth is relative, making nothing true.

<u>Modern man should instead consider the following</u>:

1. The "divine" — while certainly not some kind of anthropomorphic personal guardian or human caretaker — is scattered across the entire cosmos and is proven daily in the world if only we knew how to see — or listen.

2. While the brain and the body interact with one another, the *mind* is the animating "spirit" of mankind.

3. All truth is either true or untrue by degrees and this is only so because we are inferior perceivers. Truth exists but we cannot ever know it with certainty. Humility, then, should be the caretaker of the day.

3

Humility is more of a perspective than a feeling of any kind, a way of seeing the world and one's relation to it. It does not arise from a sense of subservience but rather a spirit of strength, an expression of respect. It is the proper understanding of our potentiality as well as an awareness of our most serious limitations.

4

We don't know how the mind and body interact but they most certainly do to some extent, as evidenced by the individual's will to act upon his environment. Should I decide to lift my arm, for example, the action will occur because there is some relation between the mental idea and the physical act of lifting the arm. It turns out, we don't even agree on the existence of "mind" as such or what the term really means. Mind, like thought itself, is an abstraction hiding within the willow trees. It is, in essence, an idea linked to the notion of selfhood. Yet, the self, too, suffers from its own ambiguities. After all, it is merely a narrative mish-mash of ever-changing interpretations of fragmented experience that lead to something of a broadly generalized identity. This sort of understanding though often breeds anxiety and restlessness resulting from the loss of some psychological certainty. However, what we *don't* know should lead to even greater achievements in intellectual humility and inspire us to some new understanding or perspective. As a result, the hope then is to find less frequent expressions of the inhumane.

5

Man is generally not going to alter a belief that he holds strongly because of the arguments of others. The ancient notion that reason proceeds to some common agreement among differing minds assumes that men are not somewhat inherently ignorant, arrogant, and obstinate. Furthermore, man possesses an almost pathological need to utilize the reasoning and argument of others to support his own perspective. So he will not be swayed by what he can easily rationalize away. His knowledge of this particular tendency, though, this quirk in his character, can startle him into developing a kind of intellectual humility which might then prevent him from one day abdicating or encouraging the inhumane in any way.

6

We learn to trust ourselves in the same manner in which

we come to trust anyone — through an extended period of acquaintance. The more time we spend getting to know ourselves in a variety of circumstances — confronted by a whole host of public and private challenges — the better equipped we will be to find our proper place in the world.

7

Treat everyone as if they were noble, humane, and righteous — not because they truly possess these qualities, but because *you* do.

8

The majority, it seems, really want little to do with life, choosing instead to reject it as a nuisance, dreaming of ultimate release from what is perceived as a prison. All the more reason that there must exist at least *some* humane and noble creatures on the earth. Otherwise, humanity itself will slowly fall into extinction, emerging once again as an unrelenting beast. So it's the duty of the individual to remain committed to the noblest virtues — those most estimable contents of our character — in order to maintain some semblance of the humane on earth.

9

We are not generally by nature a progressive creature. In other words, we do not just naturally improve ourselves morally, intellectually, and spiritually. Instead, we must make a conscious effort, a *choice,* to mollify our instinctual response in order to generate a more humane one.

10

We are entirely limited as far as our animal-selves are

concerned. We are an animal, after all, possessing the same drives and urges to which all mammals are subject. Yet, we *can* choose to fashion our own character into one worthy of admiration — a creature simultaneously refined, humane, and noble.

11

In times of war, all of our private and unspoken nightmares become quite vividly true. The terrors we normally fear to even *imagine,* those lurking in the dark corners of our slumbering unconsciousness, all seem exaggerated and surreal to a well-rested and rational mind. Yet, in war, such horrors are quite common, nightmares running amok in the brilliant light of day. We must understand this aspect of our nature though, the brutality of our species — if for no other reason than to protect us from ourselves.

12

While immediate justice may content man's passionate commitment to vengeance, true justice — the endeavor toward a more rational, impartial and evenhanded judgement — satisfies a higher, more noble aspect of our character, requiring an extraordinary amount of faith in the enterprise and exceptional patience with its results.

13

The next evolution of man will be one for which we will set the course. If we are to survive as something quite unique in nature — as an animal of a higher kind — we must first strive to overcome most of our own evolutionary prejudices and instinctual proclivities. We must transcend these natural conditions and create a cultured world best suited to the needs of such a noble creature.

14

Contrary to what Goethe writes, in the beginning is *not* the deed. Instead, it is the *impulse* that is the origin of all deeds: the inspiration, the intuition, the instinct, or the compulsion to act. So if we are to improve upon the morality of our actions, we must first make noble these more fundamental — and mysterious — elements of the human constitution. It should be the higher task of the humanities and the arts to develop and enhance the quality of our internal motivations, moving them further away from those purely instinctual and beastly drives.

15

The higher individual is not distinguished from the beast by her rationality. In other words, reason alone is not some special power that immediately propels a creature up the ranks toward distinction. After all, the rational can be utilized for a variety of horrific deeds that no other animal could possibly imagine. Instead, the sage, the more humane individual, is established through her treatment of others. Her status depends upon how humanely she *acts* in the world. Rationality, of course, is a valuable tool for determining the kind of humane response appropriate for any particular situation, but ultimately it is the humane *act* that distinguishes us as a creature of singularly unique significance. Otherwise, the animal outranks us quite handily.

16

The life of everyone is composed of an amalgamation of various experiences — some of which end quite happily while others close in a flood of tears. Ultimately, of course, all narratives end in death, but our own individual character — our nobility in the face of whatever fate we must confront — will determine if our tale is a great work of art, or simply the end of a rather contrived, overwrought, and avoidable piece of theatre.

17

An individual with character wastes very little time judging the qualities and weaknesses of other people. Instead, she serves the majority of her days — or should so spend them anyway — reflecting on her own generous limitations and attempting to understand the conditions of her existence. Her primary condemnation of others is that they seem to have little concern in pursuing this same noble goal.

18

The seeds from even the mightiest oak will rot without the proper light and soil. If it receives these advantages though, the growing tree then must withstand the winds that seem heaven sent to bend and break it with howling indifference. Once ascended to its proper height, it must then stand as something like patience on a monument, exhibiting to the younger saplings how they too must grow. However, the only reward that the grand old tree might eventually come to receive is some precious time spent overlooking the view.

19

The spirit often knows where to find its flame. It is our responsibility, however, to ignite it and ensure that it remains forever lit.

20

The person out searching for love will find many "loves" perhaps, but seldom the ideal prize he seeks so desperately. Yet, the individual who carries on with the day committed to some other, more essential, passion will find her way as effortlessly as destiny intended.

21

We must now find our own individual purposes in life, those which sustain us in times of great turmoil as well as peace. Our time, after all, no longer affords us a belief system that unites our passions in one overarching narrative anymore. We must instead, as Nietzsche notes, become something of an artist ourselves — the architects of our own lofty character.

22

An individual must commit themselves passionately to those aspects of existence which possess the most significance for the spirit and pursue these private treasures no matter what fate or consequence arrives to otherwise distract them from doing so.

23

We need not spend much time in search of our own unique path in life. Intuitively and over time, if we remain committed to the goal of bettering our character, we will learn to recognize where we should properly direct our devotion. We will eventually reach these cultivated passions as urgently as a baby stretches for its milk. In such a case we cannot help but bump into our destiny from time to time. The question will be whether we possess the courage to follow it home.

24

Our souls *should* be alight with desire, but not set ablaze by just any passion. We need to cultivate a desire for the right things at the right times — those that provide greater enlightenment as to how we should best live our lives.

25

Self-discipline is necessary because it's the tool by which we achieve moderation in all things. If we should possess little to no self-control, even our happiness will quickly turn to misery when it reaches excessive proportions.

26

The only means by which we might truly find peace or some semblance of happiness in our life is through an understanding of the distinction between our needs and our desires. The person who desires more than their due will quickly discover that Nature is working against them in most cases. Their passion to proceed where they were not invited — to force the issue — is often a desperate attempt to avoid what they perceive to be an unwelcomed fate. They naively imagine that they can substantially alter their fortune. Yet, the individual who desires to achieve *nothing* more than what destiny will allow — surrendering to fate at the slightest appearance of discord — can't possibly develop into anything unique or significant either. Such a person is purely a creature of instinct, an animal relying on the kindness of strangers. So, a balance must be established between what we truly need and what we merely wish to be the case.

27

All of us should passionately commit ourselves to a meandering education, perusing as much of lived existence as possible while imagining such ancient figures as Socrates, Aristotle, Confucius and their ilk as something of contemporaries instead of strange figures from an unfamiliar and distant past. The great texts of antiquity truly direct the growth of our spirit in the manner most appropriate to its nature.

28

Love does not survive us because of some special quality that it possesses. Love is a kind of passionate commitment like any other. If it survives us, it will be as a result of the quality of our commitment and the amount of effort we expend cultivating it to fruition.

29

We forge our own reality but live it no less passionately or sincerely because of its apparent fictitiousness.

30

We have no *need* for the company of others if we develop a relationship with our own soul. This is not to say that we are *unable* to interact with others or even that we don't genuinely enjoy such interaction, only that the obsessive *need* for company will be absent. This allows for much greater reflection and insight into the constitution of our existence. In the end, we are quite alone at any rate, no matter how many friends, relatives, or lovers we might cheerfully gather in attendance around us.

31

All of history, including one's own, is fraught with the inherent difficulties of interpretation and narration. The more popular tales eventually become myths of a sort which are then strengthened and improved — or weakened and ruined — with each new subtle translation. In fact, the simple rehashing of history creates the possibility of forming entirely new myths while solidifying the old. In any case, truth is something quite far removed from the notion of an objective reality.

32

Reality is something of an abstraction — a convoluted mess of fluids, solids, gases, and light. It is only human consciousness that gives it rationally comprehendible form.

33

Man still remains quite conscious in his sleep, but it's a different manner of awareness altogether. Death, too, may be just a simple shift in perception — returning us back into the stream of universal consciousness from whence we first arrived.

34

There are some problems that are simply intrinsic to the human condition — the limitations of consciousness, for example. Problems such as these cannot be adequately resolved by the vast intelligence of science nor the appealing wish fulfillment of religion. Yet, they still must be addressed — honestly, without the destructive force of ego that normally intrudes upon such proceedings.

35

No one can ever hope to perfect themselves in any way. In fact, the whole notion of perfection is nothing more than a construct of the human mind which forgets that it has no experience with such a concept. Yet, we are all in need of varying degrees of psychological, intellectual, or spiritual improvement. There is no end to such development, of course, but this is precisely one of its virtues. It is a pleasure most profound to explore the many possibilities of awareness. And as the understanding grows, so too does humane consciousness and moral action.

36

The human brain, of course, is the original source of ideas — higher consciousness of any kind seeming quite impossible without it. Yet, this physical entity produces — when conditions are right — a non-physical result: thought. The brain in this sense works as something of a magic wand which causes a seemingly illogical effect — a sort of big bang of consciousness.

37

Life is the experience of consciousness while death is the seeming withdrawal of awareness into the state of the unconscious. Yet, even the unconscious may come to light from time to time. Dreams, for example, regularly splash upon the dark canvas of unconscious sleep. Intuition, as well, springs from some deeply unconscious source. The loss of one's body then may just be the transformation of awareness into dream.

38

Death is not the absence of consciousness or awareness but, instead, a reunification with the "divine" consciousness of nature.

39

Death is merely the transference of consciousness into the realm of dream once and for all. The dead live permanently in that state which the living visit nightly but from which *only* the living are summoned back in the morning once again.

40

Essentially all life struggles to acquire some form of consciousness. Even the dying individual will not surrender before becoming aware of one last thought — no doubt focused on something quite trivial, made brilliant by the moment. In such states of heightened awareness it becomes quite difficult to behave inhumanely.

41

Our eyes provide Nature with a way to view her own creation. Our voices supply the means by which to sing her song, our ears a method through which she might hear the melody, and our heart, the organ by which Nature feels the experience of being alive. What greater purpose might we realistically expect of life? Nature has not the means to consciousness herself. Only we have potential access to it and only we might achieve enlightenment, which is essentially just a higher state of awareness. What a gift is love to one forsaken — taste, to the salt sea; touch, to the wet stone? What have we to offer the sun but these? What need have we in vanity and pride? In luxuries and somnambulistic minds? The greatness of humanity lies far beyond such narrow measures. We must not, above all else, allow the rusting of our souls.

42

We stand unique — or should so stand anyway — in the world of the semi-conscious animal. For us, dishonor is imposed on every writ of empty prose, every breath of wasted air, every prayer uttered that seeks to gratify some foolish wish.

43

There are many who believe that something is untrue if it cannot be empirically verified and repeated. Yet, the means by which we arrive at such a conclusion is through the medium of thought or consciousness — themselves the product of an unverifiable and somewhat miraculous existence.

44

Thought is like the empty space within the atom — essentially nothing, but everything nonetheless.

45

We become merely a thought after we have gone — an abstraction, or a memory, or a narrative, or maybe just a vague sense of loss. We remain among the living although our form is not the same. We become something of an apparition, now beheld by the physical realm in an entirely different way.

46

We transcend the physical when we ponder the notion of

whether we are able to do so — or whenever we thoughtfully ponder anything at all.

47

We cannot truly love our fate unless we can imagine that we have had some hand in its creation.

48

We should not be judged for our early years any more than we should be judged by our final ones. We are, after all, the sum of *all* our parts.

49

We need to have some concern for the opinions of others of course, but we must be prepared for those opinions to be quite contrary to our own — many times extremely so. In the end though, we must rely upon the approval of our own sane and sensible heart — the metaphoric organ that will ultimately sit in judgment over our life, rewarding us for our proper service or punishing us for our lack of faith.

50

What one age rewards as exemplary, another age may discard as trash, or treat with extreme derision. Nevertheless, the things most worth keeping in any age should be those which best develop, maintain, or inspire the humane in some fashion.

51

In order to properly ascertain man's character — including our own individual nature — there must be quite a bit known about it. Nevertheless, this knowledge will seem rightfully insufficient without at least considering how we treat other creatures. Yet any attempt to judge *these* interactions truthfully must admit that every situation — however humdrum and conventional it may appear on the surface — is unique in some aspect of its composition and each individual contributor unique as well. Furthermore, any assessment of character requires private and personal knowledge of a good many thoughts and factors that are difficult for even the participants themselves to determine. This understanding should inspire us to humbly examine our own character and forever renounce the terrible authority we enjoy by sitting in judgment of others.

52

Any moral judgment is dependent on what occurs at the right time to the right person in the right situation for the right reasons. This is the complex nature of morality and such contingencies explain why it is so incredibly difficult to assess. The person who thinks otherwise simply doesn't understand mankind or morality. Only a god *would* be able to judge such a thing since it requires omniscient knowledge of a kind that even the individual involved will find quite impossible to understand fully. This is not to say that we can't *be* moral, only that we are rarely ever entirely sure of ourselves in this regard — or at least we have no cause to be, even if we are so.

53

The Greeks thought that a person should keep quiet about his misfortune since he cannot possibly judge if such things are ultimately good or evil. While this may be true overall, we *can* assess whether something is good or evil to *us*, more or less, using the proper tools of reason and understanding. We cannot possibly know the objective truth of the matter but we may arrive at a subjective conclusion that is somewhat morally correct nonetheless. The difficulty, of course, is that an accurate assessment of any moral dilemma requires the establishment of character in the individual who would make such a determination. After all, we shouldn't expect the person who lacks fidelity to be a suitable exemplar for devotion or allegiance — or much of any other virtue for that matter.

54

We rarely possess the power or opportunity to change our external reality in any significant way. However, it *is* within our power to alter our *internal* character to a certain degree. We are unable to influence genetic factors, of course, but our perspective *about* these inherited features — as well as our attitude with respect to our external condition — is often entirely within our control. So if we are existentially miserable we often seems to have no one to blame but ourselves. We have *chosen* misery in this sense when we might have otherwise favored joy. It is our perspective that determines the overall judgment of our internal condition.

55

Perspective is a more valuable commodity than the acquisition of material possessions. Imagine, for example, a set of twins who each hold a particular toy in their hands. The toy itself is essentially identical in every way to the toy of the other twin. The only difference — if one is to exist — is the individual perspective by which each twin perceives, interprets, and judges the toy. The first twin may squeal with joy and wholeheartedly embrace his newfound plaything while the other twin remains entirely indifferent to it and may even desire the toy of the first child instead. The value is determined by the perception and perception is often the manifestation of character.

56

Any action, belief, or perspective inconsistent with what we hope to be our ideal future self — the realization of our best character — threatens the very formation of such an achievement.

57

The narrative of our lives continually intersects with that of other's — sometimes colliding violently, sometimes caressed with love, oftentimes unnoticed or forgotten entirely. These narratives all overlap one another and lace together to create the fabric of humanity — that noisy, fragile, and infinitely complex mesh of tissue, spirit, and happenstance. Yet, from the perspective of the moon, all the world is silent.

58

The development of a variety of perspectives, the ability to understand the same event or experience in a number of different ways, makes it so that we don't drown in any particular one.

59

In order to achieve the *proper* perspective, one must attempt to broaden consideration to include as many differing views as possible. After all, the earth can be only fully seen if perceived from the moon or, even more precisely, from the perspective of some far away galaxy.

60

The state of divine perspective is, like a god's, removed from a mostly self-interested interaction with the world. We must consciously disengage from the tumultuous — and so often quite petty — needs and desires of all human societies to contemplate those aspects of existence which reside in stillness and quiet. We need not make ourselves a hermit of any kind, but serenity and poise will elude anyone who fails to engage the world thoughtfully.

61

We should immediately cease our struggle with other people and begin to wrestle with ourselves instead. Only then might we amend the world in any significant way, through the development of our perspective. In many cases we must even learn to rebel against our own natural instincts since these largely revolve around the animal's obsession with procreation and survival. Yet, civilized man — not to be confused with domesticated man — arises as a manifestation of that which is most unique in the character of the human: the expression of higher culture and thought. This feature of our existence distinguishes us in nature from the eagle or the snake, each of whom have distinctive attributes of their own.

62

Most things in life are a matter of perspective. We can grumble about our feelings of isolation when we find ourselves alone or we can focus on the feeling of peace that it might provide. It all depends upon how we choose to proceed at any given moment. We might groan and complain when surrounded by a crowd or we can imagine ourselves at a gathering of friends. It's the person who can accept the circumstances of his life with joy — for the most part — who lives with joy in his heart.

63

During times of extreme hardship the Stoic perspective best serves us. If we have lost much of what had previously sustained us or we feel hopelessly trapped in a destiny which provides us with little satisfaction, then it's better to imagine our own individual life as something of little concern. We can find great comfort in ridding ourselves of all hope and fear for the time being and simply accept fate as it arrives to us without much care for our own providence. Yet, we should be careful to avoid this perspective during other times in our lives. After all, to remain stoic in the presence of great beauty or amid the rush of feeling that arises for great ideas, great art, or passionate devotions seems rude and churlish, an apathetic rejection of life's significance and profundity. We must stand knowledgeable and enlightened against any force which might rather extinguish our spirit.

64

Humanity is the collective effort of the living and the dead to develop a more humane perspective and a greater understanding of existence itself. All other activity is either the concern of an animal or the foolishness of a beast.

65

The more perspectives that we can come to perceive, the better we will be able to understand ourselves, our world, and others.

66

Nietzsche rails against the negating force of resentment that fuels the Christian perspective. In other words, he thinks that the Christian worldview arises as a reaction of the slave against his master. The slave, because he so resents his condition, inverts the morality of the masters to something undesirable and promotes, instead, the morality of the slave. Of course, Nietzsche would like us to recognize the bitterness with which Christian morality arises; however, one might charge that his philosophy emerges from a similar hostility toward the Christian. In fact, it should be noticed that the evolution of human character develops from just this kind of Hegelian struggle to synthesize a new understanding from the conflict that naturally occurs whenever we are faced with a variety of opposing viewpoints. Thus, if the master morality conflicts with the desires of the slave, Christianity arises as a new solution to this conflict. In the same manner, Christianity exists for Nietzsche in tension with what he feels to be true and his creative work emerges in response. Rather than an unnatural occurrence, this sort of interplay is essential toward the cultivation of character in both individuals as well as nations.

67

The study of science, the humanities, and culture in combination with probing the depths of the individual human psyche allows for the best understanding of how one should go about living a good life. Insight and perspective do not arise from intuition or some special talent of mankind but through a concerted effort to understand.

68

True diplomacy results when we are able to conceive of another person's perspective as our own. Otherwise we are generally engaged in a struggle for power with others who are similarly focused on gaining their own advantage.

69

The divine is an understanding — a particular perspective — rather than an entity of any sort.

70

All vice arises from some state of psychological sickness. So virtue will not consistently express itself — beyond perhaps a few superficial, meaningless, and egotistical gestures — unless we are wise enough to attend to our own psychological well-being.

71

We should set aside time in our day for quiet solitude and reflection. This need not occur with any precise regularity, but its absence can be felt as a certain spiritual bloat on the verge of bursting. A nation of such distended individuals cannot long hold without being rocked by great moral confusion and violence. The Catholics — as well as many other religious views — understood the need for reflection and quietude. Their magnificent cathedrals were designed for meditative prayer to occur in the presence of Christian art, great sanctuaries for a communion with the divine. Yet, there exist many contemporary asylums such as these which allow for a similar encounter with art — libraries, museums, galleries; none less holy for possessing a secular view. All temples, in general, seek to inspire thoughtful reflection.

72

Be aware! Look around you and allow the color and texture of your hand to amaze for a moment. Recognize the smell of your own breath! Take in the glorious sunrise with a sense of awe and gratitude — gratitude for the experience. Perceive that which is divine and you will find it before you, as if waiting all along.

73

If we attempt to isolate ourselves from the profane world of the everyday to become some kind of aesthetic monk in unadulterated communion with the "divine," we will quickly find that something quite essential has been removed from the sacredness of our quest.

74

"Morality" is merely a bloated and extraneous word in the absence of human action.

75

Some faith is a necessity for everyone, though it need not be a trust in an anthropomorphic "god." Faith in the future of our own projects will suffice. Or faith, for example, in one's spouse or one's children. In any case, everyone needs confidence that the future possesses meaning. Even the suicide finds respite when he starts to plan for his future demise. He who was once despondent and depressed, absorbed in his own mental suffering and quite unable to conceive of any moment but the present one, suddenly discovers something of the divine with the hope that relief awaits him soon.

76

Our own spirit unfolds to us like a flower from the bud. It takes a great deal of care, coaxing, and patience to convince a sprout such as this to blossom, yet it is an object of such "divine" beauty once it does bloom.

77

The perception of a true divine would require us to have all possession of the world taken away from us. When we remove all of our concerns, all of our desires, all of our needs from the world; when we no longer perceive from the vantage point of the subjective "I"; when our ego has lost its iron grip, then might we achieve "divine" understanding — at least momentarily. Yet, to live in such a way would be equivalent to *living* not much at all.

78

We must be awake enough in life to recognize the synthetic, mechanistic, and inhumane elements of existence as merely the inverse expression of something more alive, undecided, and humane. So, we should primarily focus our attention upon catching a glimpse of the divine in the periphery of our vision.

79

Personification of the divine makes a fool of any god.

The divine, while not an entity in any sense, *does* exist in one particularly profound respect — as a figurative device designed to provide insight into something otherwise incomprehensible. We have only language to help us understand ourselves and our world. Yet language has obvious limitations. How well might the simple word "love," for example, label or define a complex and ethereal phenomena such as the notion of love? How many words would be enough? Language possesses a certain ambiguity inherent in its construction that never seems to quite satisfy our needs for it — at least with respect to those matters which exist beyond the practical and everyday. The use of the word "divine" similarly might serve as a reference for that "presence" which most of us feel when encountering a great work of art or some beautiful speck of light dancing on the windowsill. The energy or force that mathematically or mysteriously drives all bodies in the universe might also be considered divine. The "spirit" or the "soul" is often thought divine as well. Nevertheless, the "divine" is merely one example of a word that points to something quite varied and inexplicable and, for better or for worse, provides a more concrete comparison or label. The metaphor of the divine as something of a great father can allow us to contemplate our relationship with the cosmos and all of creation, for instance, while the word itself provides a label to discuss important philosophical and ethical notions vital to the cultivation of a more humane species. Of course, we might also spend our time amusing ourselves to death and quibbling over the concrete and definitive "truth" of a word.

81

Beyond the pale of words rests the divine.

82

The "divine" walks among you — often quite closely — but is dismissed or ignored a great majority of the time.

83

Only in context with death does life possess any deep significance. The person who fails to think much about their own mortality will eventually find life to be something rather dull and superficial. Yet, it's also quite dangerous to explore the heights and depths of the human psyche. So, we should attempt to cleanse the windows of our perception and open all six of our senses to the awareness of each eternal moment.

84

The beauty of science is not as some definitive ideology; its magnificence, instead, arises from its faith in a method of understanding — a way of deriving answers from the physical (and sometimes the moral and spiritual) universe which may not be otherwise evident. Scientific proof is not the end to some as yet undiscovered truth, but the beginning of a voyage toward greater awareness.

85

We have the remainder of eternity to be unified again with the unconscious spirit of space, time, and matter, so we should feel no guilt in attempting to explore our conscious awareness while we are briefly afforded the opportunity.

86

The person who escapes the confines of Plato's cave does not gain a greater understanding of truth, but an increase in awareness of the world around her, an enlightening of her perspective. The cave allegory illustrates the evolution of human maturity which inevitably leads, if we continue on this path, to an understanding of the "other world" of pure abstraction.

87

Our fate is rarely, if ever, changed in any significant manner. Yet, while our destiny remains the same, the paths which lead to it are numerous and varied.

88

Only the petulant child demands retribution for the wrongs inflicted upon him by pure fate or circumstance, refusing, as he often does, to accept their decrees. He naively imagines that his presence in the world somehow guarantees him any fundamental gifts bestowed to others. So he wishes to exact revenge for those injuries in his life which disgrace him in any way. After all, he still foolishly believes that existence is a meritocratic process that naturally rewards the good and punishes the wicked. Meanwhile he feels slighted in some way since he considers himself undeserving of his fate, no doubt quite rightly. Nevertheless, a more mature perspective might be to perceive an adverse experience as a means of deepening one's own individual consciousness.

89

We can begin to reorder our lives by first reimagining them, perceiving of existence as something fundamentally different than previously conceived.

90

We have no idea whose lives we will touch but we must have faith that it will be many. We will know with certainty of only a very few — if any — but this should have no influence on our fidelity to the notion that it matters that we were once here. A smile at a random passerby can cure a mood quite depressively bleak, causing a complete stranger to remember us rather fondly as the angel who provided an example of humanity's goodness at a time when it was needed most.

91

The second hardest lesson for anyone to learn: that we must surrender and accept what we cannot control. The hardest lesson is learning to accept the fact that so little lies *within* our control.

92

Destiny is a notion that can be determined only through examining consequences — a perspective derived from the benefits of hindsight alone. Yet, in this manner, we can help to consciously shape our fate to a slight degree, applying lessons gleaned from mistakes previously committed.

93

Anyone who enjoys good fortune at any particular moment should be prepared for its reversal in the next since the enterprise of fate is predicated upon change.

94

We need to develop the inner fortitude to overcome whatever impediments that fortune might cast before us — and there will be many. We must possess the kind of strength that allows us to surrender our desires to fate when the outcome is beyond our reach. Yet, we must nurture a persistence to work daily in order to improve those circumstances which *are* within our grasp. And we must resolve to laugh and face the pale darkness of the future with the wry courage of a sage who knows that all will pass eventually, yet none will pass at all.

95

Chance is merely the right opportunity at the right time for the right person. One's entire existence is often governed by this quite privileged norm.

96

Our character does not become immediately exceptional with one act of charity or a single instance of benevolence any more than one flash of lightning constitutes a storm.

97

It is quite necessary for us to look inward, but we should not expect to find any fixed and immutable elements to our nature from which we might construct the foundation of a solid and unflagging character. Rather we will discover certain qualities, tendencies, and themes that echo through the broad and empty caverns of our lives. The resulting sound — fleeting though it may be — will be the faint call of character.

98

A virtuous individual — the person of character — cannot sit and wait for the right time to act with virtue. Otherwise, she may sit in quiet contentment while the remainder of the world burns outside her window.

99

The feminine influence — whether embodied in male or female form — exerts its power over life and nature. The masculine influence is directed towards building and governing civilization. The feminine is spiritual energy while the masculine is the force of the physical world. Yet, we have dressed ourselves in robes and worn the masks of gender instead of perceiving of the masculine and feminine as two separate energies of our character, each providing assistance within their own individual domain.

100

We should keep our focus trained on the overall long term goals of developing character and accumulating wisdom. Otherwise, we will eventually discover that we have corrupted our better selves and so now obediently serve those forces which arouse the frivolity of our nature.

101

We should concern ourselves with more than simply *developing* good character. We need to fortify it as well. We must strengthen it so that it might stand against the brutalities of the world and the inequities of other men.

102

Just because we are perpetually in the process of becoming doesn't mean that we never become *anything*. It simply means that the final determination of our character is still in question.

103

Our character, while generally quite consistent over time, is never really fixed until our death, when the matter is finally resolved. The development of character requires the practice and pursuit of virtues — those traits of the individual which defy our more base and aggressive instincts. Otherwise, we become no less driven by our environment than an animal who vastly overvalues its possession of rationality and language.

104

Our most meaningful work — generally the labor of our souls — will, if chosen well, strengthen our fortitude, open our mind, and develop our character. Whether this work is ever of value to others is beyond our capacity to control. Yet, we must, whenever appropriate, share our work with those who might honestly benefit from an exposure to it.

105

Our work is only truly meaningful if it serves some humane principle. Working to establish justice, tolerance, humility, reason, and other similar virtues is a commendable and quite noble pursuit. Yet there are many who work merely to gain some material advantage or nourish an ego that is already far too grandiose. These are the young fools who, while standing in a puddle, imagine themselves to have reached the ocean's depth.

106

The Declaration of Independence in America is dedicated to the *principle* that all people are created equally, not to the universal *truth* of it per se. It is a document that calls us — inspires us really — to a higher state of being than our instinctual personality will want to allow. We must commit ourselves to such noble pursuits if we wish to rise above the primitive circumstances of our birth. Morality works in much the same manner. There exist humane principles that we must dedicate ourselves to realizing, the same qualities found in the character of any good human being. In many cases, these are the same relatively few virtues which humanity has praised for generations.

107

If we are to be humane — cultured and civilized — we should maintain a certain set of ideals that we assemble from the work of our ancestors. We must lift our eyes to the heavens of Socrates to receive guidance for ourselves since we will find mostly banality and foolishness among the majority of our contemporaries. A traveling band of clowns for example, though perhaps a pleasant diversion, cannot contend with any of the plays of Shakespeare for depth and profundity of spirit. Yet, all of them can still contribute — some more acutely than others — to the development of our character wherein we might grow to reflect and become conscious of the highest ideals.

108

We often refuse to confront the truth of our own mortality in contemporary culture. In many cases, death is removed from us – out of the streets and into hospitals and homes. We only rarely witness such a thing ourselves and then only briefly, in our youth perhaps, where we quickly learn to put it from our mind in one way or another. Death itself becomes something of a ghost – a terrifying phantom that strikes without much warning and despite all precautions. How we address this issue will reveal something about the truth of our character.

109

We do not simply join the ranks of the humane by virtue of our birth. We must make ourselves worthy of such a distinction first and only then might we claim any special privileges afforded to humanity in general. We are *born* as something of a peculiar animal and remain so situated until we might demonstrate a tendency to *act* humanely.

110

We must learn to persevere regardless of our circumstances. The term "persevere," however, is not equivalent to the notion of remaining steadfast in order to gain some material advantage. It should not be, furthermore, purchased at *any* cost as there are certainly times when one needs to surrender. Instead, we should persevere for the sake of developing our character. All experiences in life — even the most wrenching and tragic — can be understood as offering a variety of opportunities for the growth or deepening of character. Hardship, for instance, can strengthen our spirit as well as bring us to our knees. It has the potential to inspire and motivate as much as to destroy. No wonder so many elect to renounce their soul to the mob in exchange for a little relief from such maddening duality. Yet, we must learn to persevere nonetheless.

111

A true friend is one never to be abandoned. Yet, knowing who *is* a true friend requires quite a lengthy process of character evaluation — a task requiring both intelligence and insight. It behooves us then to choose our friends wisely from the first. It also behooves us to evaluate our own character in the same meticulous manner, improving ourselves as we find inadequacies.

112

We can endure much more than we believe we might and even the unimaginable can seem a tad blasé when encountered often enough. If perceived as opportunities for such, these incidents of suffering can help strengthen our character so that we can be better prepared for what is sometimes a cruel and indifferent world.

113

We oftentimes come to find our character through the sheer elimination of what it is *not* — much as a sculptor may chip away at a rough slab of marble.

114

The story of Moses illustrates the notion that a good and righteous individual will generally not receive the rewards of her labor. As Moses is not permitted to reach the Promised Land with the rest of the herd, the person of character often must forgo any concern for recompense or acknowledgment. Such noble souls pursue virtues for their own sake and for the sake of developing their own virtuous spirit.

115

One of the things that cannot be taken from us is our spirit — the animating energy of our very existence, the wellspring of our character and talent. Death may hold dominion over our physical being, but it merely transforms the ethereal expression of our spirit. After all, the spirit isn't our own individual memory and consciousness but the fuel that ignites and directs it.

116

Sorrow and hardship can forge a person's character into steel — able to withstand even the harshest fate — but the sage must not allow such adversity to harden her compassion and spirit as well.

117

We should not expect some external reward for the demanding labor of developing and cultivating our character. Compensation, of course, will accrue but only of the private sort, the kind of gift valued for the merit of its intrinsic nature.

118

Only when we look back on our lives do we find our past suffering connected to some kind of larger destiny and this is merely because we're looking at the evidence with that conclusion in mind. We assume that our torment must have a reason for its existence because we assume that *everything* must have a rational explanation. It is inconceivable to us, being creatures of the enlightenment, that our suffering is often a condition of our very existence and must simply be endured. *How* a person shoulders these afflictions, of course, may eventually reveal the content of their character and may even help to develop it, but the concept of destiny as some prearranged role that a person must play is merely a literary interpretation and one which must be superficially imposed upon the life of any individual.

119

Greatness of character quite often arises from some inequity of circumstance.

120

Darwin notes that the accidental changes that take place in the life of any organism are sufficient to explain the gradual transformation that leads from the simplest form of life, a protozoan, for example, to the more complex system of a human being. Something similar takes place in the evolution of the individual as well — the evolution of the spirit. Chance encounters occur in the life of all children and can sometimes lead to the gradual transformation of character. A song heard in passing, for instance, can spur a profound interest in music or a book encountered serendipitously could instill a higher sense of purpose to someone's life. Regardless of the means, such accidental encounters can lead, if conditions are right, to lifelong commitments that now serve to at least partially define us.

121

We will not simply "become who we are" through some natural process, as if by osmosis we should learn to recognize what was there all along. While we are born, no doubt, with essential dispositions, our essential character is something that will need to be cultivated through education and experience.

122

Mankind often hates science because it suggests too much of the truth, namely, that in the grand scheme of the universe we possess little more consequence than the rabbit, the turtle, or the bug. Such an insight, of course, is a tremendous blow to an already substantial ego. Yet, we must accept these conclusions if we want to demonstrate any rare value to our existence. Then might we exhibit the kind of greatness that shows itself within the majesty and magnificence of the wolf, tiger, bear, or lion — a greatness of character that is connected to who these creatures are within — they cannot be otherwise. All animals naturally possess their own unique greatness of character. Yet, for us it is an attribute that must be keenly cultivated and developed. We must first wrestle with our consciousness of death, put aside our fears, and reject the magical lies that are generated to make us feel distinctive and somehow immune to ultimate defeat. Only then can we be considered heroic and worthy of mention, fleeting though our time may be.

123

We should strive to establish a moderation of our own instinctual drives in order to properly develop our character and maintain a sense of justice in the world.

Otherwise, justice simply fails to exist as anything other than the unleashing of vengeance and the lopping of heads — all the satisfying expressions of instinct.

124

We should practice emotional restraint and self-discipline given an appropriate opportunity. Whenever we find ourselves in circumstances beyond our control, we might use the event as a chance to hone our skills. Whenever, too, our patience is challenged, or our temper tripped, or our desire so enflamed that we feel the need to stoke it further, we might imagine such conditions as testing our self-control while also shaping our overall character.

125

Character is developed through a process of work and practice — the same requirements needed to improve any natural inclination: educate, incubate, experiment, practice, and produce.

126

Organized religion, as consequence of its mass appeal, generally only communicates a simplistic understanding of the world. A deeper comprehension arises from a concerted effort to cultivate the sort of character that can perceive complexity as an opportunity rather than a curse. Such a perspective can be gained by all with the proper care and guidance — although few of us will choose to crawl when a stretch-limousine is parked nearby.

127

There would be no need for governing principles — or few at any rate — if each individual arranged their character to excel at humane pursuits, if each individual, in other words, did what was required to *act* humanely in an everyday interaction with the world.

128

Corinthians 1:13 states that "love is patient, love is kind. It does not envy, it does not boast, it is not proud. It is not rude, it is not self-seeking, it is not easily angered, it keeps no record of wrongs. Love does not delight in evil but rejoices with the truth. It always protects, always trusts, always hopes, always perseveres. Faith, love and hope, but the greatest of these is love." These are not characteristics of love though. These are the characteristics of the individual who loves *well*. Love is only patient if a person makes the concerted effort to *be* patient while loving; the individual who develops his character in such a way so that *he* is patient in love. Love is only kind if we mold ourselves toward that end.

129

All of us should seek to spend some time in quiet contemplation every day. These sessions are not escapist bunk meant to provide a means for killing time. They are instead an intense focus of one's intellectual and emotional power toward some issue of existence, detached from the petty concerns of daily life and the demands of society. Contemplation is a time when we spend our energy improving some aspect of our understanding, which, as a result, often leads to the development of our character in the end.

130

An artful contemplation is a necessary component to any *good* human life. Yet, contemporary societies don't generally encourage reflection. After all, survival often depends on the contemporary individual's ability to keep the mind fixed on the task at hand — and for good reason given the kinds of perilous tasks we are often required to perform. Yet reflection is so necessary to the development of our character that a lack of it in our life will show a deficiency in spirit as well.

131

The evolution of our spirit is not a natural process; that is, it will not occur unless we undertake the sometimes arduous task of improving upon our more *natural* character.

132

None of us is a completely helpless slave to our own nature unless we so choose. We will be bound, of course, by certain instinctual drives outside of our control, but often these are merely ambitions of the animal, habits that can be thwarted with a commitment to the more humane aspects of the human character.

133

A good person must develop a strength of character as well as explore its depth if her type is to withstand the world, like the giant redwood tree buries its roots toward the center of the earth in an attempt to grow ever larger.

134

Our own reputation is merely the gossip that surrounds

us. While we may have helped to shape the discussion through actions of our own, it's largely something that we should ultimately ignore since it generally provides little more than fodder for those who wish to gorge themselves on the lives of others rather than improve upon their own character.

135

All of us should, as Aristotle suggests, act in ways that realize our own particular nature. The acorn, for example, usually grows to complete its transformation into the oak. Yet, the only way to comprehend the true nature of any human individual — something quite unique in itself, like a snowflake — is through an almost obsessive — or at the very least, committed — pursuit of that understanding. Otherwise, our own individual actions are likely to arise from conditions external to our more native soul.

136

Our animal nature cannot be denied, but it must be refined if we are to be considered fully human.

137

Any society — even one honestly ruled with the protection and prosperity of its people in mind — will generally only act humanely when it becomes a demand of its citizenry. So, each individual then has a duty to cultivate a humane character, a most virtuous soul, and act according to its desires. Otherwise, the humane itself threatens to sink into a quite self-indulgent extinction and one's culture and nation decays as a result.

138

All of humanity should strive to be kings and queens without a crown, that is, noble and wise characters without the egotistical need or desire for the glitter of royal prestige.

139

We need not concern ourselves with what *might* have been since what exists now is all that can ever be — so far. Character determines destiny more than the mere cause and effect consequences of choice. After all, our decisions generally derive from the content of our character.

140

The standard for living a good life must be set by the individual of good character. After all, only she will be able to actually evaluate the appropriateness of the standard itself; she having more privileged access into her own true thoughts and desires. Yet, the standard for living among others often conflicts with our attempt to live our lives as we would have it. How we resolves *this* issue will ultimately reveal quite a bit about our character and confirm whether our ideals are worthy of consideration in the first place.

141

We do not mold our destiny through the formation of character alone. There are just too many factors that occur outside the control of even the most powerful individual to imagine that we might somehow hold sway over the very disposition of Nature. However, the development of our character will enable us to take advantage of the many-layered opportunities that *are* available to us, those possibilities that belong to us alone. In this sense, character can guide us to the heights of our own potential.

142

We need to direct the unruly, violent, irrational, and moody aspects of our character into those activities which cultivate and enrich the spirit. We must be shown that our own self-interests are more deeply satisfied when attained through the development of virtue and the training of the sensibilities. Otherwise, we tend to fix our desires upon things much less likely to lead to something healthy or inspiring.

143

Greatness of character doesn't generally have a distinctive feature other than as a gleam in the eye, the soul's radiation. This type of individual alone can count herself as rich, the rest are often little more than auditors of gold, measuring their lives in increments of fine and precious grain — though none of it adds up to anything particularly weighty.

144

The tree spends its infancy rooting more deeply than growing upward. The process is reversed for humanity. We spread roots only later, when attempting to prevent ourselves from toppling to the force of even the slightest breeze.

145

Virtue without humor is no virtue at all, just another instance of vice in the service of fanaticism.

146

Knowledge is generally a virtue as we must ultimately know how to proceed in any particular situation with integrity, wisdom, and excellence if we might hope to consider ourselves possessing some quality absent in the brute.

147

The true test of our morality should be the unity of our virtues and vices together so that the former do not significantly exceed the latter in quantity and quality.

148

Monogamy may not be the natural state of man but it is the state of the higher man, the more humane man — the man who has not repressed his natural tendencies, but who has grown beyond them nonetheless. After all, man is quite aggressive and violent by nature too, yet this would not convert war into something of a virtue.

149

You will find your virtues reflected in the shallow or vast pools of your commitments.

150

The old fool who dispenses wise quotations he's memorized over the years often counterfeits these as understanding of some kind. Yet, if he fails to embody these virtues in his own life, he possesses little more than a collection of children's rhymes.

151

The project of the last century or so has been to unleash

us from as many burdens as possible. If freedom is a most valuable commodity — it's often poorly reasoned — then we should gather as much of it around us as we are able — the more, the better. However, leaving aside the fallacious nature of such an argument, we must still cultivate the virtue of self-restraint in all things. Self-restraint is the mean that lies between the two extremes of freedom, namely: slavery and depravity.

152

Only by performing virtuous deeds or by acting morally do we bring morality or virtue into the world. This alone should motivate a just person to begin the practice of *acting* with virtue. Otherwise, ethics becomes nothing more than the sad dream of artists, philosophers, and priests.

153

In order for the virtue of tolerance to emerge, there first must be a considerable effort to achieve a sense of understanding through the contemplation of a wide variety of views. It's difficult for us to feel compassion, after all, for something that we find entirely absurd.

154

Ideals are necessary models to help us assess our own character and guide our future goals. They are not commandments of any kind. Kant's notion of a Categorical Imperative, after all, — an absolute, unconditional requirement — is categorically wrong. Ideally we should live our lives according to the noblest archetypes of humanity rather than adopt some maxim for use in all occasions.

155

We need almost as many mentors as we have passions and interests.

156

A mentor to aide in the acquisition of simple skills isn't a difficult thing to find. The more simple the skill, the less talented need be the master. Most of us, for example, can learn to tie a shoe and can teach it to another. Yet, the more abstract the notion under consideration, the more agile and knowing must be the guide. After all, any fool can lead us off the edge of a mountain.

157

At some point in our life we will encounter a number of spiritual guides to help us on our way. We must, of course, remain open to these forces in our lives or we may neglect their discovery altogether. Without such counsel we can easily slip into the rut of the common fool who lives lacking the benefit of wisdom. A guide, on the other hand, can provide just the right means of inspiration or admonishment. Advisors such as these are often found in art or rhetoric. Nevertheless, all great counsel arrives like an offering — a gift — or a speech that reveals some great idea, directed, it seems, to us alone.

158

Our *best* friend should be the confidant and ally that we develop and create within ourselves. This "voice" or daemon becomes our chief companion and moral guide throughout the entirety of our lives. Lacking such an important friend — one who must be coaxed from the nest if it is to fly properly — we will continually find that we feel ourselves to be profoundly alone in the world.

159

Distrust all who seem to possess a zealous desire to lead for they will often lead you to your grave. Yet, follow those excellent spirits for whom leadership is something of a chore as they will guide you only as far as it is necessary for you to go.

160

No misery exists that can't be at least slightly assuaged by the mind and perception; no event so tragic that can't be somewhat alleviated by imagining it otherwise.

161

There is no final destination to life, no spiritual enlightenment that will remain fulfilling and constant throughout the course of one's existence. After all, life is in a continual state of flux and the goals that anyone might hope to achieve are immediately usurped by the emotional verve supplied by more pressing aims. We may look back from time to time and view the past from the perspective of someone above looking down on a village below, but still the trek up the steep slope of life must continue — until, of course, we are no longer here to perceive anything at all.

162

The contemporary individual often does little in his life but prepare for a future that he hopes will end more or less happily. In so doing, he relinquishes the only thing that he truly possesses: the present moment. Children should be imitated — to a certain degree anyway — for their ability to live primarily in the now. The glee of children derives from their playful and committed engagement with some task agreeable to their own particular spirit.

163

Jealousy arises from quite a narrow gaze. If a writer, for example, were to examine the exemplars of literature, he might feel greatly slighted by Nature that he were not given gifts as plentiful. Yet, ask him to recall a superbly talented pastry chef or carpenter and he will be, no doubt, at a loss. These endowments are not as important to him because his perspective is so narrow. He feels no jealousy for things beyond his constricted view. If he were to widen the horizon of his concern, however, he might perceive that no contribution can be counted insignificant.

164

The practice of detaching from the world and thereby lessening our allotment of suffering is, in fact, quite effective at relieving psychological pain. Our perspective, after all, largely determines the posture of our spirit. Yet, in so relieving ourselves of torment in this manner, we can likewise weaken our overall involvement with life, choosing instead a kind of living death as a feasible alternative. We might miss a significant opportunity for growth as well if our indifference leads us to elude some important existential conflict with which we should necessarily struggle. If we have no truly deep attachments in life — as heartrending as those affections may be at times — we essentially renounce our existence as a human being to acknowledge our kinship with the rocks. While there are certainly times when detachment is quite essential, we must nevertheless meaningfully engage with the world in some fashion, let the fires of experience forge our character, if we are to ultimately arise better fortified to challenge the inhumane.

165

At some point, the genius must consider whether the faith in her own convictions isn't just some delusion that conveniently arises to provide her with an artificial sense of purpose for her life. Otherwise she might live an entire lifetime with the same brightly tinted lenses that so often affect the perspective of the fundamentalist who sits eagerly waiting for Santa Claus to rise again.

166

Our own true opinion — at least while we are alive — should be known to but a very few of our closest friends, among whom should be only those who have proven themselves to be sufficiently virtuous — that is, a trustworthy friend is one who possesses enough kindness, wisdom, intelligence, patience, loyalty, and the like to confirm our confidence in him. While holding out one's hand in friendship should signal a commitment rather than a hollow gesture of custom, we must also recognize that inside another person's sleeve might hide a newly-sharpened dagger. Therefore, the wise will extend their hand when they intend to bring someone into their inner circle.

167

Our sixth sense is nothing *extra*sensory but rather a perception derived from the very heart of our own constitution, an insight that resonates from the intuition, a recognition or awareness of a "reality" existing beyond the reach of the other five senses.

168

Our perception is shaped by the kind of creature that we are. We do not view the sunset in the same manner as the eagle, the butterfly, or the mouse, though they all notice it in some fashion. Anomalies aside, the creature *man* finds some things to be good and some things to be bad merely because he *is* a man. It is his natural prejudice and one which he cannot ever fully escape. These affinities are largely dictated by his biology and should serve as a further reminder (as if we had not enough) that man is quite limited in what he truly knows about himself and the cosmos.

169

We are only victims if we perceive ourselves as such. Otherwise, suffering and tragedy inform the lives of all of us at one time or another. It is the nobility who stumble forth heroically nonetheless, as a glorious example of humanity at its most courageous.

170

Our perception of the world is shaped by our desires. A large rock, for example, is an inanimate and misplaced hindrance if sitting in the middle of the road perhaps, but a welcomed relief if one needs a place to sit.

171

One of the greatest aptitudes that we can develop within ourselves is the ability to recognize when forces in our lives are within our control and when they are entirely beyond our influence. Even our own will, we may come to understand, is not remotely within our power to manage at times. There are many desires, for example, that we would no doubt wish we didn't possess. Therefore, we must rely on our own perception and intuition to determine the nature of any choice we face — that is, the understanding of whether we hold any choice at all. This "knowledge" can save us years of pointless frustration and lead us to a more direct route toward our destiny.

172

Reading, at least reading books of substance, allows us to walk around in the collective unconsciousness of humanity and share in the intellectual pleasure of genius. *These* are truly the sacred books.

173

No one can expect to read a book and find comprehensive knowledge of any subject. Yet, even the knowledge which *is* ultimately obtained from a great text — sometimes quite significant — requires further reading and annotation to more fully comprehend. There is immense value to this method of engaging with the written word as it opens the possibility for the higher attainment of insight and inspiration — assuming, of course, the work possesses any to express or generally has anything much to say at all.

174

Some spirits burn so strong that they cannot be smothered by the cold indifference of the physical world.

175

A person who does not ruminate when they read has chosen the wrong material on which to spend their time. They will receive little insight from reading something that doesn't inspire them somehow. Yet, so many people merely read to "pass the time" and lose themselves in the salacious distractions of rumor and innuendo. They seek escape instead of understanding. They want satisfaction rather than passion, wisdom, or love — all qualities which require a great deal of struggle to first acquire and then sustain. Reading well, however, is essential for the proper interpretation of life.

176

The postmodern of the 21st century is due for a renaissance of sorts. He has been too long wedged into the finely-worn groove of technological optimism and entertainment industrialization. Eventually he will demand a spiritual revolution. A person can last only so long immersed in the promise — or actuality — of some superficial reward. While the life of such a materialist may become something more enviable and luxurious, the spirit often starves from a lack of its proper food.

177

If our most prized possessions fall into disrepair or become broken or rusted, we will do our best to have them fixed. In fact, we take great care to maintain these goods to ensure that they don't decay in this very manner. The same is true of the body. Our health, quite rightly, is of some importance to us. Here some of us will even go to great lengths to exercise and eat well in the hopes of preventing future decay. Yet, so many of us will rarely take such precious care of their spirit. They do little to feed it well or provide for its need of deep reflection. In fact, they often know very little about the soul at all, even reasoning it out of existence on most occasions. However, woe be to he who does not realize the significance of the spirit. It informs everything that we are and do, yet few of us give it any credibility at all. The hollow pleasures of materialism pale in comparison to the profound effects generated by the contents of our inner character, but most of us never come to realize this feature of our spirit and so will not be aware of an ideal beyond the comprehension of our own quite limited experience.

178

The life of any individual, great or small, exists as an individual layer of material seamlessly sown into the abstract fabric of time and history.

179

If we are to take Wittgenstein's caution seriously to remain silent about those things which cannot be known with any certainty, then all things possessing some level of abstraction — often the very best things of life — will be expelled by an almost religious devotion to mathematical proofs. Yet without the benefit of words — especially those words which attempt to define or clarify impossibly complex and abstract concepts — mankind would forever remain an ignorant brute and the very idea of goodness, love, or art — to name but a few — would eventually perish from the earth. While we might be able to imagine such a bleak scenario, we cannot possibly flourish in such a world, fashioned as we are by both matter *and* spirit.

180

What is lost to our external control generally leads to an achievement in the construction of the soul much like the blind person can develop exceptional hearing with the loss of sight. After all, the human spirit, that energy force that moves us toward our fate, often — if not exclusively — mobilizes in times of need or poverty rather than abundance.

181

Many imagine freedom as purely the absence of external restraint, but spiritual freedom is the independence of spirit which arises from liberating the mind rather than the body.

182

Freedom is largely an illusion, although, to be sure, a person can certainly be chained more or less severely than others. One individual, for example, may find himself in a prison or born under the rule of some fierce regime while another subsists with the kind of wealth previously reserved for royalty. Yet, all of us, to varying degrees, are restrained as well as liberated by our experience, our environment, our upbringing, our biology, and the sheer randomness of our own good or bad fortune.

183

Repression is believed to be a substantial vice in contemporary society since it appears as a significant limiter of one's freedom. In a sense, of course, this is true. Fanatical governments using repression as a means to oppress are rightfully condemned — no matter how peaceful they might seem on the surface. Yet, the other extreme — unrestricted freedom — destroys and degrades as regularly as oppression. Thus, we need to remain vigilant that we repress and liberate what is necessary for the proper development of our spirit. Repression as a means of individual growth is fine as long as it is somewhat freely undertaken. In any event, it is the responsibility of the individual to pursue the goal of sculpting one's own character into something rather exceptionally humane.

184

We are not free to determine our essence, but we are welcome to build upon it — to shape it into a thing quite refined and extraordinary.

185

The free spirit is free in spirit alone, the remainder of our lives are as subject to the laws of physics as is the rest of the physical universe.

186

Each new freedom brings with it a new responsibility as well.

187

The business of intellectual liberation must always remain unfinished.

188

Even if we free ourselves from all of the constraints that keep us chained to our society, we will nevertheless remain a subject of Nature who often demands that we shall bow — or die for our insolence.

189

The Kantian principle requires that we treat individuals as ends in themselves, and not as merely means to some other end. This entails that we treat such individuals as beings that possess dignity, who can freely choose how to act as well as decide what ends to set for themselves. Children, of course, do not strictly meet Kant's criteria since most of them don't possess the ability to freely choose what ends to set for themselves and they are only somewhat rational. Thus, their parents must often decide *for* them. However, the state of the child is merely a stage of life rather than the description of a different being altogether. Children, for instance, still possess the *potential* to do all that Kant's principle requires. Yet the question remains as to *when* exactly the child matures to such a degree that he might be considered sufficiently rational, such that we can bestow the full range of Kant's privileges to him. After all, it would seem that some people arrive at this distinction at a rather young age while many otherwise quite capable old men exhibit childish attitudes and beliefs for the entirety of their lives, suggesting that they did not possess the potential in the first place.

190

Seneca writes that no one takes delight in what is destined to perish. On the contrary, most delight deepens and becomes more profound when its longevity is threatened.

191

Every death should serve as a reminder for those left standing to *live*.

192

We often yearn for death when our lives become far too overwhelming for us. If we live long enough we will eventually reach the point when existence demands more of our energy than we have left to exert. Severe pain, too, can weaken our resolve to remain on our feet. Yet, quite often we will find ourselves surprised at just how much suffering we are willing and able to withstand.

193

Eternity, for the dead, occurs almost instantaneously. So, in a sense, the death of any individual predates the destruction of the universe by merely fractions of a second.

194

Tragedy visits the lives of all of us. We need merely wait for that proverbial other shoe to drop. Our only recourse is to strengthen ourselves for the experience and its aftermath. In this manner we might best prepare ourselves for the eventuality of our own death.

195

Nietzsche is gravely disappointed that Socrates, on his deathbed, reveals a tendency to suffer existence — *enduring* life rather than living it with exuberance. Nietzsche laments that Socrates came so close to achieving what all great teachers or spirits accomplish: concealing the truth that life is a disease in need of relief or cure. Apparently Nietzsche imagines this to be some kind of noble omission; however, the lament of Socrates is merely the expression of a particular phase of life —

the phase of death wherein life is ultimately overtaken by injury or disease.

196

All is yet undecided until death arrives to settle the matter once and for all. In this manner there is always hope for anyone's situation or character to improve — sometimes quite significantly.

197

The individual who is easily offended is often quite easy to anger as well. Such a person actively seeks these opportunities because he generally seethes so ardently from within. So, he takes offense when he eventually perceives some reason — justified or not — to unleash this bitterness upon the world. It's a choice he makes and one from which he is not so easily removed. Ultimately he will grow fond of his indignation because it allows him to feel superior to some other man. In fact, the feeling of indignation itself can be something of an upturned nose wielded as a sword. However, the sage does not give much credence to her position of rank among her fellow men. It is simply of little consequence to her. She tries her best, instead, to find offense in very little of life — not even death.

198

The individual who attempts to cast off the yoke of his civilization once and for all will find that he has discarded a large component of himself as well.

199

Individuals must surrender somewhat to the mercy of specialists if they hope to receive what they could not possibly achieve alone. No one individual can know as much as humanity as a whole. No one can be an architect, a farmer, a cook, a doctor, a nurse, and all the many other necessary specialists needed to maintain human civilization in such a way that it sustains the notion of man as a humane creature worthy of admiration.

200

There are degenerate people in the world, to be sure, but they generally don't pose a threat to the humanizing element of civilization as a whole unless they constitute a majority.

201

Fierce competition for scarce resources may just be the force motivating the animal in man, but civilized man must live his life in rebellion against this brutish pursuit. Civilized man no longer exists in the state of nature as once before — clawing and gnashing for a tiny portion of some grub or a kernel of corn. His laws, principles, religions, and philosophies — all of the humanities, in fact — are mustered together in defense of this new fragile creature: humane and civilized man.

202

When the great mass of humanity becomes too culturally localized, provincial, or myopic, each individual must alone attempt to evolve culture and the humane toward some greater enlightenment and revelation. Each individual person must construct himself as something of a Paris or a Greece.

203

Our moral education arises with our exposure to culture — first through children's songs and stories, then through the cultivation of more sophisticated tastes. Yet, in order to actually *be* moral, we must do more than simply create, study, or enjoy works of art. We must be inspired to *act* morally as well and make of it a habit. Otherwise we do not fare well in comparison to the well-read wolverine.

204

Our very sense of justice and fairness is mostly a reflection of how our culture perceives the world.

205

The fact that Moses is denied entrance into the Promised Land is sometimes understood as a punishment for some minor offense. Instead, there is a finer point to be found in this tale. Aside from the quite tenuous notion of a reward in some heavenly afterlife, Moses isn't afforded the benefits of his righteousness. He must instead struggle and strive through adversity of all kinds without the comfort of certainty to guide him. He labors for all the right things in all the right ways and still he is denied justice in return. This notion of life's essential unfairness, more so than the concept of eternal rewards, is far more familiar to us and a truth which each of us must honestly confront individually and properly resolve for ourselves.

206

We rarely receive what we most deserve because the universe has absolutely no concern for justice. Justice and moral expectation are human considerations — and quite necessary ones too. So we must work tirelessly to ensure that justice is something properly conceived and appropriately administered. It will never be perfect justice, of course, though it must be the absolute best of which we are capable nonetheless. This requires an excellence of character to achieve since it is quite a daunting task for which not all are willing to expend the necessary time and energy.

207

While a culture is generally a shared understanding of some higher ideal, they do not have to be mindless homogenies with little intellectual dissent. In fact, a great culture can arise with a common belief in a single unifying principle, a conviction for justice, perhaps. It is the unimaginative and fundamentalist fool who insists upon homogeneity in all other matters as well. Obedience and the strict adherence to dogma, after all, remind him of the simple naiveté of his own childhood, when he was blissfully ignorant of complexity and irresponsible to a fault.

208

While justice should be blind and unbiased, she nonetheless must guard against indifference and apathy as well.

209

The fool imagines that justice should provide a comparable sensation to revenge — that it should evoke some element of satisfaction. True justice, however, is concerned with much larger issues than a single individual's pleasure or contentment.

210

Justice is played upon a whimsical flute. Sometimes it pipes loudly. Sometimes it stands mute.

211

Fortune will often crown a fool of great misdeeds or trifling abilities with wealth and fame. The sage — she who is among the most humane — should wisely view these occurrences as something to test the faith in her own resolve. Otherwise, the accumulation of these major and minor injustices can, at times, overwhelm her with disdain or bitterness.

212

The fools who imagine good and evil to be entirely relative concepts — possessing only subjective truth — are generally no less dogmatic than the religious zealot. Morality is, of course, subjective in a certain sense, given that it often fluctuates with circumstances, but it is also somewhat universal to the moral sentiments that reside in the vast majority of people. Few of us today, for example, would offer up a loved one for ritual sacrifice because it would contradict our moral instinct for justice. The ancients who regularly practiced ritual sacrifices would, of course, feel no sense of wickedness in their own character since such deeds were considered fairly and necessarily adopted. So, while some may disagree about what *constitutes* justice, the notion of justice itself is inherent and universal.

213

The morality of religion, law, and children is that of strict obedience — a yes or no proposition that generally understands only black and white responses to questions and occurrences. Wisdom is perceived as suspect because it allows for a more diversely colorful world.

214

There is no such thing as a morally indifferent action. Most of our significant decisions are moral choices in one way or another, although not necessarily conscious ones. If we decide to abdicate our responsibility toward moral action and noble principle, this too is a choice which reflects something of our true character.

215

Contemplation — as well as anything remotely abstract or intellectually ethereal — is sometimes perceived as something of an irresponsible dodge, a shirking of one's obligation to others. Yet, our duty to live well requires that we spend considerable time thinking about our lives and this will ultimately lead us to an understanding of where our responsibilities actually lie instead of where others might wish to employ them.

216

Possessing knowledge is of little consequence if we have little knowledge of the highest things. Knowing *these* requires a lifetime of careful study and contemplation.

217

The modern world is in love with its messy, chaotic, rapidly changing, and profoundly unstable environment not because it suits the nature of any living creature, but because it allows for greater and greater distraction. In this manner, the vast majority of people can blissfully speed through their lives without having to spend much time at all in quiet, reflective contemplation. While such a reflective state of being is certainly the highest incarnation of humanity, it also requires a great deal of patience, dedication, and sacrifice to arrive, remain, and, if necessary, return to the "divine" mind.

218

Meaning arises from one's commitment to a task, not necessarily the nature of the task itself. We often search for meaning as if it were out there in the world somewhere. Yet, meaning arises from within — the result of one's devotion to some project worthy of sacrifice and commitment.

219

Those brave souls predisposed to testing their spirits through marriage should first engage themselves in some larger project together — preferably one which lasts for an extended time. In this manner, each person is able to discern how the other will assimilate to an environment where cooperation, humility, tolerance, and care are essential to a successful enterprise. In fact, it's an essential environment for any commitment to the humane as well.

220

All great commitments require a sacrifice of some kind — the greater the purpose of this commitment, the greater the sacrifice. Yet, many of us seem to believe that we may take these obligations lightly and so forgo the requirement of sacrifice altogether. However, such a person should not expect to reap the benefits of true commitment and sacrifice either. They should not expect the deepening of character that arrives with devotion to a spouse, for example, or some noble idea. It's up to each individual to find those causes which inspire devotion and render sacrifice as something each will gladly accept if it allows them access to the beloved.

221

The realization of one's spirit is achieved through education, experience, and insight. These are conditions — perhaps because they require such patience and commitment — that most endorse in public while shunning in the comfort of the home.

222

We cannot adjust our preferences to cohere with the natural state of some "noble savage" any more than we might recapture our youth. The time is now gone forevermore. Once removed from the coercive demands of nature most of us will find it difficult to return living among the wolves and the whippoorwills again. Even Thoreau relied on the civilized generosity of Emerson for food and shelter. His foray into the "wilderness" of Walden Pond then was more of a retreat than a commitment to the rejection of modernity. In fact, such a condition is essentially a bucolic daydream. Generally we must alert our attention to the present obstacles and future challenges of our contemporary environment. In so doing we must also face the loss of those ephemeral possessions that exist for us now forever in the past. The past itself is something quite ethereal once the present perishes into memory. Our most natural state, after all, is a state of flux. Yet reflection allows us to recover these lost treasures and consider them for a while.

223

We must remain loyal — if we are to be virtuous anyway — to those choices in our lives which we undertake with a sense of passion and commitment. We must then continue to renew these vows in order to ensure that we remain devoted to them. Otherwise we might find we have become the person we never intended ourselves to be. Our excuses and justifications will have little influence on the disappointment of our children.

224

We must develop ourselves so that we eventually learn to understand and appreciate the arts and humanities in a manner that is simultaneously profound and fruitful, providing us with a host of thoughtful perspectives that can greatly beautify or enlighten our existence. We cannot generally make art of our own lives, no matter what Nietzsche may imagine, because we usually don't possess the artistic talent necessary to undertake such a task. Besides, the creation of character requires wisdom rather than a flair for some particular craftiness. Yet, gaining even a modicum of wisdom requires the dedication of a mature individual, a person disciplined enough to remain committed to the struggle of forming themselves as a virtuous human being. The rest will content themselves, as they surely do, with the more welcoming and mostly forgettable arts of magic and entertainment.

225

Take heart those who possess something important to

contribute to humanity for Einstein endured the ridicule of many of his contemporaries for the better part of 18 years with his notion of light as a quantum particle. He alone believed in such an idea, not because he could prove it or because it had been built by some long-standing tradition, but because he strongly felt — after much difficult thinking and calculation — that it was an expression of the world in which we live. It is only *accepted* if others begin to perceive existence in the same manner — for whatever reason. Einstein was not comforted by the rightness or truth of his idea; however, he was passionately committed to it nonetheless. He imagined that he was expressing an important observation, no doubt, but no individual of any substance imagines themselves in the possession of some universal and unchanging truth.

226

Any truth that cannot be eventually reduced to a paradox is something of a lie.

227

There are a great many truths in life that should be forgotten altogether. Yet, there are many, too, that must be adhered to almost without exception.

228

The philosopher's goal is not found in the over-generalized search for "truth," but in a consistent and passionate desire to understand — the former seeks an entity while the latter hopes to experience an invigorated state of being.

229

Finding a baby on our doorstep, we will immediately begin a search for the person who left it behind. This is the manner in which we understand our world and the way in which we are *accustomed* to it functioning. If something appears that was not initially present, a child of the Enlightenment faithfully seeks the cause for its appearance. After all, we believe strongly, *nothing* arrives from nowhere at all. Yet, while such a platitude may seem as if it were true, it largely exists as an assumption which aids our comprehension of the world. The intellect naturally simplifies its observations into ideas which are easier to understand — truths which are true mostly through convenience. However, the complexity still remains hidden beneath the simple facade.

230

Imagine the novice musician who upon picking up an instrument for the first time tries to play by simply plucking a few strings. He will find a few notes this way, no doubt, and may even strike a chord or two by fiddling with it long enough. Yet the range of music that he can play will be quite limited. He won't read music unless he studies and he won't master an instrument unless he practices a great deal. People will often attempt to circumvent the severity of these truths in order to possess something that they have not earned the right to obtain — like wisdom, for example.

231

We can never definitively know the truth. What we might recognize instead are a diverse variety of truisms.

232

The social contract is renewed by each successive generation that adopts the beliefs of their tradition. Those who choose otherwise become a new kind of expatriate, one living within the country of their exile.

233

A philosophy without contradiction is an error hidden from the naked eye. There must necessarily be contradiction in any philosophical system of belief since such a theory requires language to express itself and language inherently leads to confusion or one kind or another. Yet, even the great power of rationality, which might condemn such inconsistency in thought, must nonetheless recognize when its authority is a hindrance to a more comprehensive understanding of life.

234

The statement "he is a good man" should arise no more confidence that such a person will restrain himself from violence than the claim "he is a good dog" might instill in its owner the belief that the greyhound will forever ignore the jack rabbit if commanded to do so. On the contrary, a good trainer will always keep a watchful eye on his charge in the event of some unforeseen circumstance. So, too, should we remain mindful of ourselves.

235

Knowledge and reasoning eventually trump the intellectual corruption and ignorance necessary to maintain the closed fanaticism of ideology. However, entire generations may pass before such rigid belief becomes rightfully perceived as rather silly, and countless people are persecuted while humanity waits for its reason to arrive. Therefore it would be wiser to banish ideology from the center of the mind altogether and deny it admittance into the chamber of the soul. This requires intellectual humility, patience, and more than a little courage.

236

The maturity of the individual is a move away from ideology of any kind except the creed that one possesses a responsibility toward humane thought and action.

237

We should learn to christen ourselves anew once we've grown to reach maturity and baptize ourselves again upon retiring into old age — perhaps a new name for each new stage of life. In this manner, we may learn to respect our own development as something of a goal. After all, if it's true that we will never be able to step into the same river twice, then we might rightfully say that we will never meet the same person twice as well. Instead, we are always being transformed by either biology or experience.

238

Introversion is not some kind of disease from which someone needs to be cured or a condition of youth that one needs to overcome — a kind of immaturity that must be grown beyond. It is, rather, something that we need to grow *into* if we might ever hope to be mature. We must withdraw into reflection — at least for a time — if we ever wish to be wise.

239

Contemplation aids in the cleansing of our illusions. For example, we may often find another person to be full of faults while failing to imagine ourselves possessing these imperfections as well. Only when we recognize ourselves within the glint of another creature's eye will we truly understand ourselves in any significant way. Personal and critical reflection is a necessity if we should wish to demonstrate intellectual, spiritual, and psychological progress.

240

The better part of our nature is often found in the ideals to which we aspire. Ideals that serve the humane are praiseworthy while we rightfully admonish thoughts and deeds which are inhumane.

241

The ideal person is not a supernatural force that resembles some perfected creature, but an abstract notion — derived from individual study, reflection, and experience — of what should constitute the best of that individual's own nature, warts and all. We are each a member of a collective — unique and necessary — as much as we are remote and solitary. We must maintain a balance between our duty to ourselves and our duty to humanity as a whole. Ideally, whatever responsibilities we might possess for ourselves will eventually bring an even greater contribution to the tribe as well.

242

A person can be perceived as something dead and decaying when he is no longer *moved* by much of anything. This is precisely the Buddhist ideal though, to extinguish all desire in order to alleviate suffering. While such a technique — a quite valuable one at times — certainly eases misery momentarily, it often does so at the expense of life itself. If we have the courage, life is to be our challenge. We must live a life of excellence and nobility *despite* the suffering of the world — or perhaps because of it.

243

One person's suffering *is* the suffering of all the world.

244

Suffering finds significance only if we are creative and resolute enough to seek such meaning out. Without such effort suffering is merely something that must be endured with the hope that it will quickly end.

245

Nietzsche's resentment of the great Socrates, who seemed too eager to die at the end, sounds full of the disappointment that only a young child might experience when considering the virtues and flaws of his father. Nietzsche's perception seems somewhat grounded in the romantic notion that wisdom is a product of nature and youth and the acquisition of age merely serves to tarnish it in some fashion. He seems far too unwilling to accept the possibility that someone of advanced years — having more experience with these matters — may reach a point when he has simply had enough, when life itself becomes the greatest of burdens. Life is not, ultimately, an experience to endure at *any* cost.

246

Author Mary Roach describes the resilient moss on the barren Canadian island of Devon existing as "something so delicate surviving in a place so stingy and hard." Essentially, this is the plight of humanity as well. We live in a world that is indifferent at its very core. Oftentimes it is hostile and even downright cruel to the hopes and dreams of any individual human being, a creature so delicate that it might be undone by a single gust of wind. Therefore, we must work to develop the kind of persistent spirit that allows us to do more than just survive, but flourish as well.

247

We risk an entire lifetime of suffering and regret if we attempt to force our way along a path that is not open to us.

248

The most significant achievements of our lives are generally not duly rewarded. There occur no celebrations, no parades, little to no compensation, perhaps not even a single note of thanks. Yet, such accolades are irrelevant to profound labors. Such deeds are done, not for their own sake, but for the sake of the spirit who undertakes them. Only these are truly worthwhile pursuits.

249

If we upset the balance of our conscience through some act that brings us shame, we should perform an opposing act of benevolence or generosity to level the scales once again. The more serious the infraction, the more charitable must be the response or deed.

Otherwise, we will surely tip the delicate poise of our own inner nature and find it difficult to right ourselves without significant effort. Yet, even then, we may never quite walk the same again.

250

The desperate urge to maintain the status quo derives from a neurotic desire to force life to remain forever static and easily definable. Nevertheless, life *must* change and proceed this way into the future. Prolonged attempts to impede this change are often met with tragedy or at least a great deal of bad "luck." Still others will believe that this fluctuating mechanism of growth and advancement suggests that we should simply *rush* to progress — usually at a pace that far exceeds the tempo of Nature itself. Yet, rushing forward without the benefit of wisdom, foresight, or reflection will also generally lead humanity to ruin. So, we must maintain quite a precarious balance between the two extremes of change and permanence.

251

As early man first made the mistake of spiritualizing the vast majority of the cosmos, so too does contemporary man commit a similar error by physicalizing everything. Instead, we must strike a balance in our lives and do our best to maintain it through good fortune and adversity alike.

252

Doubt is not a force that should be purged but encouraged. Doubt shields us from the overweening arrogance of our own prejudice and gives us pause at times when we should not speak. It acts indeed as something of an intellectual fulcrum upon which balance the extremes of certainty and ignorance.

253

One of the most pressing difficulties in the life of any man, woman, or child is the learning to surrender one's desires and ego to the moment, but not the moment after.

254

We so often attempt to alter the circumstances of our birth because we have learned to love what we are not. Yet, it takes a rather unique individual to embrace the destiny that is her own.

255

A destiny is something that happens to us, not generally something that we bring to fruition. We make choices, of course, which help drive our way, but these decisions are largely benign under the circumstances. A child, for instance, may be afforded the choice of either walking to bed or being carried there. This may give the *illusion* of choice, but the end is altogether decided beforehand. The child has merely chosen the *manner* in which she will proceed toward providence.

256

We must learn the difficult task of living with uncertainty or we will find it quite difficult to live at all. Our fate ultimately is an uncertain notion, a storyline with no clearly defined or comprehensive narrative. So we should allow our fate to reveal itself to us rather than force its exposure to the open air.

257

If we should not be blamed for what the planets have decided, we should not be praised for them either.

258

Our environment informs all of our choices to a large extent. While our fate may appear to be a chosen undertaking, it is merely the collected response to stimuli that we understand to be our own. We are born, for example, and we cry without deliberation of any kind. The child's next move will depend upon whatever subsequently occurs. If she is returned to her mother's breast, she will find comfort for a time. If not, her "choice" will be determined for her here too. And this is how her life will progress, moment by moment, wrestling with whatever angels we might hope to bless us. Yet this is hardly the product of some greater design — personal or otherwise.

259

Finding one's path in life is the easiest undertaking of maturity since it is always immediately beneath one's feet. The difficulty arises in the preparation for this duty — the training, which if not properly achieved, may cause us to rush to our destiny entirely unprepared.

260

The myth of the individual is that he might rise from the depths of some dire condition to the heights of salvation through the operation of his own free, untiring will. Yet, this view ignores the influence of the collective on individual accomplishment — something that can only be really understood in context with the surrounding world. The person who rises in his profession, for instance, no matter how much of a virtuoso, may only do so if there is someone who exists to fall beneath him. He might be a genius but only in comparison to all the rest. If he should think to boast, he must forget his time spent as an infant, and a toddler, and a boy, and even as an adult — moments when he was among the "needy" and found assistance in the form of some strange communal hand that shaped his destiny.

261

Who can say what any of us may find in the deep pockets of our destiny when we venture out into the world with some great purpose in mind. If nothing else, we may discover ourselves.

262

There are times, to be sure, when we must push against our fate. For the most part, however, our fate pushes *us*.

263

Ultimately, history is a myth about the past which helps inform and guide most of our future expeditions.

264

Hope and the future are inextricably and intricately woven together so artfully that the one cannot exist without the other. There can be no hope without a future. Why, even the suicide perceives a future of some kind — one that might hopefully provide relief.

265

The present moment is the proper mean between the

extremes of past and future. The present harmonizes the other two and inspires them each to greater significance.

266

That which today generates outrage, surprise, praise, or alarm will tomorrow nary produce a yawn.

267

Life is only a dream to the person looking backward into the past or forward to the future.

268

At any particular moment life is an expression of the best of all possible worlds since, the moment having passed, all possible outcomes have been revealed. The next moment, of course, allows for improvement and growth — as well as further destruction and decay.

269

The lesson to be gleaned from the fable of Job is that an individual should not become so entangled in his plans and hopes for the future that he is unable to endure their loss. After all, fortune wields its scepter indiscriminately and what any person possesses now will be taken from him eventually. This is not to say we shouldn't attempt to achieve our goals, only that we need to prepare our minds for their inevitable loss. Otherwise, grief can press us into madness instead of inspire us to wisdom.

270

We must be wary to avoid making ourselves a slave to money, love, or even life itself. These may grace our existence from time to time, but so could we be stripped of them at any given moment. We will grieve their passing, of course, but ultimately we must of necessity be prepared to part with them all and more. Otherwise we can become obsessed with retrieving that which fortune has already seized.

271

There is no real need to be faithful to most desires of the body since the body will ultimately disappoint and leave all spirits stranded in abstraction.

272

To think, but not to do is to merely *imagine* the living of one's life. However, if we were to do, but not to think, we wouldn't have a life much worth imagining in the first place.

273

A life lived solely in the mind is as distasteful and pathetic as one lived without much mind at all.

274

The great beauty of art is that it allows for the illumination of a single spirit to flash on the canvas or the page and send out a beacon to those distant ships drifting hopelessly on the horizon.

275

Dreams are the manner in which all individuals attempt to give shape to what cannot be articulated in prose. After all, we have definitive words for only those things which can be so easily labeled, the rest must be fashioned into art of some kind — dreams are simply paintings on the canvas of the amateur.

276

Socrates proclaims that we somehow encounter a weaker version of an experience if we receive it from the written word rather than from the spoken. However, speech is quite limited by the moment in which it's released. In other words, circumstances will determine much of what is said and heard at any particular time and most of what is said — it should be observed — is purely superficial. Furthermore, we can only digest so much of all that arrives to our senses during a discussion. When engaged in conversation there is simply no time — no thoughtful pause — that might allow for deeper reflection of any kind. The best that one might hope to achieve through dialogue is the understanding that reading is fundamental to a more comprehensive — dare I say, more profound? — understanding of the cosmos and of those creatures who inhabit it.

277

There is no real justice or morality or much of anything else we might consider "good" in this world except for those virtues that we both esteem and bring to fruition ourselves. It is mankind who must define and provide goodness. *We* must create and maintain justice. *We* must wisely choose to what we should commit ourselves and then act with a passionate resolve on behalf of that pledge. Yet, we must remain vigilant as well that our commitments do not degenerate into zealotry.

278

Our dreams can reveal something about the state of our soul. These dreams serve as messages from the divine realm of the unconscious imagination which the dreamer may then interpret for guidance. This requires a subtle mind and a competent understanding — both traits sadly lacking in our more natural state.

279

Reflection and meditation may seem counterintuitive reactions to life's imperatives, but this is precisely the state of mind needed to connect us to the profundity of our spirit.

280

If we have no place of peace within ourselves to which we can retreat in times of great sorrow, we become something of a spiritual nomad without the benefit of a psychological shelter to protect us. How might such a thing be accomplished — developing a rapport with our own inner soul? In the same manner that we acquaint ourselves with any other creature that we meet, eventually befriend, and ultimately entrust with our lives.

281

Our actions should be always aligned with what we feel to be the needs of our own spirit while simultaneously serving the needs of the world entire. These two demands, if properly synchronized, generally lead to a life most beneficial and significant.

282

We are quite strong enough to endure the majority of hardships that we will face in life; however, we must first choose to do so — to prove our mettle in the confrontation between spirit and brute force. Why? In order to establish our humanity as something quite distinct from the beast whom we resemble more.

283

We cannot and should not expect that we might perfect ourselves in any way. Yet, this does not excuse us from the responsibility of developing our spirit in a manner more admirable and humane than its current incarnation.

284

The exuberance and beauty of the human spirit is often concealed within. In such a case, our creative and intellectual fierceness sometimes cannot be seen beneath the veneer of a cautious and fearful physicality. It's only in our life's work that our character is on display.

285

Observation: contemporary man — the most temporary of men — seeks to fulfill himself through acquisition and accomplishment.
Implication: fulfillment arrives by means of some physical property or manifestation.
On the contrary: our most treasured wealth lies directly behind our forehead. This is the spiritual center of all humanity.

286

The true interest of humanity shouldn't be directed at some dream of a universal human nature, but to the notion of a humane potential within the spirit of every person — the possibility inherent in each individual to rise above the brute realities of everyday existence.

287

In physics, the law of conservation of energy states that the energy in a system cannot be further created or destroyed, only changed in some manner from one form to another. The potential energy of water, for example, is not lost when it's slowed by the turbines of a generator, but transformed instead into the kinetic energy needed to produce electricity. Not surprisingly this same process holds true of spirit in the world. In the human race, the spirit or soul is the animating energy-source of the body — the thought, temperament, and character of a person. So, while our body changes slowly over time — eventually returning back into carbon, dust, and ash — our soul is transforming too, finally separating from the body altogether and returning again to the abstract ether from whence it came, that great collection of everything.

288

The reason that many of us feel so much more alive and spiritual when we separate ourselves from the modern world and all its machinations is because in so doing we limit the amount of targets aligned for our desire. This sheer lack of desirable objects leaves us no choice but to focus our attention within. The difficulty will be, of course, when we emerge from this cocoon and must return to the world once again, that environment which most inspires frivolous and inane aspirations.

289

The professional is the slave of his profession. Thus it might be more advantageous to consider oneself a professional individual at play in the world.

290

The manner in which humanity plays most profoundly is through the creation of art and the dance of intellectual expression.

291

No one can live a life in strict accordance with any particular theory — eventually a contradiction will arise to prove the rule is false under some conditions. This is not to suggest that we are just woefully ignorant or hopelessly blind, but we should remain intellectually modest no matter what we imagine ourselves to know.

292

All is won in losing if by losing one has fought to win something truly meaningful.

293

If we are to be undone by love, it should be as something of a natural defeat — an occurrence quite impossible to defend.

294

The goal of any person should be foremost to discover the individual meaning of her life and then its relationship to the rest of world. She will not be truly satisfied with the one unless it includes a connection to the other. For example, the artist who whittles sculptures will not be content if her work sits collecting dust in the basement and, likewise, she whose existence is consumed by work that is not her own will find herself wishing that she possessed some private genius.

295

One of humanity's greatest traits is our persistence in questioning the meaning of our own existence; one of our greatest weaknesses is our attachment to the answers that we derive from this inquiry.

296

Our primary concern should not fixate upon a career but on those truly meaningful projects for which choose to dedicate our lives. If we haven't any, then we need to make the search for some an urgent ambition of the life we have remaining.

297

All "good-byes" have the potential to be final good-byes. We need to be persistently conscious of this fact lest we miss some significant opportunity.

298

There can be no true source of human happiness since happiness has no foundation on which it lasts for long. Happiness, when it arrives, is generally something accidentally discovered rather than an entity to be actively pursued. To proclaim we have every right to pursue our happiness is to say that we have every right to breathe the air. We have no need to pursue what we already possess within ourselves. In fact, a person pursuing happiness is in search of something altogether immaterial — a particular state of mind that might have been otherwise accomplished without the need for a pursuit of any kind.

299

We should of course learn to follow the dictates of our own heart, but we must also ensure that we can distinguish its higher attributes from the baser nature of its more primitive desires.

300

Only patience is ultimately rewarded. Impatience tortures us to relent, and when we refuse to do so, punishes us with our heart's content.

301

We must first be a midwife to our own soul before we might take Socrates' advice and be a midwife to others. More often than not, however, the vast majority of us are found in the lobby smoking cigars and waiting for news instead of standing patiently in the birthing room.

302

We must learn to recognize fortune as something other than a big, ugly monster of change. We need to train ourselves to overcome such fears. We also should be quite patient to observe when fortune yields conclusions that we instinctively resist, for herein lie matters for thoughtful consideration.

303

The spread of technology has left us impatient with the slow and steady pace of Nature so we attempt to improve upon her to such a degree that she becomes hardly recognizable to even her oldest friends. We have artificially increased the speed of our own internal clock and we expect time to go zipping along with us. We are, in a sense, seated on a runaway train as the scenery outside the passenger car blurs against the window. However, if we were to leap from such a train as it continued to speed out of sight, we would immediately recognize just how quiet and peaceful is the remainder of the world. Assuming, of course, that we would survive the fall.

304

The greatest challenge for the survival of the anti-extremist — the thoughtful, honest, reasonable, and open character of humanity at its best — is to wage war with the varied and largely quite ignorant doctrines of extremism without fashioning a response that is itself dogmatic and extreme.

305

We need not have to practice what we preach, but we should at least attempt to reach those heights and more. Our hearts must set the bar over which our bodies will then eventually follow. Regardless, it's far better to attempt something great and fail than aspire to very little and receive significant acclaim. After all, we learn more from our failure than our success and even the most minor disappointment can provide some profound element of insight.

306

While rote and rigid adherence to practice, discipline, and technique will eventually yield a musician who can *play* music exceptionally well, it can also present as an obstacle to the *creation* of music.

307

Inspiration enlivens the soul like colors splashed upon a

clear blue sky.

308

A person who in her struggle to inspire justice finds fame along the way should not concern herself much with these consequences of her work. Her original intent remains clear whether others take notice of her or not and only this ambition truly sustains her anyway. Yet, if someone originally aims for fame and by work or luck receives it, he shall find that it cannot meet his unrealistic — and perhaps unconscious — expectation to cure those conditions that ail him most.

309

I see the moon shining just as brilliantly as when I was five; as it did in Socrates time, no doubt. I notice the sunlight on the leaves of the trees at the end of the day and it differs very little from the beauty of dusk that I've observed for these last 40-some odd years. The cool of the evening still brings the same chill to my skin as I'm sure it did Whitman, Heraclitus, or Montaigne when they sat on their doorsteps at the close of day. Nothing has changed either with respect to the cut of the mountain against the horizon; it still casts a formidable shadow and inspires awe as much as ever. I also smell the fresh cut lawn in the afternoon and this odor harkens me back to childhood when the same aroma hung thick in the air. While much in life appears to change, such differences seem relatively minor when perceived with the proper lens.

310

Imagine an afterlife which is composed entirely of consciousness released from the moorings of a physical brain. Such an experience, seemingly infinite with possibility and independent of time, would be much like an extremely vivid dream but without the storage of memory to recognize it as such.

311

Where is the child who once sat upright in my arms? And smiled so sweetly that angels felt ashamed? Where did she go? Saddled to a star and grown away? She was once no larger than a teacup it seems. Why did she feel the need to leave? We're good people. She wanted for nothing. And yet she flew to places that we will never see. Where is the child today? She no longer frolics on my knee or clings to my fingers as if they were the branches of some majestic tree. Her giggle now has faded and her clothes have passed along to someone new. Yet, where is she? Gone it seems, gone for all eternity. And in her place I see a strangely familiar butterfly.

312

We can observe the waves crashing upon the rocks for the majority of our lives and still perceive little change in the formation of the boulders in all that time. Yet the waves, as relentless as Sisyphus, will only rest to gather more force in order to resume their task. Though these efforts may persist for a few thousand years, eventually they will succeed. The cultivation of humanity requires a similar faith and persistence.

313

We cannot — and probably should not — expect war and aggression to be entirely eradicated from the earth. After all, humanity being what it is, the development of the humane may require a certain amount of violence to defend itself against the powers of cruelty and ferocity. The noble task is to act in order to encourage and inspire the humane response as best as possible.

314

While it is possible to be entirely overwhelmed with the uncertainty of life — without any hope of relief — uncertainty itself is the force that most often leads to some new illumination. After all, without the darkness, there would be no need for light.

315

Any traditional religion can stupefy the masses sufficiently and calm their skittishness about the uncertainty of life. This is an extremely necessary foundation for the person ill-equipped to build a life without it. The extraordinary individual, on the other hand, is able to assimilate all of the messy, paradoxical and abstract elements of existence into her being without it causing a major psychological revolt.

316

We generally spend so much of our time in public that we almost ignore our private accomplishments altogether. We imagine that if we are not publically celebrated, we are somehow not properly alive.

317

"To thine own self be true" is the advice of Polonius to his son, but the old man never imagines that such wisdom would actually encourage the young man to kill the prince of Denmark. Instead, we should be true to our *better* self rather than the self that is our own.

318

Repression is only a sin if it oppresses our better nature. Otherwise, it's often quite necessary.

319

It is not the *best* person who should take on the responsibilities of civic leadership, but the best leader with the best of intentions. The sage, on the other hand, provides guidance as to the best manner of living.

320

The particular manner or habit of a good life will be different for every individual. This is not to say that any approach to life is just as good as any other approach, only that traditional prescription — the voice of the law, the ritual, and the way — cannot possibly hope to regulate and define the infinite diversity of human experience.

321

We should understand that we cannot "cure" the vices of our fellow human beings. These people must do that task for themselves. So we should not attempt to benefit our contemporaries without their desiring the help. We might, after all, be quite wrong in our assessment of their need. Besides, we lead best through our example and not, as some boastful pundit, for the sake of what we perceive to be the overall "good."

322

"Brotherhood" is far too narrow of an idea to define one's

ethical duty in the world. Concern and tolerance should extend far beyond the borders of the neighbor's fence. Instead, we possess a duty to treat all of creation with the same care and reverence reserved for kings and dignitaries.

323

The first purpose of law — or what should be its first purpose anyway — is to insist that we treat one another humanely. Its secondary aim is to keep the peace, of course, but even this intention must bend to the authority of the humane which promotes the notion of a kinship between strangers.

324

A city of 10 billion people can isolate us as readily as any mountaintop. The wise soul will need to be isolated — for a time at least — in order to understand the nature of the abyss that awaits her. She must learn to live in harmony with the melancholy tune of isolation.

325

We need not necessarily detach ourselves physically from others in order to gain solitude in the city. As Emerson noted, it's difficult to maintain a sense of solitude in the company of the crowd; however, this is precisely what all great souls must ultimately do. Their greatness derives from their willingness to descend from the mountaintop to share their wisdom with the rest of us.

326

Living in the modern world of technology and luxury is similar to a person who drives their car in a heavy rainstorm. Inside the car — as inside the contemporary world — the individual is comfortably at his ease with perhaps some Mozart or Chopin on the music-player for good measure. He is dry and warm while the rain slaps against the window in loud applause for the technological achievement that keeps him so secure. Of course this allows the person to shield himself from all of the un-pleasantries of nature and the storm, but the sounds of the rain still remain a constant reminder of his vulnerability nonetheless. In fact, if he were to step outside for a moment, unprotected from the elements, he would immediately notice the thin and fragile features of his own natural armor.

327

In the end, what will be your last words? And what shall be the words used to define you then? What words define you now? What stories do you tell about your life? And what words make that life sparkle? Which make it fly? What have been the sounds of your existence (since words are merely sounds)? What words have you forgotten? Which have forgotten you? And what words have controlled you? Shaped you? Inspired you? What has been and will be your legacy? How will others speak of you in the end?

328

Man, like any artist, must face the brute facts and odd circumstances of his birth and make of them something noble and worthy of profound admiration.

Wisdom

1

There can be no definitive law or guide that can help us decide what we should do with regard to ethics, as Aristotle noted. Therefore, we will need to develop wisdom. Habit or custom are not enough when confronted with a conflict that divides the soul, as do most moral dilemmas. Only the individual of wisdom will know what she should do and she will only become and remain wise through intellectual and spiritual exercise.

2

There should be a few times in our lives when the beauty of the world forces us to our knees from a sheer sense of astonishment. In these moments of "divine" confrontation, our spirit recognizes its own reflection and must pause awhile to reminisce.

3

The sage knows that she merely holds a thing; she does not own it. Therefore, she has no need for spending much time or energy in sustaining her grip. After all, she has more significant matters to consider.

4

Wisdom will lead us to the correct path that we should travel, but only faith will keep us on it. Whether we succeed on our quest is immaterial since it is the expedition itself that will lead to our evolution.

5

Wisely and slow does the learned soul proceed or she shall find herself in the sea with Icarus.

6

Our private desire to kill — a rather common remnant from our ancient past — must be somehow weakened or sublimated. It lingers in our personality, loitering in our subconscious mind — always at the ready to explode upon the scene whenever necessary. Yet, the sage will not repress such instincts. She will merely attempt to refine these energies into something more beautiful or sublime.

7

The wise individual has little to say to his contemporaries because they don't typically understand him when he speaks. Besides, only rarely do they wish to discuss matters of any importance.

8

While old age never made anyone a whit more wise, it does provide an extended opportunity for reflection and insight which might eventually lead us to wisdom nevertheless.

9

A sage needs to develop an inner strength, a place of great reserve and patience within her soul, wherein she can always find peace in a noisy world populated by neurotic fools who wander the city night in search of spectacle.

10

Assuming a person has not been reduced to an animal state, there are essentially four different paths for him to travel in life, any one of which could easily diverge into another, and all, like a lazy river, wind through and around the various obstacles and hardships of his overall destiny. The first route is that of the pleasure-seeker who finds all sorts of distractions along his way. His path is strewn with a bouquet of sensuous delights that only fuel his desire for more. An individual gets lost oftentimes in the sheer abundance of these diversions, awash in the ecstasy of sensual experience and the spectacle of mere entertainment. Yet, he seems quite happy to tread along this trail. The second path is the way of the common soul. A person on this trail is astute enough to imagine a larger sense of duty governing his life so he travels onward searching for these obligations, rarely at rest except to briefly contemplate his next conventional undertaking. The extraordinary path, the third of four, eventually forks into a puzzling network of highways and country roads that all seem to drop off at the horizon. Yet, this does not deter the individual who wanders out so far away from his companions. This person, too, feels obliged to seek some higher purpose in life, but he has not the benefit of chart or star to guide him. His aim, as well, is loftier so the risk is greater too. Tradition and law help steady the common soul, but no such advantage directs someone through the labyrinth of the extraordinary. Such a spirit is left largely on his own — to perish or to prosper in supplication to the fate that is his alone. The fourth and final path is that of wisdom which will ultimately lead to some greater understanding, but will require great effort and struggle along the way. Nevertheless the attempt to truly understand something about the highest things — those perspectives that ignite the spirit and inspire the soul — provides quite a deeply personal and passionate commitment to study and contemplation.

11

Wisdom has always meandered along the very precipice of extinction. If it weren't for the efforts of a few noble practitioners, humanity might have banished human insight from the earth entirely. After all, if none will volunteer to be the standard bearer for wisdom, then only knowledge and ignorance will survive and these will not sustain mankind beyond a few malingering generations.

12

The wise soul knows the fool to be someone who has rendered himself so unconcerned with thought and reflection that he can only hear his own echo and see his own image. There is no point in arguing with such a person or attempting to move the planets in order to alter his opinion about anything of importance. The fool chooses to live a life free from the frustration that occurs whenever the sage attempts to develop herself into something greater. He would rather spend his days lost in the stupor and comfort of his ignorance. If he does emerge from the dense mire of foolishness, it will be only as a result of his own decision to do so. Thus, the wise soul will make no effort to convince such a fool directly, yet she may still exert an influence by the example of a life spent in service and sacrifice to "divine" wisdom.

13

The difficulty with wisdom is that we must be well versed in a wide variety of perspectives and understandings in order to apply the correct judgment to the appropriate situation at any given time. The Buddhist, for example, is admirably able to persevere through the most extreme of circumstances by detaching himself from his own concerns. He is quite correct, after all, that desire has a strong tendency to lead a person to suffering. So the Buddhist way will serve quite nicely under certain conditions. However, suffering itself can sometimes lead to a profound epiphany which in the absence of suffering might have never arisen. The child must necessarily suffer frustration in learning to walk or to read or learn much of anything else. So a whole cluster of different views may be needed in determining what to do in any particular situation. The wise individual is she who knows when to apply what for whom.

14

The sage employs philosophical theory when appropriate to the circumstances. Stoicism, for example, can be utilized primarily by the terminally ill and during extended times of pain and suffering. Utilitarianism on the other hand is a view designed for crowds and those times in our lives when consequences will matter most to the dispensing of justice. The Kantian approach meanwhile might be best applied when a kind of ethical absolute is needed. In any event, any particular circumstance still requires someone to employ the theory wisely.

15

As the belief in religion — as opposed to its mere outward display — faded over time, humanity began to seek justice on its own. If someone perceives he has been wronged in some manner he will blame the government, or society, or his fellow citizen and demand or exact retribution accordingly. Yet, this same individual imagines himself as exceedingly moral, his vengeance merely a consequence of what justice requires of him. The sage, on the other hand, wishes to inspire forgiveness and mercy when she has been wronged because these virtues embody the merits of true justice; these are the virtues — among others — which rouse humanity from the luxurious cradle of the inhumane.

16

Introspection, reflection, and study are meant to aid in leading us to a larger understanding of ourselves and our world. In this manner we will have a better comprehension of exactly *what* desires we must surrender to fate and *which* passions we should cultivate and pursue. Yet, these results will be slightly peculiar for each individual. The path to enlightenment, as they say, can be lined with thorns as well as roses and the bones of many high priests and kings lie littered beneath a field of weeds. Thus the need for the cultivation of wisdom — a kind of passion, too, brought about through introspection, reflection, and study.

17

The individual of wisdom and true genius is defined by

the uniqueness of her perceptions rather than the singularity of her talents.

18

Wisdom, even of the most dour and unfortunate of life's features, reflects the highest form of humane activity, an intellectual pleasure that humbles the ego and cautions one to pause before leaping into battle or proclaiming some eternal truth. All of the other virtues derive in some sense from wisdom. Benevolence, for example, will not arise until someone can be inspired to fully understand and feel its significance. Courage, too, without wisdom, is merely the rash or instinctual deed of a fool. Intellect, if used unwisely, is a dangerous tool for all sorts of rationalized immoralizing. So, the virtue of wisdom bestows an understanding of what one should do in a particular situation from the imagined neutrality of the "bird's eye view." Yet, the "proper" or wise evaluation will be the one which best appreciates the circumstances involved and this is generally accomplished through the moral imagination — imagining the world from the scrutiny of someone else's perspective.

19

While the wise soul contemplates what should be done in any particular situation, the rash fool arrives to enforce his own less considered view. Yet, there are times when a rash response is necessary. The wise then must also learn to recognize when urgency is needed since not all circumstances allow the luxury of introspection.

20

The lovers of knowledge differ significantly from lovers of wisdom. Lovers of knowledge are engaged in the acts of acquisition, collection, and categorization of information in order to uncover what passes for "truth". Lovers of wisdom, on the other hand, concern themselves with how this material might inform living the best life possible. It's a relatively easy task to stuff the head of any common fool with knowledge from a vast array of sources and, through practice, have him remember it all again. It is far more difficult indeed to teach him to reach a wise decision with such learning.

21

The wise souls of any society are generally those who are well versed in the humanities. After all, wisdom arises from experience and the humanities provide familiarity with the very best and worst that humanity has so far thought or achieved. The sage then, in a sense, lives a thousand lives while engaged in the process of developing her own singular identity.

22

Governments, groups, and mobs fear the individual sage because she is so engaged in refuting theories and scoffing at other pet projects of Truth with a capital "t" — the very sort of notions that ideologists and idiots tend to serve and revere. Yet, no such fear is actually necessary since most ages generally ignore or dismiss their wisest spirits altogether.

23

The great stench left behind by war is Nature's method

for discouraging the practice entirely. Humanity, however, merely invents the mask and smelling salts so that we can proceed to places where people might otherwise struggle to keep their nerve or their appetite. In fact, a great many of our inventions are designed to overcome what might be wiser to simply accept — although, of course, this too requires that we first develop the virtue of wisdom.

24

There is no political action or movement toward reform without the will of the people. This is as true of dictatorships as it is of democracies. Any large body of people properly united in agreement to enforce their will shall eventually arise to adamantly do so. Similarly, if the people haven't the will to bring about reform, no matter what the moral issue, there will be no change. This wisdom can save the neck of a great many untimely revolutionaries.

25

The truly serious individual, she who is immersed in the profundity of existence, should expect ridicule from her contemporaries. She does not think as they do — although by all means these traits alone should not determine her wise. The masses are generally slow to recognize wisdom. Their concerns, instead, rarely extend much beyond the conventionally practical. The dull cancer embedded within their spirit, however, continues to metastasize and eat away at their souls — leaving behind merely the outward signs of a creature unique and admirable. Such people then stumble onward purely through the mechanisms of biological necessity and instinctual habit, often quoting chapter and verse from their favorite religious encyclopedia.

26

The poets and philosophers of today are more concerned with words and language than they are enamored with wisdom.

27

Democracy requires a great *many* virtuous people while tyranny requires none at all. In fact, tyranny best thrives in this condition.

28

It often takes greater courage to stand *against* the horrible current of war than face the many horrors awaiting at the end of the stream.

29

We must learn to develop a wise perspective in order to determine the right course of action and the best perspective is only gained through experience and knowledge. Perspective is, of course, the manner in which we perceive the world, the lens through which we filter all of existence. The lens itself, of course, is in need of constant maintenance and innovation in order to remain relevant, therefore, the true individual must spend the majority of her life gaining wisdom through the acquisition of knowledge and experience.

30

Any type of friendship or marriage should be first heated in a crucible to find its boiling point — even the strongest metal, after all, will submit eventually. Assessing character during times of tranquility and peace generally provides merely the nicest and most congenial of perceptions. It's usually during times of stress when we reveal our true nature and unveil the manner in which we intend to treat others. Some of us, of course, can modify our demeanor and change our behavior accordingly, but this requires the kind of insight generally reserved for the wise, a condition quite often lacking in the vast majority of human beings.

31

The sage learns to endure the offenses of her contemporaries by imagining their transgressions as the trespasses of little children. Yet she should also see that such immaturity is a condition that these small spirits have largely chosen for themselves.

32

No one can permanently ignore the truths of their own moral failings. The transgressions must be justified or otherwise sufficiently explained. If not, these offenses awaken us at night with a persistent cry for recompense. Such pleas do not originate from the universal heavens but from within the soul of humanity itself. Morality, after all, is at the heart of human character — or, at the very least, it is integral in developing a truly human disposition. A person cannot help but judge some things "good" and others "bad" since it is a component of our own nature that moves us to such assessments. If we are to make *moral* judgments, however, we must acknowledge perspectives and considerations beyond our own individual prejudices.

33

There are plenty of higher souls in the world. However, there exists no higher *type*. The sage can arrive in a variety of different forms while possessing a host of unique talents and perspectives. It's a mistake to imagine that the wise and noble spirit fits exclusively into the mold of artist, philosopher, or saint.

34

In the current age of whirring spectacle and technological miracles we often have little time to sit or think or read or simply ponder the quiet beauty of a winter lake. Our world is so overwhelmed with the deluge of entirely superfluous, and often downright contradictory, truths that we are at a loss as to how to make sense of it all. Usually the task is too great and many of us will simply surrender to our fate as something of a fleshy automaton for king and tradition. It is the wise indeed who know where lies the most peaceful and profound condition of human nature: the state of thoughtful reflection.

35

We all want different things at different times of our lives, but *that* we want is fundamental to our nature in some important way. We cannot simply banish such a fundamental element of our character without it surfacing again and again in an obsessive want to eliminate wants. We should contemplate instead upon the refinement of our desires, the virtue of our passions, so that we might better live according to some higher purpose than our own individual existence. Yet this requires a wisdom for which most won't even bother to attempt.

36

If someone develops a reputation — well-earned or otherwise — as a malcontent, they can expect to spend much of their time alone, sequestered away from the vast majority of others who would rather not hear the incessant complaints. Yet, the improvement of mankind — as well as each individual — will never arise without a great deal of constructive criticism and protest. Critiques of this kind, however, are often conducted by a large mob of inferior minds whose shrill and ill-informed voices frequently rise to a din that overwhelms the more thoughtful and learned responses of the sage. So, while everyone should be entitled to an opinion, only the judgment of the wise possesses value beyond her own individual existence.

37

Wisdom is gained through experience but an experience derived from a certain kind of ambition — a manner of living according to the highest values of humanity, those most humane qualities which can arise from even the most brutish of hearts. Unfortunately there are more brutes on earth than excellent spirits dedicated to the lonely pursuit of wisdom. This struggle for a kind of spiritual survival, of course, will always be the burden of the enlightened soul. She must be strong, then, who will be wise. Yet, she must be soft as well at times and it is wisdom that serves as a proper mediator between right and wrong decisions.

38

The government of the people, by the people, and for the people idealizes the common individual to such a degree that he becomes imbued with qualities that he can't possibly possess. Yet, he will be afforded the same opportunity of opinion as the sage whose thoughts on almost any matter are far superior to his own. This is not to suggest that the common man's interests should be dismissed, only that he may not be the appropriate person to understand how these might be best employed.

39

It makes little difference how long the words of a sage must remain quiet on the silent page because they are quite deafening to the inner consciousness of those who will read him eventually. Great souls may hibernate for a time but they never fade from existence entirely — at least not while humanity itself remains.

40

A life lived in the robes and costumes of another person will always seem quite ill-suited to the individual who wears them.

41

The philosopher's job should be to contemplate rather than prove. A sage intends to meditate on a wide variety of differing perspectives since these intellectual snapshots can provide some insight for when he must confront the vast array of life's challenges entirely alone. The academic philosopher, on the other hand — that professional picker of nits — desires to prove some benign point through logical induction that is of concern to his colleagues, perhaps, or to those who enjoy a good game of tiddlywinks, but to no one else. This is not to say that academic philosophy is a useless exercise. As with the majority of perspectives, the academic view has much to teach and everyone would do well to partake of the rich banquet found within those hallowed halls, but few philosophers today have much to say to those attempting to live a meaningful life. The best that they might offer is a proper introduction to some ancient master.

42

Our spirit will never feel at rest if we aren't engaged in a process of self-actualization. This requires that we possess the intention to cultivate our character rather than impose our will upon the world. We simply have no greater responsibility than to form an appropriate meaning to our lives. However, we must balance this duty with the needs of others. There will be times, for example, when we must declare our superiority and times when we must bow to the will of the community. Only wisdom can provide guidance in deciding the proper path to pursue — wisdom generally gained through encounters with those divine elements of art, culture, and nature.

43

The aesthetic monk is quite a different creature from the sage. While the aesthete — in the name of the good, no doubt — denies himself food, drink, property, dress, sex, and sleep in an effort to somehow transcend physical reality and commune with the divine, the sage attempts to lift her spirit and character through contemplation and study alone.

44

Our character will be tested a number of times in a variety of ways. Smaller pre-tests occur almost daily in little scenarios, conditions that provide practice for the more difficult challenges sure to appear later in life. However, true tests of character generally go unnoticed until we reflect on a particular situation with a keen eye and a contemplative disposition. We must gain a suitable perspective through which to view an event for it to possess profound significance in the narrative of our lives. In this manner, all of us are offered the opportunity of wisdom, but very few ever expend the necessary effort to achieve it. The majority of us prefer that someone else sample wisdom for us and pass along the information in a small pamphlet or nursery rhyme. The vast majority, it should be observed, are far too busy to be troubled with notions that don't generate food or income.

45

The wise should avoid the very human temptation to surrender to any of the extreme conclusions that so easily stir the emotions and lead us to believe that we know more than we possibly might. After all, we barely know our own constitution. Do we possess something like a spirit? What breathes life into our deeds? Are the soul and body intertwined together until one returns as ashes to the earth while the other aids in the animation of the mountain wind and the illumination of a star? These are metaphorical questions which do not speak to empirical truth of any kind, but neither do they refute it. The anxiety brought on by such complexity and the resulting confusion in determining truth from illusion, fact from fiction, can often make the primitive notions of extremism seem more attractive since the fanatic at least provides the comfort of superficial certainty.

46

"Fools rush in," the aphorism cautions, "where wise men fear to tread." Yet, it should be remembered that sometimes wisdom arrives directly as a result of undue haste and even a bit of risk. There exists no edict so fine and universal that it occurs without contradiction or exception of any kind. The commandments of Moses himself are not applicable to all circumstances. The individual who honors a father and mother who abuse him is a fool while he who refuses to kill in self-defense is a fool now dead. Wisdom requires a flexibility of mind that seems sadly lacking in the greatest majority of people.

47

The secrets of our dreams are all neatly woven together and one thread, loosened from that sacred weave, could leave the entire fabric a limp and tattered web.

48

The wise person will eventually realize that all prophets, seers, and sages are generally ignored by the majority of their contemporaries. The soothsayer's cry that Caesar must beware the ides of March is mostly dismissed as silly superstition while Oedipus pushes Tiresias away with a gale of laughter and mockery. The cost of wisdom is often isolation and ridicule, but the individual benefits far exceed these rather paltry expenses. In fact, isolation is something we often *need* in order to function as we must. It is commonly the obstacle of collective indifference that oppresses the genius and causes her to spend her days working on something other than her work. Contrary to Nietzsche's pronouncement, it is not religion that prevents the genius from flourishing, but the communal and oftentimes quite natural demand that she spend her days absorbed in tasks of little consequence.

49

Happiness is not some delightful feeling that overtakes us and washes away the troubles in our lives — momentarily or otherwise. Instead, happiness is the balanced state of wanting no more than one already possesses and needing no less than what fate has bestowed. This kind of stability requires wisdom and virtue in order to maintain the equilibrium. True happiness, after all, can be found lounging beside a pool of misery as well as loafing in a penthouse cabana along the golden shore. One's external circumstances rarely produce the kind of profound satisfaction established from the wisdom to know and the virtue to persist in the proper manner. Happiness arises when we develop a wise and virtuous character.

50

Power permeates into all things so we must learn to utilize those powers now coursing through our veins. There is no "will" to powers such as these; they are so much internal lightning or psychic force — features better channeled than controlled. The wise will endeavor to encourage those powers which arise naturally from the requirements of their soul, those powers which seem to most animate them toward a more humane existence.

51

The wise sit grounded to the center of the earth — unmoved by even the greatest wind.

52

The person who toils without reward will eventually imagine success as something largely random and providential. Similarly, the realization of one's dreams can seem as final confirmation that such achievement is quite obviously attainable to all. In each case perspective is defined largely, if not entirely, by one's environment. The wise should know the prejudices of their own heart as well.

53

Religion often assumes that an object must be *made* sacred through some contrived ritual or proscribed law. The wise know, however, that all things already possess a part of the sacred within, including humanity itself — though we attempt through actions both evil and ignorant to demonstrate that the opposite may be more reasonably true.

54

It does not seem possible for us to influence the very nature of reality. We are, after all, fatefully born into so many established traditions and institutions from before the time of our grandfathers that our entire life can appear a rigidly determined affair. Yet, as we engage with these apparently inflexible forces and shape ourselves in relation to them, our own unique character slowly begins to emerge and so do our higher ambitions. While the vast majority of us aspire to things unworthy of conscious attention, the individual of true character pursues wisdom. The wise know that the ultimate goal for any human life is the evolution of the excellent individual away from that part of the self which is most inhumane and bestial. The more souls who so admirably hope to achieve such a feat, the more quickly does humanity as a whole elevate — at least for a time. To this end, art — if it is to be something more than just puerile amusement or sensuality — provides a depth and richness to experience that may further deepen the understanding.

55

Perspective is the foundation of perception. In other words, what we see is quite often determined by our own particular vantage point. A religious zealot, for example, is not likely to imagine life as something of a purposeless affair. Moreover, a poem might be found amid an advertisement for laundry detergent while misery and depression can follow even the most beautiful of days. One man's horse, it seems, is another man's ass. Yet, there appears to be no truth of the matter either, no definitive authority which could provide the final say. The best that one can hope to achieve in this regard is a genuine appreciation for the complexity of human thought or action. We must confront a wide variety of differing perspectives in order to even remotely understand our species. The wise know, or come to know through study and experience, *how* to perceive any particular circumstance that they encounter. This is not some mathematical formula by which to calculate the sum of "wisdom." Instead, it is a manner of living in the world that prefers tentative understanding to confident ignorance.

56

The sage exchanges those flashy, immediate, and superficial pleasures of life for the serene and patient joys found in the better part of anyone's heart. It is here that the wise may transcend the veneer of the everyday to witness the eternal. The true self arises with a commitment to what is most excellent and humane in any particular individual.

57

The collective unconscious is the notion that beneath the thin veneer of the conscious mind exists a kind of symbolic dreamland of humanity's repressed desires, epic struggles, and every wonderful and horrific thought and deed of mankind as a whole — Eros on the rampage. The wise know, however, that while they may not have much control over their own unconscious thoughts and fantasies, they must still act so as to minimize their more destructive nature and maximize those elements which most reflect the humane features of human existence.

58

Imagine the great souls from antiquity to be not merely your contemporaries, but your peers as well. Who might then still boast of his accomplishments? Only the fool.

59

It is not enough to merely labor to achieve some semblance of happiness. The sage understands that labor must be directed toward some great project of her own choosing, one that serves, as much as possible, to benefit herself as well as mankind as a whole.

60

Patience should be one of the first virtues cultivated by any individual who hopes to be wise. Wisdom, after all, requires careful reflection and this is not achieved when we are rushing along.

61

The vast majority of people find the greatest expression of the divine to be a congregation of others, all loudly proclaiming the shared values that were given to them in youth. The less communal individuals — generally these are the wise — perceive divinity when the distractions of daily living are put aside. Such disruptions and amusements are often merely idols of a kind, the sort which divert humanity from the task of civilizing itself.

62

We will generally become more interesting, wise, and profound when we are no longer counted among the living. Until then, we are as much of a fool as everybody else.

63

In the great fabric of time an individual life is but a single, invisible thread.

64

We must be willing to labor, wait, fail, sacrifice, succeed, and begin again if we wish to experience the kind of wisdom held in conservatorship by the great sages of the world.

65

Nations and groups — all mobs really — must preserve the interests of the greater or stronger numbers. This is the nature of group reasoning. So, the individual, if she is wise, must certainly assess where she stands amid the group and try her best to at least give the impression of assimilation, but she should remain especially steadfast to the interests of her better nature since only she will look to them.

66

It requires a significant amount of knowledge in order to make a chair well. No one comes to such a task for the first time and masters it in a fortnight. Instead it requires years of instruction and effort to consistently do the job well. The construction of character arises in a similar fashion — demanding knowledge, experience, effort, and wisdom.

67

The sage is obligated — for reasons the wisest already know — to return to the tribe, the hamlet, the church, or the city and teach what he has learned — to reach the millions of lost spirits who search for meaning in their lives. However, the sage is not a missionary of any sort, converting heathens and nonbelievers, but instead merely a fine example of spiritual excellence.

68

The best life is the one most free of self-generated disturbances, the wise soul being she who maintains the harmony of her spirit even amidst the chaos. Fate, of course, sweeps all of us along its current, but the person who struggles will tire much sooner than a similarly situated companion who floats.

69

Only with a true and realistic understanding of our own

limitations might we prevent the flowering of our arrogance. Socrates was the wisest, remember, because he knew his limitations best of all.

70

Wisdom is the beacon which offers safe passage to those ships who seek the shore.

71

It is already the corrupted spirit who imagines that excess leads to wisdom. While of course we may learn from the mistakes of excess and apply these lessons to the living of our lives, the same is true of all experience — excessive or no. Nonetheless, we must maintain a sense of equilibrium in order to perceive beyond the banal and ordinary understandings of a distracted humanity. Otherwise, we are likely to be, ourselves, overcome by the *fumes* of excess.

72

Wisdom shall never evolve without the virtue of compassion to guide it along the proper path. Wisdom, after all, derives its power from the ability to comprehend a multiplicity of varying perspectives. This can be only achieved by projecting oneself "outside" of the subjective experience in order to truly understand the perspectives of another.

73

A sage cannot predict the future — he is not, after all, a prophet of any kind — but he can recognize when to proceed with caution and when to venture out with passionate force.

74

In order to instruct a child as to the ways of living an authentic and moral human life, parents will turn to some form of art — usually through the civilizing force of parables or fables. As the child matures, however, her tastes should mature as well and the art which inspires and informs her most should become more abstract and ethereal in nature. Yet, the average contemporary fool remains committed to a perspective unencumbered by notions of complexity or gradation. He has shaped his life upon the lessons and ideals taken from the hedonistic "culture of delight" that informs all immature understandings. Thus, for him to gain wisdom of any kind he must necessarily move beyond the few superficial offerings of his society. He must instead sail onward with his own heart as a compass and fully prepared to set a course against the current of the sea.

75

The notion that great souls eventually receive the award of fame is naïve and misunderstands the true value of possessing such a character in the first place. Wisdom guides the spirit along the journey of understanding where the blesséd soul travels in quiet delight. This sort of enterprise has a tendency to transform a person's life entirely and cause him to renounce the very thought of fame as something insignificant altogether.

76

The will of humanity — that gross collection of desires and impulses which course through our veins at any particular time — must be governed by the only power capable of such a rule: wisdom. Otherwise, willing slips all too easily into the fierce tooth and claw of beastly competition.

77

The sage is generally wise no matter what the age. After all, the very old can be much more foolish than the very young and youth alone should not preclude the comprehension of Socrates.

78

The mere presence of a good person in the world — even in her most benign daily interactions — is enough to inspire a resiliency and hope in others while providing a model by which to shape one's own life. One good deed often multiplies into thousands, spreading faster than any contagion in our nature and these deeds reproduce exponentially as long as good people so remain in the world.

79

The wise must know — sooner rather than later — that their contemporaries will only tolerate wisdom when it is spoken by the dead. However, even then it is often interpreted as arrogance by those of limited imagination.

80

In order to perceive of humanity as by nature either good or evil is to not truly see us at all. We are both, of course, and more — not so easily defined in simple terms of yesteryear. Yet, we should still have no need to aid or abet the inhumane nonetheless — this coming quite naturally to our more beastly instincts anyway. It behooves humanity as a whole instead to cultivate the good as much as possible. It is the cultivation of the good in us which requires the most consideration and labor. A good person is often just an individual who tries to *be* a good person, no matter what their instincts. How does one know or define what is good? This is why wisdom is so necessary to the development of character.

81

Carl Jung imagined sixteen different types of people. Nietzsche, too, in his doctrine of types, states that each person has a fixed psycho-physical constitution which determines them as a particular type of person. If this is so, then the attainment of wisdom will be different for each of the differing types. In fact, some types won't be drawn to wisdom in the least. Yet, each type must find the manner in which they best flourish — based upon their own individual talent and temperament — and serve the needs of all humanity as protectors of and advocates for humane practice.

82

Wisdom is not some final state or destination that a sage achieves after much determination and labor — as if wisdom were something of a house to be constructed. If one does arrive at what he perceives to be such a "palace" of wisdom, he may find that he has lost his way walking in the door and must begin anew to seek the same entryway. After all, true wisdom can fail us at any time and often will if the sage does not remain prudently balanced upon the beam. Patience and attentiveness are necessary conditions for even the slightest amount of insight.

83

The wise know that even the most tragic of heartbreaks

will one day subside and give rise to some new vista hitherto unfathomable.

84

We should all strive to become the wise adjudicator of our own lives — the honorable and cultured judge who evaluates the evidence put before her and makes informed decisions accordingly. Yet, in order to do so, she must first learn the laws governing her own existence and then enforce them with a kind of passion generally associated with children at play.

85

Speaking "truth" to power isn't a pathetic and childish attempt to reveal the lies of some corrupt administration. Such a goal is not merely unwise, it borders on the moronic. After all, real courage is not an act of fear or recklessness, it possesses instead a kind of insight that understands how one should proceed in any given situation. The truth then that we must speak is not a foolish act designed to expose the conceits of some other fool. The sage knows that political and social concerns, while certainly important, are generally transient in nature and their context — along with their "truth" — often becomes meaningless over time. Speaking the truth though is something of a metaphysical — or rather, metaphorical — expression. Such truths are related to notions of humane values rather than the refutation of petty and superficial lies. They are truths concerned with how we should live our lives no matter what our circumstances. Yet, too often the world is governed as if our existence were to feed the great machinery of the state.

86

Metropolitan cities must necessarily exist in a state of dangerous — and often violent — tension because there are so many various groups living closely together. Over the course of thousands of years smaller groups of people learned to live tenuously in peace with one another, while larger contingencies — only quite recently formed — have had less time to evolve solutions to complex issues with diverse perspectives. A cosmopolitan individual — she who has developed a certain sophistication and maturity with respect to a wide range of ideas and perspectives — has learned to accept and endure the dread of uncertainty that is occasioned by the introduction of some unique experience or innovative notion. So, in order to live properly in the contemporary world, we should follow the example of the cosmopolitan.

87

Science may free us of fearful superstition but it likewise damns our spirit with the illusion of certainty. However, this is not the fault of science; it is a failing of humanity that we are so stunted and provincial. After all, science does not intend — nor does it accomplish — the elimination of wonder and imagination. It merely alters — or should so change — the context of our consideration.

88

Everyone will decide for themselves — consciously or no — as to whether life is something worth the effort of living it. Yet, the vast majority of people endure far more hardship and turmoil than even they might imagine themselves capable because — often to their own surprise — the question, "is life worth living?" is decided by some inner subconscious drive rather than by will or reason.

89

The person who intends to truly inflict evil yet refrains from doing so — for whatever reason — possesses a far more noble sensibility than the brute who simply forces his will upon the world. While perhaps not a saint of any sort, the individual of restraint still ranks as a more humane specimen than many of his less thoughtful contemporaries. Such is the nuance of moral judgement and the reason why perspective is so significant.

90

Evil is not the *cause* of the goodness that often arises in the aftermath of some hateful and wicked deed. Thus, it should not be considered as something of a necessary link in the great chain of an inflexible destiny. Evil is, instead, a judgment about some disturbing occurrence, an assessment that serves to make sense of that which defies understanding. It also serves to help define and refine our perception of what we value as good.

91

Ideals, like the stars, can help lead us to many great and noble destinations, yet we must first know how to read them. We must know how to recognize those stars or ideals that can lead us astray, to know when the way can be trusted and when the lights are but flickering illusions. In any case, the sage must be, above all else, an effective and skilled interpreter of experience — the cosmopolitan connoisseur of many differing perspectives.

92

There exists little distinction between reality and virtual reality other than our imagining there to be one. Reality, after all, is a construct of the human mind — no less fabricated than a computer simulation — assembled from the projected truth of one's own individual perspective and experience.

93

A particularly American psychosis is the notion that no one should have to suffer the indignity of fate — whether by choice or providence. It is the sad hope of significantly altering the physical reality to which we were born so that it might better suit our needs and desires — as if desire itself possessed some special kind of privilege. Instead, one is wise to recognize when destiny has been written into stone and when it is merely etched in sand.

94

In the end we must trust the conscience of our convictions, but only if we have troubled ourselves to develop one. After all, here, too, wisdom must prevail to prevent a stubborn faith in nonsense.

95

Life is something of a wave. It can be seen to grow over time to either overwhelm the coast or lightly tap the shore, but when it breaks, it is gone forevermore. Yet, the spray merely returns to the sea once again to be gathered by some other force — as the force that drove the wave onward now pushes some other form. Life, the wise all know, is a process rather than an incident.

96

We must, of course, surrender to those forces which exist beyond our ability to wisely control them. Yet, we must also stand resolute against that which encourages or otherwise directly supports the proliferation of the inhumane. This delicate balance — as with so much else — requires more than just a little trace of wisdom to maintain it. Thus the need for everyone to develop their character in such a way as to make the best of choices.

97

There exists no substantial thing or object named gravity. It is, instead, a mathematical formula used to predict and explain certain physical features of the universe. It was not really discovered but rather articulated in such a way as to render it intelligible. As with all scientific notions, had the concept of gravity not allowed for prediction and control, it would have been rapidly discarded by any age that seeks to possess that power. In other words, if gravity had no "use" it would have no meaning either. In such a case, gravity may as well be the force that impels one into the grave, it possesses something of a magical quality. It is magical in the same sense that the rising sun is magical — while it may be predictable and understood to a certain degree, it is entirely inexplicable nonetheless.

98

The only immaterial substance is thought. So, in other

words, the idea — or consciousness if you prefer — is the only spiritual "thing" and so provides some insight into the composition of the soul.

99

Those who don't believe in chance and its randomness must deny the arbitrary and indiscriminate nature of death as well. Yet, we should prepare ourselves for just such shocking, fateful occurrences in our lives or they will arrive to overwhelm us instead.

100

The significance of understanding a variety of differing perspectives is that these views as a whole improve the moral character. Unless one has the opportunity and ambition to truly understand another human being — and this is only achieved through the act of perceiving circumstances with the eyes of another — then the instinctual condemnation of differences will rule the day.

101

Hostility is not defeated by some vague feeling of love but through an understanding of why such aggression arises and how best to confront it. Sometimes aggression merely leads to more aggression so a calm and thoughtful response to the violence might actually diffuse the situation. After all, war cannot commence if we refuse to fight our enemy. However, we should not dispense with ferocity altogether since we may need it to face the inhumane opponent who dispatches people as he might rid himself of ants. Thus, a certain wisdom should be developed in order to select the proper means to pacify hostility for a time.

The fundamentalist, the jihadist, the literalist, the evangelical, the political or religious zealot and all other fools of such absolute faith in their own certainty — those beasts unleashed in Eden — are indeed the enemies of humanity as a whole. They are the proud adversaries of free thought since a superficial homogeneity is their overall aim. Combatting such forces often requires great restraint, labor, and wisdom. Each individual, if she does not wish to join these enemy ranks, must develop a host of humane virtues within herself. She must form the type of character that has been educated in the classics, informed through experience, enlightened by philosophy, art, and music, inspired by noble sentiments and emotions, and made wise through the lens of multiple perspectives. Then she must pass her wisdom along to others so that it becomes something of a genetic trait flowing out to future generations. Otherwise, the humane itself may very well perish from existence entirely, stricken by loneliness and malnutrition. What would remain on earth after the demise of the humane — assuming humanity doesn't *physically* extinguish itself from the planet as well — would be a Hobbesian nightmare of tooth and claw, man reduced to his most savage nature — a raging beast among the animals. In order to avoid such a fate for humankind, it is the duty of all wise, courageous souls to elicit, encourage, and express the highest values of humanity whenever possible. Only then might we hope to see an improvement in the overall nobility of the human species.

What if this was the only world you were to ever know? What if it were true that when you die you are simply banished from existence for eternity? Let us imagine that there is no god. Whose life then would still hold meaning for them? Would it not be those exemplar spirits, those eternal rebels who would press onward regardless – morally, excellently, not out of some delusional denial but, instead, from a profound, heroic sense of self? Is that not what we mean by "god"? Faced with the abyss, surrounded by isolation and meaninglessness, she created meaning.

About the author

Emile Benoit is a writer and teacher living in California with his wife and two daughters. He holds both B.A. and M.A. degrees in philosophy from San Diego State University. His other books include: *Essays and Aphorisms on the Higher Man* and *The Artistic Perspective*.

www.ingramcontent.com/pod-product-compliance
Lightning Source LLC
LaVergne TN
LVHW051726080426
835511LV00018B/2905